THE
Unlucky Country

The Republic of the Philippines
in the 21st Century

Duncan Alexander McKenzie

BALBOA.
PRESS

A DIVISION OF HAY HOUSE

Balboa Press books may be ordered through booksellers or by contacting:

Balboa Press
A Division of Hay House
1663 Liberty Drive
Bloomington, IN 47403
www.balboapress.com.au
1-(877) 407-4847

ISBN: 978-1-4525-0335-6 (sc)
ISBN: 978-1-4525-0336-3 (hc)
ISBN: 978-1-4525-0334-9 (e)

Library of Congress Control Number: 2011961197

Printed in the United States of America

Balboa Press rev. date: 01/09/2012

CONTENTS

IN MEMORY AND IN DEDICATION

This book is dedicated to Dr. Jose Rizal, the National Hero of the Philippines. And to Filipino Journalist Romeo Olea, who was murdered while exercising his democratic right to speak and to report on matters of public interest, an essential element of a true democracy. And to Catholic Priest Father Cecilio 'Pete' Lucero, who was gunned down while engaged in human rights work for his church and his Filipino flock. And to Benigno Ninoy Aquino, murdered on his return from exile, and the carrier of so much political hope for this land. And to the 14-year-old boy who was shot and killed in Cebu while out on an errand, killed by men robbing him of his simple cell phone. The blood of those above was spilt on the soil of this nation, the Republic of the Philippines. You are true patriots of this land. Of the above, only Dr. Rizal was killed by a foreign occupying force. The others were killed, not as a result of accident, and not by the will of God. They were killed as a result of the treachery and evil in the hearts of a few of their fellow countrymen. The enemy is within.

INTRODUCTION

This book is about a cluster of 7,107 islands that lie in the South China Sea, the Republic of the Philippines. It is about the culture of the Philippines, its economy, its history and its future. For anyone coming to the Philippines for the first time it is a useful introduction to the nation, and a primer in regards to cultural variations in contrast to the West. For the Filipino reader it presents a useful insight into their character and culture from the perspective of a Westerner. For those Filipinos wishing to go overseas it is a primer in regards to the cultural differences that they will encounter, and how Westerners think. For anyone with any interest or connection to the Philippines the book presents an overview of the nation, the problems it has, and how these problems can be overcome. It is part comedy, part tragedy, part hope and part despair. The hope that it engenders is important. There is no point in writing a book that will leave the reader depressed or despondent. The Philippines can respond and overcome the challenges it is exposed to. This book contains, in fact, all of the variants and elements of life within the Philippines, where the same, hope, despair, comedy and tragedy are being lived every day. The opinions that I give in this book are frank and honest. I owe it to the reader to be this way.

Actually, the first fact to know about the Philippines is that, strictly speaking, at any given time the Philippines may have fewer than the above-mentioned figure of 7,107 islands, as some experience periodic submersion by the sea. Indeed, it is reported that in the future, due to higher global sea levels, the number of submerged islands will increase. Thus, there is an inherent imprecision in regards to the physical parameters of the land and number of islands composing the nation. Contemporary concerns regarding the rise in global sea levels, as a consequence of global warming, and the subsequent immersion of increasing numbers of Philippine Islands, is an issue of concern. Consistent with the Filipino trait of finding humor in just about anything, this has given rise to the joke that the Philippine insurgency group, the New People's Army, will have to change its name to the New People's Navy. Beyond the very number of islands making up the nation there is also the factor of the shape, or morphology, of the nation's land mass. It has been evident throughout history that the boundaries of a country, and the shape of the land that it encompasses, can disadvantage a nation, or it can help to unify it. The morphology of most countries can be divided into five major categories: *compact, fragmented, elongated, perforated, and protruded.* A compact state with a circular shape is the easiest to manage. Compact states are also easier to defend than states of other shapes. Nations such as Indonesia, which is composed of more than 13,000 islands, are known as fragmented or, because they are composed of archipelagos, archipelagic states. It is difficult to govern such a country composed of islands (and more than 200 million people). The Philippines is an archipelagic country. That is highly significant and has economic and political consequences for the nation. An elongated or attenuated nation, such as Chile, makes for difficult governance of peripheral areas in the north and south, away from the central capital region near Santiago. Vietnam is also an elongated state.(1) Therefore, the morphology of a country can contribute to its fate, its capacity to be ruled by a central government, and as we shall discuss in chapter 3, the nation's morphology can also have a significant impact in regards to its economic development. At the start of World War II, Hitler's forces marched across the European continent. Through the use of a tactic of war they developed, called the *Blitzkrieg,* or 'lightning war', they captured everything in their path with incredible speed and efficiency. They invaded France, and intended to invade their old enemy, Great Britain. But they hit a problem, a natural barrier to any further progress.

It was a barrier for the Germans, and a protection for the British. This barrier was the English Channel. A body of water separated them. The Germans planned to invade, but were prevented by adverse weather conditions. What prevented the Germans from invading England, the hindrance of a channel of water, prevents the free flow of trade and goods between the islands of the Philippines. The Philippines has many barriers of water hindering economic activity, allowing piracy to occur, and hindering effective contact and communication. The dynamism of an economy, and economic growth, is dependant principally upon the free flow of goods and services. With a fragmented land mass the free flow of goods and services is constrained to some degree, and noticeably so within the Philippines. The internally inefficient transport system of this nation exacerbates these constraints in relation to the free flow of goods and services. On the political level, there is also a weakly felt projection of power and influence in the southern regions of the Philippines from the central government in Manila. It is very important to note how these factors, how the very shape of a nation, can influence its prosperity, its capacity to be effectively ruled, and its fate.

This book is titled 'The Unlucky Country' in reference to a 1964 book, 'The Lucky Country', by Australian social critic David Horne. Unlike the Philippines, Australia is essentially a huge contiguous land mass, (with only one State, Tasmania, being separated from the mainland), and Australia is the world's largest island, and smallest continent. It is blessed with abundant resources, and is in the fortunate position of having a very stable political system, little corruption and a highly efficient economy. It has stable climatic conditions and, apart from the north of the country, is not subject to the destructive typhoons and extreme weather conditions that so plague the Philippines.(2) It is, in so many ways, the antithesis of the Republic of the Philippines, and therefore the title of this book is the antithesis of the phrase 'The Lucky Country.'

The Philippines is highly populated, with an estimated population of 101,833,938 in 2011. The bulk of the nation's population lives on just 11of the islands of the archipelago. The urban population comprises

49% of the total.(3) In terms of population density the nation is ranked at number 45, with 307 persons per square kilometer, out of a list of 241 nations, with the nation at number 1 being the most densely populated(4). The first census in the Philippines, in 1591, yielded a figure of 666,712 people in the islands. In 1799, Friar Manuel Buzeta estimated the population count as 1,502,574. However, the first official census was carried out by the Spanish government, pursuant to a royal decree calling for the counting of persons living as of the midnight of December 31, 1877. The 1887 census yielded a count of 6,984,727, and the 1898 census yielded 7.832.719 inhabitants(5).

The birth rate is the highest in Asia, and forecasters have stated that the population could double within three decades. The issue of birth control within the Philippines has always been contentious, and in the chapters ahead, this topic will be discussed in detail. It is a highly important issue.

In the Philippines, there are between 120 and 175 languages, depending on the method of classification. Consistent with the shrinking number of languages globally, four of these languages no longer have any known speakers. Of all of these languages, only two are considered official in the country, that is Filipino (Pilipino), which is the national language that is based largely on the Tagalog dialect, and English. Although most state that the Philippines was named after King Philip II of Spain, the precise course of events is that the islands of Leyte and Samar were named in 1543, by Spanish naval Commander Ruy Lopez de Villalobos, 'Las Islas Filipinas', in honor of Prince Philip of Spain. He was then heir to the throne, and did not ascend to the throne as King Philip II, until 1556. (6) Further Spanish expeditions then incorporated the other Philippine islands into the body of the nation. Spanish was the original official language of the country for more than three centuries, and became the lingua franca of the Philippines in the 19th and early 20th centuries. In 1863, a Spanish decree introduced universal education, creating free public schooling in Spanish. It was also the language of the Philippine Revolution, and the 1899 Malolos Constitution proclaimed it as the official language of the First Philippine Republic. The national hero,

Dr. José Rizal, wrote most of his works in Spanish. Luciano de la Rosa established that it was spoken by a total of 60% of the population in the early 20th century as a first, second or third language. Following the American occupation of the Philippines and the imposition of English, the use of Spanish declined gradually, especially after the 1940s.(7)

Under the U.S. occupation and civil regime, English began to be taught in schools. By 1901, public education used English as the medium of instruction. Around 600 educators (called "Thomasites") who arrived in that year aboard the USS Thomas, replaced the soldiers who had functioned as teachers. The 1935 Constitution added English as an official language alongside Spanish. A provision in this constitution also called for Congress to 'take steps toward the development and adoption of a common national language based on one of the existing native languages.' On November 12, 1937, the First National Assembly created the National Language Institute. President Manuel L. Quezón appointed native Waray-Waray speaker Jaime C. De Veyra, to chair a committee of speakers of other regional languages. Their aim was to select a national language among the other regional languages. Ultimately, Tagalog was chosen as the base language on December 30, 1937, and evolved into Filipino (Pilipino).(8) Although it is the national language, Filipino, or more correctly its base language, Tagalog, is mainly only spoken as a first language in the Luzon region where it stems from. Otherwise, the population uses their regional language or dialect most of the time. They are expected to be proficient in the national language, Filipino, but this proficiency varies between individuals. Manila is, without question, the economic, political and cultural center of the Philippines, and the national television programs produced here are broadcast in Tagalog or English. Philippine languages are often referred to by Filipinos as dialects, partly as a relic of the inaccurate vocabulary used in literature during the American period (1898–1946). While there are indeed many hundreds of dialects in the Philippines, they represent variations of no fewer than 120 distinct languages, and many of these languages maintain greater differences than those between established European languages like French and Spanish.(9) English is an official language of the Philippines, but the proficiency of Filipinos to speak it varies widely between individuals. In everyday conversation, often the informal "Taglish" is frequently spoken, and is that dreadful mish-mish of English and Tagalog words, sentences and phrases. It has become increasingly prominent in movies, on television, and in ordinary conversation. So Filipino (Pilipino) and English are the two official languages of the Philippines. Eight major 'dialects' are in use and these are—Tagalog, Cebuano, Ilocano, Hiligaynon or Ilonggo, Bicol, Waray, Pampango, and Pangasinan. The laws of the land, as enacted by government, are formulated in English, and it is also the language of the Judiciary.

The Philippines is a nation, one nation, therefore we refer to it, as a national entity, in the singular, although it is composed of many islands. There is always some confusion and discussion over this, just as there is over its languages. I researched this point and found a fascinating reference to the Secretary of State for the USA, Hillary Clinton, stating the following, "Look at what the Philippines have done in a change of administration," Mrs. Clinton told Jim Clancy of CNN International's Freedom Project. "The Philippines probably export more people of their citizenry than nearly any other country in the world."(10) Mrs. Clinton uses the plural form in her statement. It should actually be the singular form, as in, what the Philippines *has* done.(11) Also, her statement should read, that the Philippines probably *exports* more of *its* citizenry. Some individuals also like to capitalize the 'the', as in, The Philippines, and that seems to be an acceptable usage, as far as I can determine. The Philippines, as a nation, is certainly referred to in the singular, though, whether you use 'the Philippines' or 'The Philippines.'

Public health problems abound within the Philippines, They principally relate to the major infectious diseases with a high degree of risk evident for food or waterborne diseases, such as bacterial diarrhea, typhoid fever, and hepatitis A. Vector borne diseases such as dengue fever, malaria, and Japanese encephalitis are problematic, and major outbreaks of dengue fever are occurring at the time of writing in 2011. Rabies is still present and problematic in the Philippines and causes between 200–300 deaths per year. According to the World Health Organization, the Philippines has the ninth highest number of tuberculosis cases in the world and the highest in Southeast Asia. The WHO estimates there are more than 14 million people living with TB, which kills 75 Filipinos each day.(12)

The Republic of the Philippines presents a unique culture and a unique face to the world. It is the only Christian nation in Asia. and its history of colonization, by Spain and then by America, for over 300 years and then over 40 years respectively, has stamped a unique cultural template. Catholicism is the major evident enduring legacy of Spanish colonization while the American presence and administration of this land, which ended in 1946 turned the eyes of the nation towards Hollywood. Filipinos have an obsessive fascination with American culture and foreigners in general. They are hopelessly star-struck. This cultural fact has been of major significance, and has shaped the mind-set of the Filipino, a mind-set that will be explored in detail in this book.

This book provides a comparative study of the culture of the Philippines in contrast to that of the West, specifically in contrast to my British and Australian background. In engaging in this analysis of the cultural differences between the West and the Philippines, there is no implicit attempt to make a value judgment about what culture may be "better" than the other. My view is that such value judgments, relating to which culture may be "better", are meaningless. They are certainly different cultures, but one is not superior to the other. To engage in such thinking and such value judgments is a dangerous exercise, and arrogant. Such value judgments between cultures have led historically to disasters, such as with National Socialism in Hitler's Germany, where German culture was considered superior to all others. The people of other cultures, and nations, were viewed as being sub-human. This is dangerous ideology.

I engage here in an examination of Filipino culture and Filipino behavior, and postulate as to how the cultural and behavioral norms of the Filipino will contribute to the economic success or failure of the nation. It is my premise that the behavioral and cultural traits of individuals within a nation are factors relating to the economic success, or otherwise, of that nation. Examined also will be the systemic issues surrounding such behaviors, those factors relating to the political processes and to issues such as crime and corruption.

This book provides a wealth of information in regards to statistical and other data, but it also documents real-life experiences, situations in which the author has found himself while in the Philippines, and which illustrate cultural differences and reveal significant issues and factors relating to Filipino life. This experiential approach allows a true understanding and an accurate reflection of things as they are, and as they would occur on a day-to-day basis.

So above we have a snapshot of pertinent facts relating to the nation, as it exists at this time.

The Philippines is a land of exquisite beauty, fascinating history and unique culture. For the foreigner, it is both a challenge and a delight to live in the Philippines. An increasing number of foreigners are visiting the Philippines, for leisure, for work, or perhaps to find romance or adventure.

I am an Australian living in the Philippines. I hope my book will prepare the foreigner for their journey here, and I hope it will provide the Filipino with insights into their culture and behavior, from the perspective of a foreigner. Goethe, the German poet and playwright, once said that one can never truly understand one's own language until one learns another language. That is, one requires an external frame of reference. As Robert Burns, the Scottish poet once wrote, 'O wad some Pow'r the giftie gie us, to see oursels as others see us! (And would some power the gift give us, to see ourselves as others see us!) Filipinos will be fascinated to see how others view them, and an understanding of cultural differences will prepare them for any travel to a Western country.

Composed of interesting facts, an overview of the nation, stories from everyday life, and discussion concerning future challenges for the Philippines, this book will be of interest to anyone who lives in this nation, visits the Philippines or has any connection with it.

25% of the profits from this book will be donated to Plan International, which is an international aid organization that is active in the Philippines, and assists those living in poverty.

The author wishes to acknowledge fully any sources that were mentioned or quoted in this book and has done so, to the best of his knowledge, in the bibliography section. Please contact the author, via the email address at the website given above, if further acknowledgement, or amendment, of any sources is required.

CHAPTER 1

Cultural norms—coming to terms with a culture of contradictions.

KEY POINTS: Filipino culture has evolved out of a mixture of other cultures and influences. Filipino cultural traits perfuse every aspect of civil, political and economic life.

THIS CHAPTER IS written to offer those who are new to the Philippines an insight into Filipino culture. It will also provide Filipinos themselves with a view of their culture from the perspective of a Westerner. Life and culture in the Philippines is kaleidoscopic and multi-layered. It is often confusing and frustrating for the foreigner attempting to come to terms with it, the variations from culture in the West being so marked, and yet in so many ways, so similar. Philippine culture may be viewed as a culture of contradictions. So much of what Filipinos do is contradictory. For those foreigners who sometimes feel unsure about how to behave and how to fit in, and how to act authentically, just remember: *Filipinos themselves have had exactly the same problem.* This is essentially because Filipinos were never free to develop and live their own culture in a truly independent way. For centuries, they have had other cultures superimposed on them, and their identity is multi-faceted. From the Spanish decree that Filipinos must have Spanish names, (just to pick any Filipino name at random, Mario Mendoza does not sound particularly Asian!). And the name of the nation itself originating from a Spanish monarch, to the adoption of English as an official language (which most Filipinos do not speak as a primary language), we can see that external cultures and influences have shaped their lives and their thinking, and pressed on them obligations that may never have really resonated deep in their soul.

During our discussion, we will not only use factual and statistical data, but also real-life examples. That is, anecdotal experiences. The first thing to remember, when discussing anecdotal events and everyday experiences, is that we, through these, formulate *generalizations*. We are discussing what is typical of a Filipino or of Filipino culture. Variations occur between people and the behaviors they exhibit. There are always variations to the norm. However, for the most part here, we capture Filipino culture as it presents itself to us in everyday life. Culture may be defined as the set of shared attitudes, values, goals, and practices that characterizes an institution, organization or group.(1) Like everything else in the Philippines, if we discuss the culture, things can get complicated because the same culture is not consistently displayed between the various regions. Within the Republic of the Philippines, there is certainly a very different culture and set of behaviors between the Christian north of the country and the Muslim far south. However, we will generalize for the purposes of our discussion. Again, I must stress here that these are only cultural comparisons. There is no "better" culture. Cultures are simply different. There is no value judgment stated or implied in this examination of cultural differences between the Philippines and the West. However, it is contended that certain cultural traits and national behavioral characteristics are adaptive or maladaptive, and predispose towards global economic success, or failure, in the 21st Century.

We will take at this point a little scenario that has likely played itself out between various foreigners and their Filipino host a number of times. It was 9.30a.m. on a hot, sunny morning in the Philippines.

The foreigner felt like an easy day while on vacation. Wanting to do nothing more than get a haircut and a cup of coffee at the local mall, while his wife was visiting other relatives, he was asked by an in-law at the family home where he was staying what he planned to do that day. He explained that he was going to walk on his own to the local mall, to get a haircut and a have a nice cup of coffee. An immediate display of consternation was expressed by the foreigners' Filipino in-law. *"Going to the shopping mall alone!"* *"You can't, it's too hot. It's too dangerous!"* The foreigner is somewhat puzzled by this assertion of it being too dangerous. He looks out onto the street. Passing by at that very same moment is a speeding motorbike with four Filipinos perched on it. None of the riders is wearing a crash helmet. As it whizzes by, he thinks, "Now, *that's* dangerous!" While this is going on the foreigner's in-law has been busy texting on her cell phone. *"It's all arranged,"* she then states to him. *"My cousin will come here. He has a car. He will take you to the shopping mall. He'll be here at 11a.m."* The foreigner waits patiently. At 11.20a.m. the in-law receives a call on her cell phone and talks in her regional Filipino dialect to the caller. On finishing the call, she turns to the foreigner and says, *"My cousin has to take an aunt to the doctor, so he can't take you to the mall, but he has asked his friend to take you instead. His friend is a jeepney driver and will be here at 12 noon, because he finishes work then."* At 1.10p.m. a jeepney arrives at the residence. In the back of the jeepney are a group of people who are excited because they are all going to the beach. The foreigner sees that everyone seems really happy, and dispenses with any notion of going to the mall. He joins the happy throng in the back of the jeepney, and they all have a great afternoon at the beach.

The first lesson that the foreigner learns in the Philippines is that time and arrangements are often fluid. There is not the same degree of commitment that one experiences in the West. In the West, when making an appointment, one expects the person with whom the appointment is made to strictly follow through with the arrangement set. In the Philippines, this does not always happen. Secondly, it is not considered normal to want to go out on one's own. Filipinos have a far higher degree of sociability than Westerners do, and being accompanied is the norm. In the scenario above, reflected also are the variations in the perception of danger between cultures. Filipinos, out of a protective sense and fearing danger, will caution the foreigner not to go out on one's own, but taking their family members out on a motorbike without a crash helmet does not raise any particular anxiety. They will also fill up their gasoline tanks while smoking a cigarette, and try to fix electrical equipment while it is still plugged in! However, they will not let the foreigner do it. As a foreigner, should one adjust to this, or should the foreigner continue to behave in ways that is normal and expected for him? We will explore that point later. The foreigner in the example above decided to 'go with the flow' and joined in with events as they turned out.

When we discuss the day-to-day experiences of living in the Philippines, and the traits and mindset displayed by the typical Filipino, we must explore all dimensions of this, and below we list and discuss other dimensions of the Filipino behavioral template. Shopping malls are usually crowded in the Philippines, and it is best to be there immediately when they open if one does not like crowds. The perennial security guard at the entrance to the shopping mall will provide usually a cursive inspection of one's bag, and then you're in, to consumer paradise. One day I chose to go to the shopping mall at the wrong time, on a Saturday afternoon. At this time, the mall is always crowded. Full of adults and children. Just like in the West, they wander around, talking, shouting, singing silly songs, chewing on food, engaging in tomfoolery and blowing bubbles with their chewing gum. And that's the adults I'm referring to. The children are far worse. Yes, shopping malls on a busy day can be compared with the madhouses of 18th. Century London. Needing to purchase some bread, I made my way to the bread shop within the mall. The shop was awash with people. It is sometimes difficult for the foreigner to get used to the sheer mass of individuals that inhabit the Philippine nation. Attempting to stand in line, or what passed for a queue, people jostled for position and interrupted the sales staff with their demands. Waiting for as long as I could to be served, while unsuccessfully attempting to maintain my place in what passed for the queue, I was just about to be served when a Filipina to my side interrupted to request her order. My patience being exceeded I turned to this lady and stated firmly "Would you please wait your turn and take your place in the queue." Her face immediately displayed a reaction of shock and horror. In the Philippines, queuing in an orderly manner and allowing sales staff to complete the orders is not commonly practiced. Usually the Filipino will march up directly to the counter, make their presence known, and interject even if the sales assistant is busy, without any consideration of who may be waiting there turn before them.

This propensity to have oneself served before others, or to only consider oneself, is a well-recognized Filipino trait, and is referred to in Tagalog as *'Walang bigayan'* (No consideration, or an aversion to being considerate). For the foreigner, especially someone who was born in the United Kingdom, or Australia for example, where queuing in an orderly manner is rigidly enforced, it is very difficult to adjust to this behavior. The exception seems to be at the ATM where orderly queuing is enforced, either by the bank security guard or by the people waiting to use the ATM machine. There are just some things that one cannot queue-jump for, and *pera* (money) from the ATM is one of them. By the way, be prepared to wait a lot longer at ATM's too. Filipinos seem to take forever to transact their business at these machines. An inherent behavioral contradiction becomes apparent when one experiences how Filipinos, as mentioned above, deal with appointments and scheduled meetings. In contrast to the appearance of being in a rush at the supermarket or in shops, and seeking to be served first, the average Filipino will dawdle along to meetings and is frequently late. The manifestation of *walang bigayan* on the part of the Filipino is startling when one considers the extraordinary depths of consideration and sacrifice that they will make for their families. This contradiction between inconsiderateness as a trait displayed in public, and the extraordinary consideration the Filipino displays for his or her family, is just one of the contradictions inherent in Filipino culture and behavior.

We have noted above that punctuality is a nebulous concept to the Filipino. They are known to have 'an imprecise or diffusive consciousness of time'. (2) In the Philippines one jokes about "Filipino time" when an appointment is made. It means that an appointment scheduled for 09:00 hours is likely to result in the individuals concerned meeting at 09:40 hours or 10:10 hours. One takes ones luck. This trait of the Filipino and others will be discussed later in regards to adaptive or maladaptive traits *vis-à-vis* the economic position of the Philippines, and regarding its economic future. In contrast to this propensity to be late in the Philippines, other cultures have a different attitude towards time, and there are certainly marked variations in business culture between nations. The Japanese, for instance, are considered to have a very high degree of predictability and reliability. This is reflected in their business practices and everyday living. With bus or train timetables, for instance, if a schedule reads "arrival 11.47a.m.", then the bus or train would arrive exactly at that time. Being efficient and organized is considered a way of life in Japan. This efficiency and detailed organization is evident also in the mindset where, if a meeting is due to start at a specific time, then individuals will arrive five minutes beforehand, due to the requirement to be seated and prepared prior to the meeting starting *exactly* on time. (3) They certainly do plan ahead, in every detail. Moreover, their capacity for self-organization is remarkable.

In contrast to the West, and as highlighted in the opening scenario above, there appears to be a lesser degree of *individuation* within Filipinos. What I mean here by individuation is that *separateness* between people, their degree of independence, and tendency to engage in activities on one's own. Filipinos live in extended families, not nuclear families as in the West. From birth until death, they are usually surrounded by family members. Grandparents, brothers, sisters, aunts, uncles and cousins often live together in the same house, sometimes in the same room even. As a consequence of this personal space is limited. Noise levels, due to large numbers of family members engaging in their day-to-day activities, are high. Stimulus levels, and background noise levels, can often be troublesome. People talking, televisions blaring their incessant noise, usually from the inane entertainment programs that are present on Filipino commercial television, karaoke singing, children running around shouting and crying, dogs howling and barking, and interruptions from visitors are a constant feature of Filipino household life. The noise in the urban areas of the Philippines is incessant and all pervasive. There is little opportunity for any peaceful solitude or meditation, unless one employs successful noise-blocking measures. Essentially, the urban environment and the households therein are often chaotic places, with excessively high stimulus levels. An acquaintance of the mine, a High School student, mentioned this to me, stating that the noise levels in the boarding house where he resides are sometimes so high that it is difficult for him to think properly and pay due attention to his homework assignments. In Philippine urban life, noise is everywhere.

This extended family system and this lack of individuation in comparison to the West has ramifications even for political life within the Philippines. For those in positions of political power, the fruits of political influence appear to be as far as possible distributed within the family. Political dynasties are created, and spouses and other relatives of those in political power are often given free reign to use their position for financial gain. The concept of conflict of interest is largely an alien concept in political life within the Philippines. And this is to the detriment of the country. In contrast to the West, and this point will become evident again and again, the boundaries are blurred. We will discuss this issue in detail later.

In contrast with other nations that have a plethora of rules and regulations, which are enforced, the Philippines does not seem often to set effective limits on matters. Whether discussing noise levels, or the number of children born, or the large numbers of dogs roaming the streets, or alcohol drinking hours, matters seem to take their own course. There are certain areas where regulations are promulgated and enforced. An example relating to road safety is that of motorbike helmet use being enforced in Manila, with motorbike riders being fined if not wearing a helmet. These measures are important health and safety matters and their regulation and enforcement are to be applauded. However, in other regions the necessary laws are absent or enforced haphazardly, or not at all. Filipinos seem sometimes to have a problem in setting boundaries and setting limits. The boundaries between the individual and their family interests, between the Catholic Church in the Philippines and the State, between the military and the political organs of power. The Philippines, of course, is not the only nation where this is occurring, but those nations with highly successful economies and highly effective political systems have very clear boundaries in place between the various sectors and interests of society, and on a political level relating to family members and conflict of interest. As we will discuss later, the Church and the State are deemed by the Philippine Constitution to have an 'inviolable' separation. But time and time again, they find themselves enmeshed. This has had very important consequences for the nation, primarily relating to issues such as birth control and family planning.

We stated earlier that due to the high density of population and the large numbers of extended family members in the one household, that background noise and activity levels are very high. The ability to engage in quiet study, or even to concentrate or think clearly is compromised. My experience of some Filipino households is that of a chaotic environment, due to the sheer numbers of people present, and the number of simultaneous events and interactions occurring. The noise levels are often troublesome. The rule of thumb is that the lower the socio-economic status of the family, the greater the degree of chaos. The elite of the Philippines, and many of the clergy, live a genteel existence, in orderly and peaceful environments. Environments that offer the capacity for solitude and quiet reflection, for undisturbed rest, and allow one to concentrate with full mental powers on what one may be doing. I am not critical of these groups having this living environment. I just wish it were available to everyone else too.

While living in Cebu I was a member of the local Salvation Army Church. The branch of the Church that I attended, and completed some voluntary charitable work at, was run by two Filipino Salvation Army Majors. These two extraordinary individuals were exceptionally dedicated, and were tireless in their efforts to help others. They also ran the education center for young children attached to the Church. It was one of my duties to read English stories to the children there. The Majors at the Church and the congregation are the sort of individuals that one never forgets. During my time there, I had occasion one

Sunday, after a service, to visit alone what is referred to as a 'squatter's area' in Cebu. I did not tell anyone I was going. Out of this sense of being protective, that we mentioned above, they would not have let me go. A squatter's area in the Philippines is an area of public land, or private land that is not being used, where large numbers of families that would otherwise be homeless, reside, or maybe we should use the term exist. In comparison with conditions in the West, or in the higher classes of the Philippines, it is not much of a life. One enters the area and becomes enveloped in a labyrinth of narrow alleyways, with ladders leading up and down to various living quarters. The walls are bare concrete, dull and defaced with grime; the buildings and structures are a mish-mash of concrete, wood, tin, cardboard and any other material that can be cobbled together to resemble a home, and the people who live there have rummaged what they can to serve as their possessions and the material elements of their lives. There is noise, activity, and the smell of cooking and sometimes of sewerage everywhere. The person that I visited was very apologetic because on my way to see this person I passed a group of men who were apparently celebrating a baptism. Filipinos are always celebrating, wherever they are. As I passed by these men, I got the usual calls of "Hey Joe", and "Where you going, man?" As a foreigner in such an area, I stuck out like the ears of a monkey. It did not bother me. As a foreigner, I am used to being so addressed. The person that I visited lived with family members in a few rooms of living space that was home for a large extended family. As is always the case, the hospitality was immediately apparent, and these people who have basically nothing, offer you food and drinks and try to make you as comfortable as you can be. Filipinos have this habit of closing around you as a foreigner. If you have any connection with them, they immediately become protective of you. I felt completely safe. To visit a squatter's area was something that I knew I had to do to really understand the Philippines. To understand the poverty, and the living conditions of the masses in this nation. There were children everywhere. Happy, bright, inquisitive little faces, and other, tear-stained little faces, were peering out at me from behind pieces of cardboard, from behind old bits of furniture, and from behind the adults that were present and to whom they were clinging onto. They were dressed in old T-shirts, some very large fitting and thus dispensing for the need for shorts or underwear. Children were appearing out of nowhere. Oops, there's another one. Sorry kid, I nearly stood on you. Curtains or screens separated the rooms and there was a ladder leading up into what appeared to be another room upstairs. And more children appeared and came down the ladder, just to have a look at the strange, white-skinned, long-nosed foreigner that had turned up in their otherwise insulated world. The various medical conditions that the children suffered from would have covered every page of a compendium of medical conditions. It was a fascinating, but sad experience, to see so many adults and children live this way. Especially the children, the *future* of this nation, who as soon as they left the womb of their mother's in this place, were disadvantaged from the first day of their lives. The living circumstances were indeed absolutely chaotic. Let us examine just one of the consequences of this. I have mentioned above the noise and stimulus levels, to name but one dimension of the adverse living conditions of the poverty-stricken in the Philippines.

In a study conducted in 1959 it was determined that 'When young children are exposed to speech interference levels of noise on a regular basis (the actual volume of which varies depending on distance and loudness of the speaker), they may develop speech or reading difficulties, because auditory processing functions are compromised. Children continue to develop their speech perception abilities until they reach there teenage years.' What the evidence has shown, is that when children learn in noisier classrooms, they have a more difficult time understanding speech than those who learn in a quieter setting.(4) Another study in 1993 determined that, 'Children exposed to noise in learning environments experienced trouble with word discrimination as well as various cognitive developmental delays.'(5) We know about the material, the nutritional, and the academic deprivation, but what is not often discussed is the way noise and chaotic environments, like the squatter's areas, adversely affect cognitive, or thinking, processes and development. This is one of the reasons as to why the primary resource of the Philippines, its people, are disadvantaged and under-achieve. The environment in which they live has a negative impact even on their cognitive processes, to mention only one dimension of this experience. The others adverse factors, of course, relate to malnutrition, and a lack of educational opportunity.

Moving back to the discussion of general culture, and the environment within the Philippines, as I mentioned before within the urban areas of the Philippines, noise is everywhere. It seems to be a maxim with Filipinos that the noisier it is, then so much the better. Within households and within shopping malls, at political rallies and on entertainment television programs, on the street and in the supermarket the noise levels are extremely high, far higher than in general in the West. Typically, western music is played, at the decibel level of a jet engine, and Filipinos have a propensity to play the same music repeatedly. Usually, some catchy tune will find itself embedded in the psyche of the Filipino and it will then be played at every available opportunity. For the foreigner this repetitiveness is downright annoying, especially as the tunes are of the commercial pop variety. During most of 2011, it was the song with the title *'Waka Waka This time for Africa'*. Now this song, after hearing it wherever one went in the Philippines, really began to get on my nerves. I was considering taking out a one-page advertisement in the Manila Bulletin newspaper, along the lines of 'Please turn the damned volume on that amplifier down! And pick another tune!' But now that I am writing a book, people will read my complaint here. Yes, I know, *'gago Americano'*. 'Crazy American'. I am actually Australian, but then we do all look the same. With these kinds of tunes, Filipinos sing them repeatedly, on the karaoke, at baptisms, weddings and funerals. And then they dance to the same tune on talent shows, and so it goes on *ad infinitum*. In previous years it was Whitney Houston's *'I will always love you'*. That one is still a perennial favorite of many of the Whitney Houston wannabe singers in the talent shows. The Filipino obsession with silly musical ditties reached an all-time high in previous years with the homegrown Taglish song *'Otso-Otso'*. *Otso* means in Tagalog the number eight. God give me strength, where are my ear plugs? More to my liking musically Filipinos also have a taste for the heavier dance music with a strong beat, and often a jeepney and even motor-tricycle would be fitted with stereo equipment that would belt out the strong bass of many a good dance track. One of the most astonishing things in regards to being in the Philippines is how rarely one hears any classical music.

For the foreigner, being in the Philippines can be an intoxicating experience when the right ingredients come together. Walking down the urban street in the hot tropical weather, there is often this incredible background noise of thumping dance music, the constant and never-ending movement of Filipino life, the smells of the food being sold on the sidewalk stalls, and the Filipino men and women themselves. These beautiful, dusky, innocently sensual creatures with their almond eyes, slim physique and graceful movements. For the foreigner the dusky skin of the Filipino is beautifully attractive. The color actually varies markedly. For various reasons. Some Filipinos are *mestizo* (male) or *mestiza* (female), meaning they are of mixed descent. Those that may have Chinese or Spanish heritage may have a lighter skin color. Their facial characteristics will also display some variation from what might be called the 'typical' Filipino. The same applies to what is referred to as Eurasians, or individuals of mixed European and Asian parentage, or Amerasian, those of mixed American and Asian descent. Large numbers of Amerasian children, some 50,000, were one of the lasting legacies of, for instance, the huge former American Subic Naval Base in Luzon. (6) Local Filipinas gave birth to these children after forming transitory relationships with American personnel from the base, or otherwise it was a case of the Filipina call girl, and her client, not taking appropriate precautions during their brief and passionate liaison. These Amerasian individuals, now adults, have reportedly had a very difficult time. They have been the victims of social stigma and discrimination within Filipino society, and have suffered identity problems as a result. In terms of skin color, Filipinos will almost always attempt to lighten their skin, rather than darken it. The lighter skin tone is seen to carry a certain class superiority. The laborer or lower classes are likely to toil outdoors, in the sunshine, and therefore be darker in color. Whereas the upper classes are spared this drudgery in the elements and have a lighter skin by being mostly indoors. For the Westerner of course this sense of what is attractive is reversed, and the white skinned foreigner will often try to become darker and get a good suntan, viewing this as more *chic*.

As a foreigner in the Philippines, one is downright conspicuous. If from the West, whether because one is usually taller than the average Filipino, or whiter, and has a "long nose", the foreigner stands out and will attract a lot of attention, especially in the provincial areas. During the Second World War American troops were stationed in the Philippines. The individual American forces conscript was referred to as 'G.I. Joe' and the name seems to have stuck, with every foreigner visiting the Philippines likely at one time or another being greeted with a Filipino calling out "Hey Joe" as he haplessly walks by. Then he wonders if he does in fact know this Filipino who is calling out to him, and perhaps got his name mixed up. The foreigner could simply reply with a "Hey Jose" if one felt so inclined. For some foreigners this "Hey Joe" greeting is considered a term of endearment, a friendly greeting, and a welcome. For other foreigners it is considered impolite and offensive. In addition to "Hi Joe!" or "Hey Joe!" one also is subject to other questions, asked in a fake American accent, such as "What's up, man?", or some other banal question that attempts to typify American conversation. I have traveled to many parts of the Philippines and am amazed at how widespread this custom of calling out to foreigners is. The contradiction here is that for the most part Filipinos are very reserved and polite. For those foreigners who happen to actually be named Joe things could be really get confusing! For a foreigner actually named Joe it would be difficult to determine if one actually knew the person addressing you or not. In any case, the use of the greeting is widespread. In addition to "Hey Joe" being called out, some middle-aged male westerners may be subject to the greeting "Hi Daddy". This is usually made by a teenage Filipina out with a group of female friends. The friends will share in a giggle, and it is really about adolescent group behavior, and the Filipino practice of having a "gimmik" (gimmick in English). The gimmik, as it is called in the Philippines, is basically what would be called in the West tomfoolery. It might also be called fun or silliness depending on one's point of view. Every nation has its share of silly people and the Philippines is no exception. There is often an immaturity evident in

Filipinos. When so greeted by the term "daddy", personally I really feel like saying "If I *was* your daddy I would discipline you for being so impertinent!" Of course, it is pointless attempting to communicate with these individuals, especially in the adolescent group situation. They would immediately become "shy", bashful and even sillier. God give us strength.

Personally, I find this common practice of being greeted with "Hey Joe" to be impolite and annoying. It is not a genuine attempt to engage in meaningful conversation. It is important to analyze why this phenomenon occurs, and let us engage in conjecture as to what is really being communicated by the Filipino with this behavior. It has to be stated that Filipinos hold contradictory and ambivalent feeling about foreigners, and these feelings are sometimes played out on an unconscious level. This may well relate to the "Hey Joe" syndrome. Filipinos are, on the one hand, absolutely fascinated by foreigners, and the assumed wealth and power that all foreigners possess. Foreigners have a charisma in the mind of some Filipinos. All white foreigners, in their mind, come from Hollywood, are rich, and might be famous or a movie star. This is what the media and the entertainment industry portray. Hollywood, and its ethos, exerts a mystical hold over Filipinos. For those Westerners who may become arrogant and conceited to be considered a movie star when visiting the Philippines, keep in mind that the movie star the Filipino might be thinking about in relation to you might be Frankenstein or Lassie. So on the one hand foreigners possess a charisma, and Filipinos feel attracted to them. On the other hand, Filipinos often feel inhibited, shy and intimidated by foreigners. One must bear in mind that the Philippines, as mentioned before, has throughout its history been subject to invasion or colonization by foreigners. By the Spanish, by the Americans, and by the Japanese. The "Hey, Joe" greeting that some Filipinos use is a mask, a false projection of confidence and bluntness that hides, if only for a moment, the insecurity the Filipino feels about foreigners, and about themselves in comparison. Were one to approach a young Filipino who calls out a "Hey Joe" greeting and attempt meaningful conversation, it is likely the Filipino would immediately become uncomfortable. If the foreigner said "Actually my name is Alex, and I'd be really interested to come to your school and meet your classmates, and we could do a question and answer session about who I am and where I come from. You might find that would help your English skills also", it is likely that nothing fruitful would come of this offer. If the foreigner followed-up on this offer it would likely transpire that the event proposed would not happen because the students are "shy" or the teacher is "too busy" or "gone to the provinces" or some such other excuse. I have heard other foreigners complain that Filipinos do not make use of the foreigners that are here, in terms of tapping them for their experience and knowledge. There was a situation that I heard about recently where a foreigner, who was retired, and highly skilled in teaching English, offered to give his services free to teach English, and the vernacular English, to Filipinos. For those wishing to work in Call Centers, for instance, this should have been a golden opportunity. English-speakers sometimes revert to using slang or the vernacular, informal English, to communicate and it would be essential for a Filipino working in a Call Center environment, for instance, to be knowledgeable about the variants of the language. An Englishman might say, for instance, "Hold on a jiffy, I'll just whiz down the local for a quick jar, and then I'll be back before my better half gives me grief". Translated into formal English this would be: "Just wait a moment, I will go to my local bar and have a quick beer, and then I will be back before my wife complains about me being absent." This foreigner in question, who offered to teach English for free, was bemoaning the fact that Filipinos did not take him up on his offer. This important offer of teaching not only formal English, which English native speakers don't always speak, but the vernacular and the slang language. This was a wasted opportunity for Filipinos. This "shyness" that Filipinos display, as a character trait, is a hindrance. Filipinos must take every opportunity they can to improve their skills, their knowledge and their expertise, *wherever and from whomever that may come from.*

In an essay by Dr Eddie R. Babor LL.B., a Filipino scholar, entitled 'Heidegger,s philosophy of authentic existence and the Filipinos: a social dimension',(7) Filipino character traits are analyzed and discussed. It is stated therein, and he sources Foronda as a reference, that 'the Filipino has frequently been diagnosed as suffering from a value crisis. That is, he is ambivalent in his convictions and distrustful of his competence. He is Asian by birth and geographical setting, but matured within a western matrix.'(8) This maturation within a 'western matrix' being due to the Spanish and American colonial presence. And the text quoted from Dr Babor's essay captures succinctly an emotional complex present in the Filipino, and one that the Westerner must understand. It is perplexing initially for the foreigner to experience this attitude, this insecurity, which many Filipinos have about their competence, because professionals within the Philippines are highly proficient and highly knowledgeable, and dedicated to their profession. However, like other Filipinos they generally seem to share this basic fear of making a mistake when they speak in English. or of appearing less than perfect, or of embarrassing themselves. As a foreigner living in the Philippines I really do wish Filipinos would use any knowledge and experience that I might have for their own ends. Having traveled widely, being a native English speaker, and having trained and worked as a Registered Nurse, I would like to think that I might have a mentoring role for some Filipinos. I have tried to be available for this purpose but, like the foreigner who was highly skilled in English mentioned above, I have had no success. I did suggest to my niece, for instance, that I attend her school to perhaps have a question or answer session about Australia. Nothing came of my suggestion. I did also try to become a voluntary mentor at a Nursing College. I knew one of the students at this particular nursing college and I stated to her that I would really like to attend the college as a voluntary mentor. This would entail having the occasional informal tutorial, and to talk about my experiences as a nurse, of nursing overseas, and to assist students with any question they might have about working overseas, or of the English language, or of the different cultures, or of nursing as a profession in another nation. This was to no avail. I had to chase this matter up, and eventually the student I had spoken to did raise it with the College Principal however, the answer was "maybe next year we could do that". This raises another issue. For the foreigner there is always more of an urgency about such matters, and usually less of a tendency to delay or postpone events. While in the Philippines I would often say, "There is no tomorrow", meaning what can or what needed to be done today should be done today. Filipinos sometimes like to delay matters, or are so insecure in regards to their own competence, that they do not like to get foreigners involved in case they are negatively judged. This very self-defeating and maladaptive attitude is in contrast to that of other Asian nations, the populations of which will seek knowledge wherever it can be found. Other Asian countries, for instance, will unashamedly take apart a device manufactured in the West, analyze it, and then reassemble it. They will then copy it and manufacture the same device themselves. They will often be motivated to ask questions, to study deeply, to seek knowledge wherever it can be found, and to use it for their own purposes. This drive for economic success and ascendancy in some Asian nations is remarkable, however this same drive and appetite is lacking in the Philippines. Part of the reticence in approaching foreigners, or of seeking and sharing knowledge, is that they believe that foreigners are magically gifted, talented and superior. As always, perception is more important than the truth. Of course, nothing is further from reality. As a foreigner, when I introduce myself, I will sometimes say, "By the way, I can't dance, I can't sing, I can't play basketball and I'm not good at Math". That's all true. However, foreigners can share their experiences and assist with languages for example, or provide mentorship and support. Use them. Consider foreigners who live here a resource. If you seek help from any of them in regards to a question or a project the worst that can possibly happen is that they say "no". But many will be happy to help. 'Nothing ventured, nothing gained', as the saying goes.

When discussing professional groups here in the Philippines, in addition to teachers, health professionals are also very well trained and generally highly competent. I have undergone dental procedures within the Philippines and also minor surgery, and found the standards to be comparable to the West, with the cost a fraction of what one would pay in Australia for instance. This is one particular area that the Philippines could capitalize on, and indeed does. 'Holidays' for medical or dental procedures are increasingly common. The combined cost of the airfare to the Philippines, a stay at a nice hotel, and the medical or dental procedure, is often far less than the cost for only the procedure itself in the West. And with comparable results. The surgical procedure that I underwent took place in Manila and I will mention it as it also illustrates a point about the culture here. I had had a consultation appointment with the surgeon and a date for the surgery was set. I paid for the consultation appointment at the office of the surgeon by using my American Express card. No problem. I also knew that the cost of the surgery would be US$800-. The secretary to the surgeon kept in touch and reminded me about the appointment. Prior to the due date for surgery, I traveled up to Manila and lodged in a hotel. I had been instructed to be at the hospital at 9a.m. I arrived there at 8.15a.m. A little apprehensive before surgery, I sat and tried to calm myself. I had assumed that following the procedure I would be billed in the normal manner for payment. While waiting I received a text from the secretary to the surgeon asking if I had arrived. I advised that I had. She then stated she was reminding me that the cost for the surgery was US$800—and that I should have the cash ready, in US dollars, to pay *prior to the procedure.* This was the first time that pre-payment had been mentioned. So it is before 9a.m. on a Monday morning, I am waiting to have surgery, and the secretary to the surgeon advises that I need to have US$800—in cold, hard cash before any surgery can take place! A series of text messages then transpired between the secretary and myself. I advised her that I had assumed I would be billed for the surgery, and that I could pay by American Express. The payment would therefore be in Philippine Pesos, but American Dollars had been the sought currency. I became annoyed about all of this, especially when the secretary advised that I should travel from the hospital to the surgeon's office, pay there and then with my American Express card, and then return to the hospital for the surgery. I made it clear that I was not moving from the hospital, and that I was annoyed and considered it inappropriate in regards to this stipulation that the bill be paid in American Dollars prior to any surgery and without being previously advised of the need for prior payment. In addition, I expected the surgeon to be there at the appointed time for the procedure to take place. I also advised her to inform the surgeon that I was very annoyed and upset about this turn of events. I did not receive any more text messages. The surgeon later attended, and he greeted me and we spoke about general matters. I do not know if he knew about the altercation I had had by text with his secretary, but he was too much of a professional to raise the issue of money with me before surgery. As he went to prepare for surgery, his secretary, who had accompanied him to the hospital, asked if I could pay at that point with my American Express card. This I did, and they got the payment in Philippine Pesos, not the coveted American Dollar that Filipinos are often so obsessed about. It is a currency that has lost value in any case, but Filipinos still consider the Greenback as the only real world currency and superior and more valuable than any other. The surgery went ahead as planned and it was successful. As Shakespeare once said, "All is well that ends well". The reason I mention this is that the Filipino surgeon was as skilled as any in the West, however for anything that might be considered straightforward and simple in the Philippines there is always the potential for a drama surrounding the event. The potential for a racy episode of a Tagalog drama is there; an up-class suburb of Manila, the beautiful secretary of a surgeon, American Dollars, furtive text messages, and a bed, albeit a hospital one! With Tagalog dramas there are a few elements that are indispensable, one is that someone has to be crying every five minutes, and one of the others is someone being mortally ill lying on a hospital bed. Unfortunately, there occurred no association between my hospital bed and the beautiful secretary, and the surgery itself proceeded, due to the skill of the surgeon, without incident.

The essay by Dr Babor cited above demonstrates that there is an intellectual presence in the Philippines, and an academic tradition, but sadly, there does not seem to be a widespread pursuit of intellectual advancement within the general population. Some of the population are highly intelligent but uneducated. Young children are educated well and there is a great deal of effort expended in basic education, however there seems to be very little emphasis on adult education and further study. Once Elementary, High School and College education are completed there seems to be little emphasis on studying beyond that. The books are set aside and life goes on. Or so it seems to me. I would think that many of these well trained, highly educated and highly devoted teachers within the Philippines must shake their heads when they see how little reading, writing and educational pursuits their former students engage in when college is finished.

I have traveled extensively within the Philippines and have found a marked variance within the population in the ability to speak English fluently. Surprisingly, in the cities the command and understanding of English is sometimes not good. English is an official language of the Philippines. All of the laws of the land are formulated, written and passed in English. I was traveling once in the provinces of Masbate. Masbate is one of the poorest regions of the Philippines. Stopping at a provincial *Sari-Sari*, or mixed goods store, I engaged in conversation with a local woman who was obviously poor. I was amazed that this woman had no hesitation to ask me where I was from, and converse in English. On discussing local politics she mentioned the phrase 'pork-barreling', which is, a political concept relating to politicians favoring there own regions when it comes to the allocation of federal money or grants or projects. She was obviously not financially capable of pursuing an advanced education, but was certainly intelligent and possessed the intellect to have benefited from this. She also obviously had good linguistic intelligence, and a mindset and attitude that allowed her to attempt conversation in English without feeling inhibited or embarrassed.

In contrast to the West, within the Filipino culture there is far less of a sense of control over one's fate. Sooner or later, a foreigner is going to experience situations where this attitude is evident. The following sad story illustrates this. I adored my niece ever since my first visit to Cebu in 1981. She was like so many of the gorgeous children one sees in the Philippines. She was a favorite of mine, a beautiful child. Growing up into a beautiful woman, she married a Filipino and they decided to start a small business. This business tasked itself with the soldering of metal support frames for such items as lampshades. She and her husband produced four children. In Filipino terms, there life was normal and they busied themselves with the everyday concerns that one has caring for a family and running a small business. One night my niece and her husband were out on their motorbike. They had to visit someone. At some point in their journey, control of the motorbike was lost and my niece and her husband were thrown from the machine. They were not wearing crash helmets, which is not unusual in the Philippines, and suffered serious head injuries. My niece died the next day as a consequence of her injuries. Her husband survived. I attended her Wake. It is common in the Philippines to have a Wake where the body is displayed in the coffin, giving relatives and friends the opportunity to view the body and say goodbye. Family members and friends will set up camp around the body and stay with the deceased for a number of days. Attending this I was present when a friend of my niece visited to view the body and pay her respects. She stated to those present, after viewing the body, "It's God's will that this happened." Those present accepted this without comment. I felt like saying to her, "No, it was not God's will; it was because she wasn't wearing a crash helmet." It happened for reasons not related to any will of God." I stopped myself from saying that because I knew that I would likely get the same reaction from this lady as I did from the woman in the shop that I mentioned above, who displayed what I considered inconsiderate behavior. The lady at the Wake was expressing a cultural belief and attitude common here. To believe in fate is comforting to the Filipino. Due to Filipino religiosity, they also call this "Gods will". This is expressed in Pilipino, the national language largely based on the Tagalog dialect, as 'kapalaran' (fate) or similarly 'bahala na!' (come what may!). I, as a Westerner, do not have any right to directly challenge this. In the West, we talk not so much about God's will, but more about individual choice and responsibility, and how such accidents can be avoided. Thus, Westerners view themselves as being in control of their fate and seek an understanding of how various factors will operate, and controlled, to steer their fate in a direction of their choice. If a disaster happens in the West, someone or something is accountable for that. It is not simply seen as "God's will".

Poverty is endemic in this nation and the daily struggle for existence that plagues the average Filipino is a never-ending source of tension. The typical Filipino is driven by a desire to help their families, and displays a mystical attachment to their family unit. There is nothing the

Filipino would not do for their families. For those parents who have the responsibility of caring for the typical large brood of offspring that is common in the Philippines, it is a daunting task to provide money for food, clothing and education for their children. Despite this never-ending struggle for existence and the desperate poverty that many Filipinos live in, the suicide rate is one of the lowest in the world. In a statistical table representing suicide rates worldwide the Philippines is ranked 89th from a total of 106 nations, a nation being ranked at number 1 as having the highest suicide rate. The source used indicated a suicide rate of 2.1 per 100,000 persons within the Philippine population. In contrast, Australia, a nation blessed with great wealth, prosperity and political stability was placed 45th in the same table, with a suicide rate given at 10.55 persons per 100,000 of the population (9). Therefore five times that of the suicide rate in the Philippines. Contrary to this, and again presenting us with a contradiction, the homicide rate in the Philippines is high by world standards. Statistical data reveals a figure of 6.44 homicides per 100,000 of the population, whereas in contrast Australia has a low homicide rate, recorded at 1.23 per 100,000 in 2009 (10). Therefore, suicide is not a behavior that is particularly prevalent in the Philippines, whereas homicide is. The contradiction is that in a poverty-stricken nation such as the Philippines, where individuals will despair over where they are going to get money for food or other necessities, and live in the most appalling circumstances, this does not translate into suicidal behavior. One may attempt to explain this by considering the high degree of religiosity of the Filipino. That due to church doctrine, committing suicide is taboo. However, such an assumption would lead one to logically conclude that the same religiosity would be an effective inhibitor against killing others. However, this is not the case. As we have seen the homicide rate is high. Were religion of its own, then, an explanation as to why the suicide rate is low, and it being the main protective factor against suicide, we would expect that homicide would also be correspondingly low. That religion again, by virtue of the commandment 'Thou shalt not kill', would provide a protective factor against homicide. However, this is not the case and the homicide rate is 4 times higher, as to that of Australia, for example. Therefore, Filipinos kill themselves at a relatively low rate in comparison to other nations, but kill each other at a relatively high rate. In regards to homicide, the high rate is partly explained by the dysfunctional political system, and the murder of rival politicians, or journalists for example, who happen to probe too deeply or reveal too much about the activities of certain officials or politicians. There is also a low-level conflict going on between the Muslim separatists in Mindanao and the central government, and with communist insurgent groups also in conflict with the government, and a steady death toll as a result. The high homicide rate also relates to the culture of alcohol use amongst Filipino men, who frequently get drunk and may end up quarrelling. Alcohol impairs impulse control, and therefore with the availability of guns, legally supplied or from the black market, a deadly mixture occurs. Again, these contradictions in the behavior of Filipinos are striking. Filipinos are generally a gentle people and avoid overt displays of aggression and conflict. In contradiction to this, they kill each other at a much higher rate than Australians, for example, who are blunt and open about how they feel about a matter, and do not avoid confronting people on issues if it is so required to do so. Yet despite such open assertiveness and tendency to confront, Australians kill each other at a much lower rate in comparison to Filipinos. Perhaps it is precisely this behavioral trait that acts as a protective factor. Where open assertiveness actually leads to better conflict resolution, or the complete ventilation of emotion and verbalization of the issue, this reduces the emotional tension more effectively. Filipinos may be more prone to internalize issues, to brood on a matter, to hold grudges, and then to "explode", with homicide as the result. What immediately comes to mind, when discussing this issue, is the supposed phenomenon of running 'amok', or an explosive, homicidal frenzy that is reportedly culture bound to the Malay ethnic grouping. Personally, I do not accept this phenomenon as being culture bound at all. The frequent homicidal gun-toting, killing frenzies that, as one example, American citizens have been known to engage in, for instance, contradict the assertion that it is culture bound to any one racial group.

Another important personality trait, and that linked to the Asian cultural matrix, that the Filipino shares is the concept of losing face. Again, we look at a real-life experience, a true story to highlight this concept. The motorcycle mechanic was busily engaged in servicing the trail bike, which had been used to transport me around the breathtaking scenery of the Philippine island on which I was residing. Engaging in his work, the mechanic held in his oil-stained hand an oily spanner, both were coming into contact with the shiny new seat of the machine. Observing this, I assumed that the mechanic would ensure that the oil smudges he had left on the seat would be wiped clean before the motorbike was handed back to my companion and myself. I also thought of how better it would have been to have covered the seat first, to protect it from staining prior to commencing his work. Obviously a skilled and knowledgeable mechanic, he completed his work quickly, and advised my companion that the machine was ready for us. The oil smudges were still apparent on the seat of the motorbike. I advised my friend that I was not going to accept the motorbike in that condition, and he should tell the mechanic to wipe the seat clean before we leave. My Filipino companion seemed uncomfortable, but nonetheless asked the mechanic to clean the seat. Of significance here too, is that my companion was a young male and the mechanic was an older man. Filipinos have an inherent respect and veneration for older people. In England, where being cheeky has a certain cuteness, a young male might say in the same situation, *"Hoy, wipe it clean, Grandpa!"* In the Philippines, this is simply not done. After discussion in their dialect between my companion and the mechanic, my companion advised me that the mechanic had stated that we could buy a cloth at the adjacent shop with which we could wipe the seat clean. Yes, *we* could buy a cloth. Why not the person who made the mess buy a cloth? For a foreigner it is unacceptable that it is the customer that should buy a cloth and clean up the mess the service person made, and was being paid for. However, for the Filipino, it appears that for the most part this would be considered the end of the matter. Especially where the Filipino is older, it appears that younger Filipinos, as was my companion in this case, would have to show due deference to the older person. There is also here the concept of 'loss of face'. That is, where my companion confronts the mechanic about any aspect of his work, the mechanic would feel slighted, and suffer a 'loss of face'. In any case, as a foreigner, I considered the suggestion that we buy a cloth to wipe the seat clean ourselves unacceptable, and I stated to my companion, "The hell we are buying a cloth. *He* smudged the seat with oil, so he can clean it up. I'm going to get the manager right now. This is not good enough". I went and advised the manager of the problem. While some discussion between us all was going on the security guard at the motorbike facility, who had been observing what was going on, got a cloth and the seat was wiped clean. Everyone was then happy. No on suffered loss of face. As is usual in the Philippines, everyone in the vicinity became involved in one way or another.

The concept of loss of face is a trait that Filipinos have internalized from their occidental cultural roots. In countries across Asia 'loss of face' is a concept that drives much behavior. Causing someone to lose face would not be easily forgiven, even if this did occur by accident. It relates to the standing that an individual has within a community, and their sense of worth, dignity and honor. While in the West, we value directness and people can often be blunt, the opposite holds true in Asia. In business dealings meetings may be preceded by a lot of 'face building', before getting down to the real business.(11) The foreigner is bound to make the observation that Filipinos tend to tiptoe around the need for asserting oneself, and avoid confrontation. The Westerner, by contrast, is used to asserting themselves and their rights without hesitation. Another example related to this is when my companion and I decided to travel on a bus from Masbate to Manila. Masbate airport had been closed for repairs; the re-opening date had already been extended. The bus service leaves from Masbate and boards the ferry that will take it to Pilar, Luzon, and from there the road trip to Manila proceeds. For anyone truly wanting to understand the state of the infrastructure of this nation, I would advise this trip by road. We will discuss this issue, and its impact on the economy of the nation, in chapter 3. For now, back to the story at hand. The bus was a late model vehicle. On entering and availing ourselves of our seats, we noticed that underneath the seat in front of where we had placed ourselves there was vomit. Presumably, one of the passengers, who had alighted the bus from the previous trip, had been sick. The bus was obviously not going to be cleaned prior to the return trip to Manila. I asked my companion to advise the driver about the vomit, and to ask that a cleaner be found to clean the mess up before we started our journey. My companion replied, "He won't listen to me". I replied "He'll damn well listen to me!" I then approached the driver, pointed out to him that there was vomit on the floor of the bus, and asked that it be cleaned up. The driver replied by stating that this would be done, he then obtained a cloth and wiped the vomit from the floor and removed it from the bus. Cleansing of the residue, and the staining on the floor, was not completed. I had expected that the bus would be checked prior to passengers boarding at the depot in Masbate, and cleaned thoroughly prior to the return trip to Manila. Filipinos who are being provided with a service tend to accept what foreigners would not accept. The fare for a bus trip to Manila can be almost that of an internet-booked airfare to Manila by one of the low-cost Philippine carriers. This acceptance of poor service standards perpetuates shoddy service, and in this case unacceptably unhygienic conditions. Foreigners will complain, most Filipinos in the same situation will not.

As an aside, I will mention the economic benefits that a foreigner has by living in the Philippines. I mentioned the motorbike-servicing incident above. The motorbike was purchased brand new in 2011 for PHP67,000 (that is roughly the equivalent of US$1,560-). The dealership would only accept cash. My Filipino friend and I were laughing because we were carrying this money around in a bag. I told him it was ready money in case I got kidnapped. I'd be in the Guinness Book of Records. We'd be walking along with the bag of money and someone would stop us. "You're kidnapped. We'll send the ransom note." No need we've got the cash on us, here." "*Salamat. Paalam.*" (Thank-you. Goodbye.) Done and dusted. Fastest kidnapping and fastest release in history. My friend and I did discuss if the kidnappers would accept an American Express card these days. Just in case they do, I now never leave home without it. On a more serious note, I did tell my friend not to bother paying the ransom if I was kidnapped by a Muslim terrorist group in southern Mindanao. It's likely I'd have my throat slit as an infidel anyway. The regular NPA in Luzon would be far more reasonable, would negotiate the ransom, call me *brad*, (brother), and let me sing on the Karaoke with them. I'd sing the old song by Engelbert Humperdinck, *"Please release me, let me go . . ."* And they would sing, *"Stay awhile, stay forever."* It all depends on your luck, or lack of it, as to what kind of insurgent group you might fall prey to. Now, back to the story about the motorbike. I later had a remote start and alarm system fitted to it. This was a fun gadget that allowed the motorbike to be started remotely, and it spoke to the rider in a robotic, none-too-grammatically accurate voice, when using the indicators, or when starting the machine. It spoke such phrases as "Welcome to use our motorcycle". On turning off the machine, it said, "Remember to lock your motorcycle well." Good advice. The system cost just over PHP1,200 (US$28) and we found a mechanic to fit it. This guy was very skilled in what he did. He had to dissemble parts of the motorbike and the electrical system to link in the electronic alarm system that I had purchased. He knew the electrics of a motorbike back to front. After spending an hour getting the system securely fitted and working, he charged PHP150, the equivalent of just over US$3-. The equivalent cost in Australia or in the US would have been at least twenty times higher.

For traveling within the Philippines if utilizing such services as the low cost air carriers, for example, one finds oneself in a different world of standards and expectations. My experience of airlines in the Philippines is of well-organized enterprises, with comparable standards of operation with any low-cost carrier in the West. It is with such companies that one can see that if proper standards are set, then Filipinos can reach these standards. Not only is the bus company that owned the bus on which I traveled selling itself short, but Filipinos who accept this failure to meet acceptable standards are also selling themselves short, and perpetuating failures in proper service provision. Where service falls short of acceptable standards, Filipinos should complain and expect change to occur. That's important.

Travel in general in the Philippines is often a often-haphazard affair. Apart from the previously mentioned low-cost airlines, in which the foreigner finds themselves transported by a service comparable to Western standards, other forms of transport can present challenges and problems, as previously mentioned with the example of the bus trip.

The Philippines is a fragmented group of islands and sea transport, where one chooses not to travel by air or lives in a region not serviced by air carriers, is frequently necessary. The boats one uses vary in size depending on the destination and length of trip. One remarkable constant is that, wherever one travels by boat, the traveler will always find himself in the presence of a crate of mangoes, a rooster, which makes its presence know by crowing at various points in the journey, numerous children, and large quantities of food, which Filipinos carry and consume wherever they travel. I always wonder too about the chronological reliability of roosters, because they never crow when there supposed to, that is at dawn. As a young boy I was always told stories about roosters crowing when the sun rises, but I found that in the Philippines they crow at any time they feel like it! Consistent with the trend to medicalize every variation in behavior, I'm sure this would be referred to as 'Rooster Chronological Dysfunction Syndrome". This would allow the pharmaceutical companies to profit by then making a drug to treat this "illness". Or maybe, because they are Philippine roosters, they have the same 'diffuse sense of time' that Filipinos have too! When one comes to terms with the traveling companions that one has, that is the roosters, one finds that the facilities on the regular inter-island boats are frequently poor. The toilets, which one always refers to in the Philippines as "the CR", are often dirty and smell bad. There are often pools of water on the floor. The boat itself is frequently crowded and accommodation for longer trips, in the economy section, consists of tiers of bunk beds. Private cabins may be available and present a more comfortable and private travel experience. However, not all shipping lines offer these. There have been many disasters over the years with boats sinking in bad weather, and safety equipment has not always been available to prevent drowning. I was appalled to see on a sea journey from Masbate to Pilar various passengers throwing their empty plastic drink containers overboard during the journey. This, even though garbage bins are provided on board. Environmental awareness appears to be sadly lacking on the part of some Filipinos, despite the sea journey offering spectacular natural views of the sea, of islands that are being passed, and of dolphins that appeared from time to time. The official motto of the Philippines is, *'Maka-Diyos, Maka-Tao, Makakalikasan at*

Makabansa—For God, People, Nature and Country' and this is being ignored when it comes to nature. It must be said though, that in this regard, Filipinos are not any different from their counterparts in the West, who also pollute the environment and defile natural habitats with garbage. Even when garbage bins are nearby.

As mentioned in the introduction, the geography of this nation is characterized by a fragmented land mass, and some of the islands are periodically submerged. Thus, the figure for the exact number of islands that make up the Philippines is imprecise, and there is, within the Filipino mind, also an imprecision of thought. The Philippine nation consists of sometimes 7,107 islands, sometimes 7,104. This inherent variability, and therefore inability to determine with precision the exact number, seems to reflect itself in the Filipino, for there is often an apparent inability to state something with precision. It is almost as though fate has linked this imprecision of geography and mind together. The issue of exactness and precision of thought needs some examination, with regard to the cultural template of the Philippines. Traveling with Filipinos, we were attempting to locate an address in Cebu. We had located the town in which a relative of one of our group lived in, a town that we had never visited before. We stopped to ask directions and my Filipino friend asked in Tagalog, he is not fluent in Cebuano, for directions. On one occasion the man whom he asked directions from seem puzzled by my friend's questions. He did not seem to understand the Tagalog my companion was using. Some Filipinos use there own 'dialect' exclusively, and can be troubled by someone attempting communication in another 'dialect', or even in Tagalog, which is the root language of Pilipino, the national language. This issue of language we will further examine later. People whom my friend asked directions from would answer by pointing in the general direction of the address or of saying "*diritso*", meaning "straight ahead" or they would say vaguely "turn at the bus terminal". It was necessary to ask a number of people, all locals, until we progressively, step by step, were able to locate the address we were seeking. I have experienced this situation on a number of occasions. Often, when asking directions from a local person, in response they will just point their chin in the general direction of the location sought, and state "*doon*" meaning "over there". A friend of mine advised of a trip he made to Germany, "It's amazing", he said, "if you ask for directions, for example to a post office, they will say something like "proceed thirty meters down this road and at that point you will reach a street intersection. Turn left at that point. Then proceed for about forty meters down that street, and then you will then see a Lutheran Church on the right. Stop at the church and diagonally opposite the church, you will then see the Post Office". Precision and exactness. On seeking directions within the Philippines, or attempting to obtain information, the foreigner can be taken aback with the vagueness of the responses given. When my companion asks directions, and obtains the usual imprecise responses, I am often tempted to state, "But can you ask him *exactly* how far we have to go down this road, in order to get to where we want to go". The response from my companion indicates that it would seem impolite to press the point with anyone one is asking, and seems happy to leave the matter as it is. A clue to this behavior, and why it sometimes happens, relates to the cultural issues that we have mentioned, of deferring to one's elders, and the concept of loss of face. 'You ask someone older than you for directions to a landmark. Rather than losing face by telling you that he does not know how to get there, the man confidently points you in the wrong direction!'(12)

This attitude, this impreciseness and vagueness, also relates to arrangements or commitments one may have made with others. On taking up residence in the Philippines, I decided to enroll at the local martial arts club. After some discussion, it was arranged that my friend and I would attend a Monday, Wednesday and Friday schedule. Initially things went well. The instructor never arrived on time, but that is usual in the Philippines anyway. I would always arrive at the arranged hour of 8p.m. in spite of that. I'm a foreigner, so that's my habit! The instructor was a very good martial arts exponent. Someone that one could learn a lot from. Some nights there would be a number of students, other nights just my companion and myself. We received quality instruction and I enjoyed my training. As is usual it was seen as an honor to have a foreigner present in the class. We attended one night and no one else turned up. We made enquiries at the residence attached to the hall used for the martial arts club. We were advised that the instructors and some of the students had gone to another city for a martial arts tournament. There was never any formal notification to us of this, or posting of any message on the club door, or text to us, despite the fact that we had given our text number on the club registration form. We made repeated efforts to attend after this date; however, the club remained locked. We then heard on further enquiry that the instructor had decided not to be an instructor anymore and had gone back to his usual work of tricycle driving in the evenings. That is fine, should he wish to exercise that choice, however one would expect a notification and explanation. I did consider it odd not to receive any text notification regarding the above, as the Philippines is one of the world's biggest texting nations. However, texting seems mainly to be used for social reasons rather than business efficiency or effective communication with others over matters of importance, such as cancelled classes at the martial arts club. Thinking that this was perhaps an isolated incident I shrugged it off. But sadly, the same thing happened again at a later date. Living in a town in the Philippines, in the Bicol region, I began attending one of the local gyms. There were actually only two gyms in the town. My Filipino gym partner and I decided to attend the newly opened one. It was nice and clean, had all the necessary equipment and the owners were very friendly. We asked if a Monday, Wednesday and Friday schedule at 6a.m. was available to us to allow us some early-morning training. No problem we were told. On the first day of attendance, we were promptly there at 6a.m. Most foreigners are like that. If they say 6a.m., it means 6a.m. However, no staff from the gym were there. At 6.15a.m. I asked my gym buddy to text the owner on the number that was displayed on the gym signage at the door. He did so. The owner of one of the adjoining stores happened to walk past and we indicated that we were waiting for the gym to open. He shook his head and gestured as if bringing a bottle to his lips. The gym assistant was known to enjoy alcoholic beverage and had probably been drinking the night before. Eventually ten or fifteen minutes later the gym assistant turned up and we began our training, albeit delayed. This merry dance of unpunctuality on the part of the gym assistant, who was charged with the responsibility opening the premises, carried on. Whenever attending our training session, and he was not there, I insisted my gym buddy text the owners to tell them we were waiting. This is the issue, does the foreigner just accept that everything runs differently and unpunctually in the Philippines, or does he live as he normally does and expect others to make the adjustment to his habits? I suppose if one is paying for the service, then one is entitled to expect others will make the necessary adjustments! Eventually the gym assistant would attend. This carried on for a while. Slowly but surely this seemed to be working and on attending at 6a.m. the gym was then more frequently than not, open and ready for us. I was really pleased about this newly established pattern of predictability in our training schedule. Then one day it was the owner himself who turned up. We heard that the gym assistant had gone back to the provinces. The owner was reasonably punctual. One day we arrived there at our usual 6a.m. and no one attended to open the premises. Other gym users who also regularly attended at that time also turned up. We waited at the front of the building, but no one showed up to let us in. We texted the owners, on both cell phone numbers that they had. No response. After 40 minutes of waiting, we ran out of patience, and returned home. The same thing happened our next planned gym session. I got really fed up with this and did not return to the gym. The following week my gym-buddy and I were out walking. By chance, the owner of the gym passed us on his motorbike. He stopped to say hello and asked us why we were not at the gym. We explained that we had attended last week but that no one had presented to open the gym. "Oh," he stated matter-of-factly, "my family and I were all on a visit to another town last week." There could have been a text message sent to us to advise us of this, or perhaps a note attached onto the premises door. But nothing. He asked us if we were going to re-attend and we stated that we would if there was going to be someone there at they gym for us at 6a.m. for our usual schedule. Not a problem, we were told. We attended duly at 6a.m. but again had to leave after waiting for some time. No one turned up to open the gym. It is extremely annoying and frustrating for the foreigner, and I am sure to some Filipinos too, to experience this sort of gross casualness in regards to commitment. Many individuals seem disinterested in what they are doing, unfocused and/or disorganized. I mention these examples because I believe they have significance and importance in terms of how organized and economically efficient a nation is, and how the mindset of its people can be a precursor to the economic success, or failure, of a nation. This behavior is in marked contrast to the Chinese or Japanese or Germans who are highly organized and committed. I have been to Hong Kong, and I have been to Singapore, and in both of these places there is a hunger for business, a drive for success and a motivation to work that is astonishing. That is why they are so economically successful.

I mentioned above that no text messages were received, to explain why prearranged appointment and schedules were not followed through. And I must mention the irony in regards to this, as text messaging trends in the US and around the world, aggregated from various news sources, reveals that the Philippines continues to be the text messaging capital of the world. In 2009, the average Filipino mobile subscriber sent an average of 600 text messages per month, or 43 percent more than their US counterparts did.(13) A researcher in this field stated that SMS statistics vary widely but that the trends and comparisons are generally consistent. That is, we can be reasonably certain that the assertion about the Philippines being the world's foremost texting nation is true. Texting is extremely popular in developing countries and it has become the communication method of choice, acting as a substitute for face-to-face conversation and the use of e-mail.(14) Like 'Facebook', the Filipino has embraced texting, and incorporated it as a feature of their everyday lives. It is usual here to have text-mates and numerous Facebook friendships. With texting, a language has evolved that abbreviates common words and phrases in order to squeeze more words into the one message, which, incidentally, costs 1 peso to send. In regards to the global phenomena of Facebook, the Philippines was ranked second in a list of numbers of Asian nations Facebook members. In 2009, the Philippines had 8,387,560 members, second only to Indonesia. The growth rate for Philippine membership in the preceding year was a whopping 2046.8%. (15) There are internet cafes wherever there is internet coverage in the Philippines. It is one of the most popular businesses that Filipinos will choose to set up, should they have the available funds. On entering these internet cafes, it is likely the majority of the clientele will be accessing their Facebook accounts. Facebook ties into the Filipino tendency to sociability and to embrace any fad or device that is from the West.

We mentioned previously the very important fact that the Philippines is fragmented in a geographical sense, having an archipelagic structure and this has significant disadvantages for a nation. The Philippines also appears to be at times fragmented or divided by language. Such matters can come to the surface in strange places and in strange ways. The Miss Universe Contest would suit any Filipina to the ground. Full of Hollywood-style glitter and pomp, it gives Filipinas a chance to parade their unquestioned beauty in front of an international audience. Pageantry, and the desire to look beautiful is in the blood of the Filipino, whether it is the Filipina or the gay Filipino. The chance also to find instant fame and fortune is very enticing. For one Filipina, a former winner of the Miss Universe Contest, matters did not turn out as she had envisaged, and a storm was let loose that highlighted not only regional differences and tensions, but also the issue of languages within this archipelago.

'Gloria Diaz declared 'persona non grata' in Cebu' was the newspaper headline that announced the storm centering on a former Miss Universe winner. Appearing in the September 1st, 2010 online edition of the Manila Bulletin, the article stated that the Miss Universe of 1969, a Filipina named Gloria Diaz, had been declared as "persona non grata" ("personally unacceptable or unwelcome") and is now banned in the province of Cebu . . . .' (16) The article reported that the Vice Mayors League in Cebu condemned a comment attributed to Ms. Diaz, where she allegedly belittled the Cebuanos' ability to speak in English. Reportedly, she had stated that there may be a need to hire an interpreter for candidates in the pageant. The controversial statement allegedly made was ". . . . when you think about it, a Cebuana can hardly speak English and of course Tagalog. So maybe she should answer in Bisaya." A Cebuano official later stated that, ". . . . Diaz's remarks pierce our hearts as Cebuanos who consider our native tongue as a sacred heritage . . . ." and further, that Cebuanos felt her ". . . arrogant remark insinuates that Cebuanos are inferior breed of Filipinos." (17) Later, clarifying what she had said, Ms. Diaz stated that she had simply meant to say that if one speaks Ilocano, then use Ilicano, or if one speaks Ilocano and also speaks good English, then say it in English. Or if comfortable with speaking in Spanish, then use Spanish. Ms. Diaz reported that she was shocked by the reaction that she received, and by the anger that had been expressed.(18) She reported that she had simply meant that people ". . . say it with whatever you're comfortable with."(19) That's good advice. I can readily sympathize with Ms. Diaz. I can also fully understand local politicians defending their region against perceived insults or slights. That is to their credit. The perceived capacity or otherwise to speak English would have ramifications for the Call Center industry which is particularly strong in Cebu, and the foreign tourist industry. I have lived in Cebu, and it is an advanced, progressive and highly developed metropolis. The city is referred to as 'The Queen of the South' and is without doubt the second most important metropolis outside of Manila, in terms of economic growth and dynamism. However, the whole issue of language in the Philippines is confusing and divisive, and obviously linked with strong regional pride. As mentioned previously, there are only two official languages in the Philippines, English and Filipino. The other major auxiliary languages include Cebuano. However, in reality, the degree of fluency and competence with which the official Philippine languages are spoken varies markedly, not so much between region to region, but more between individual to individual. An example of how the issue of Filipino languages can generate confusion, and here in regards to the relationship between the national language, that is, Filipino, and the regional language, Tagalog, happened during the impeachment trial of the former President Joseph Estrada. When the presiding justice Hilario Davide, a Cebuano, asked which language the witness Emma Lim preferred to testify in, Lim promptly answered "Tagalog", to which Davide did not agree. According to Davide, nobody could testify in Tagalog because it is not the official language of the Philippines and there is no available interpreter from Tagalog to Filipino. However, Senator Franklin Drilon, an Ilonggo, defended the oneness of the two by saying that an interpreter will not be needed because everybody would understand the testimony in Tagalog.(20)

There was no common language in the Philippine archipelago when the Spanish arrived in the 16th century. The three major languages of common use throughout the islands were Liwayway (Tagalog), Hiligaynon and Bisayan (Visayan).(21) On November 12, 1937, the first national assembly in the Philippines approved a law creating a National Language Institute to make a study and survey of each of the existing native languages, with a view to choosing one, which was to be used as a basis for the national language of the Philippines. This language was to be called Filipino.(22) The Wikipedia entry in regards to 'Filipino language' makes a very interesting statement. That is, 'In practical terms, Filipino is the formal name of Tagalog, or even a synonym of it. It is sometimes described as "Tagalog-based", part of a political fiction that the national language is based on an amalgam of Philippine languages rather than on Tagalog alone'. The above entry in the Wikipedia article is given as a sourced entry.(23)

Some Filipinos rely more or less exclusively on their local language, what is usually referred to as their "dialect". When one has a language of choice, and one uses this to think one's deepest thoughts or to express one's deepest emotions, one would naturally use this, especially in situations of stress, to express ones' innermost feelings. That is, to fully *articulate* oneself. This is the point that Gloria Diaz was making. Aside from the issue of whether anyone was slighted by her comments or not, due respect has to be given to the other regional languages of the Philippines, and indeed other languages worldwide. Why does everything have to be spoken in English anyway? It is simply a part of the cultural colonialism of those most influential nations in history that is the United Kingdom and the United States of America. I have met Cebuanos who speak English fluently, and I have also met Cebuanos who seem to have great difficulty conversing in English to any reasonable degree. I have had exactly the same experience with Filipinos from Manila. It really seems to depend on the individual and not on from which region they come from in the Philippines. And it depends on how motivated the Filipino in question is to learn English, and other personality factors such as their degree of extroversion. That is, how willing they are to attempt communication, and the confidence they have in what they are doing. It is common for Filipinos, when they are attempting to think and talk in English, to state that they are "getting a nosebleed." I'm not sure of the origin of this phrase, but it may relate to the effort of speaking English is increasing one's blood pressure and an epistaxis, or otherwise called a nosebleed, is the result (24). Perhaps. But Filipinos do have a harder time, if not necessarily actually suffering nosebleeds, in regards to this issue because they are *expected* to be able to communicate fluently in a number of languages, whereas in Australia for instance there is only one official language and that is English. And may I add that some Australians do not ever make the effort to learn another language, or even improve their own English, whereas at least some Filipinos are fluent in their regional language, or "dialect", their national language, Filipino, (which is interchangeably called Pilipino and largely, some would say fully, but that was never the original intention, based on Tagalog,), and that inheritance of the American colonial administration. That is, English. In addition, some of the older generation still speaks the Spanish of their forefathers.

In addition to the area of language there is often a general rivalry felt and expressed between the Visayan region, for instance, and 'the Tagalogs'. However, this situation is not unique to the Philippines. The same kind of regional rivalry exists in many other nations. In Australia, for example, when the nation became a federal entity there was a great deal of squabbling in regards to which major city, Melbourne or Sydney, should become the capital of the newly formed federal nation. The conflict was resolved by building a separate city from scratch that would serve as the nation's capital. That city is now called Canberra.

On my cell phone, I receive regular text messages from the telecommunications company that I subscribe to. One of these regular texts relates to the Tagalog language, and is very useful for a foreigner trying to learn a little of the language. When discussing "Taglish", that mixture of Tagalog and English, there are some delightful examples.

One day on my phone, I received the following text lesson, which outlined the origin of a word. It read: 'Origin: Hello world (he-low world)-peeking'. Then below this it gave an example of the use of this phrase: 'Example: *Ang buhok sa loob ng ilong nya ay naghehello world na.* (The hair inside his nose is already peeking.)' Such delightful phrases and such illustrative examples abound! A further example that I received is the word 'Lobat'. The text ran: 'Origin: Lobat (lo-bat)—exhausted. Then, 'Example: *Ayoko na tumakbo lobat na ko.*' (I don't want to run anymore. I'm already exhausted.) Now this word, as far as I was able to determine by researching it, is not a Tagalog word at all, but a contraction of the phrase 'Low Battery', thus 'LoBatt', and finally to 'Lobat'. That ever-present connection between Filipinos and their cell phones has thus become incorporated into the language. Tagalog, or its variant, Taglish, is then, a living and growing language, even able to incorporate mutated technical terms. The moral of the above discussion is this; if you, as a foreigner get confused about the language situation in the Philippines, then do not worry, because everyone does. Even Filipinos. Get used to it.

And so we pass on from that clearly thorny and controversial topic of language to another matter concerning Filipino culture. I was attending a fiesta in a provincial area and on display were all the facets of Filipino life. The sense of community, the love of pageantry, singing, dancing, beauty competitions and an activities program that inevitably in true Filipino style never ran on time. It started late and finished, well, whenever. Foreigners who attended were, as usual, treated with great hospitality, respect and interest. The Fiesta program booklet indicated that due to occur one afternoon was a "Hockfight". I asked my Filipino companion if this was a typographical error, and should have been typed as "Cockfight". It wasn't clear if this was the case. In any event, the afternoon for the event duly came and all gathered in the usual cockfighting area of the village. Cockfighting is a Pinoy pastime with many Filipino men engaging in this activity. Referred to as '*Sabong*' in the local language, the fighting cocks are carried everywhere and a great deal of money changes hands with the associated betting that takes place on which cock will win. It is a "sport" that would be banned in any Western nation, the overall objective of it being for one fighting cock to kill the other. In Australia, for instance, such an event would create an outcry, such is the sensitivity of Australians in regards to any mistreatment of animals. Having said that, they are great meat eaters and have in general no qualms about countless cattle and fowl being slaughtered each month to feed their voracious appetite for fast-food hamburgers and chicken-burgers. Like the Australian attitude to death, what is kept hidden and sanitized does not create any problems. On attending the event, I was not able to watch the proceedings, just finding it all too gruesome. We discovered that a "Hockfight" was an all-in fight to the death between a number of cocks that were placed in the arena at the same time. The last cock remaining alive was declared the winner and its owner happily collected the pool of betting money. Observing from a distance, I observed that for the Filipino male such an event produces great excitement. It is a gory site. Cockfighting is a ritual involving the elements of life and death, of physical prowess, of triumph and defeat. It is a ritual fixed in the Filipino male psyche, especially in the provincial areas. In contrast to this gory ritual, the Filipino is, generally—speaking, a gentle and caring soul, who tends to avoid overt displays of aggression. While happily watching, and becoming excited by, the site of two animals tearing each other to death, the Filipino in their daily lives will tend to avoid overt displays of aggression. They are not by any means a nation of bloodthirsty people. Further to this, this gentleness and avoidance of aggression in the typical Filipino male is again contradicted by the homicide rate, which is high. Perhaps, for some, the cockfight is an outlet for natural male aggression, a catharsis. One can only speculate.

Apart from the pastime of cockfighting, commercial television is popular in the Philippines, with its seemingly never-ending broadcasting of drama, or rather melodrama, and variety entertainment programs. Filipinos are modest and prone to a sense of shame. When it comes to clothing, dress is usually modest and there are, apparently, no nudist beaches for instance in the Philippines. The strict moral taboos around such matters would prevent this. In 2009, the governor of the island of Cebu filed a lawsuit against the organizers and performers of a 'bikini contest.' For some inappropriate reason the 'bikini contest' was held during Holy Week. Now if Filipinos themselves cannot understand the sensitivities regarding Filipino culture and religion, then what hope have foreigners! In true Tagalog-drama fashion the 'bikini show' episode all ended in tears, with the actress involved issuing an apology. A newspaper report entitled 'Actress says sorry for bikini show' issued on February 19th, 2010, stated that a Manila-based entertainer shed tears in front of the Governor of Cebu as she apologized for a show held during last year's Holy Week.(25) "We, the undersigned respondents, would like to apologize to the people of Cebu for the wrong we have caused by our participation in and/or organization of the incident," the apology stated.(26) The show had invoked the governor to press charges against the organizers and performers. "We realize that the purposes and objectives of the laws have been transgressed and we undertake never to commit the same wrong again," the performers and organizers said.(27) For one of the participants involved her life changed after the governor filed the case. The 25-year-old show business star went back to college after the incident, and is no longer active in show business. The mother of one of the participants said she had not been informed on the nature of the show. Her daughter, she added, had texted her to complain that she was not comfortable with what the organizers asked, that is, to appear in a bikini.(28) There is still a strong moral vein in Philippine society.

The above incident reflects the clash of values within the Filipino culture, and an inherent tension between the old values and modernity, with its tendency to disregard religious convention, and host events such as 'bikini shows'. Holy Week is mentioned, whereby attention and thought is supposed to be given to religious and spiritual matters, so one could rightly question the appropriateness of such an event at that time. Despite this, the Filipino can never avoid that inherent need to socialize and celebrate, whatever the occasion or excuse.

The prohibition on exposed flesh and perceived vulgarity on a local level, and especially where the timing is inappropriate, such as during Holy Week, is in stark contrast to the commercial television variety entertainment programs. These are often vulgar, with the female dancers wearing the skimpiest of clothing and the tightest of shorts and engaging in sexually suggestive, pelvic-gyrating dance routines. Why would one want to complain, one might say! The general Filipino population seems to lap up this nonsense, especially if it has a style adopted from the West, which seems to justify everything. I really question this issue of imitation of Western culture and Western music and artistry. Within the Philippines, this imitation of all things Western is everywhere. I sometimes wonder if the term 'enslavement' might be more appropriate than the term imitation. For the Filipino, and the Filipino 'wannabe' singer or dancer or actor, American culture, or more specifically Hollywood culture, seems to embody all of what one should be. There is really less of an emphasis on individual creativity. On Filipino creativity. (Please note here, when I use the term Filipino I am referring to both genders, usually referred to in the manner of Filipino for the male and Filipina for the female, or Pinoy and Pinay.) There are a number of talent shows on Filipino television and they present a never-ending supply of acts of varying standards of performing ability. Some are dreadful, and some display real talent. The consistent thing appears to be the Westernization of the act. Artistry and creativity really ought to be about individual expression, within the unique cultural matrix of the Philippines, and including its native arts and music. Sadly, the enslavement to Western thought and entertainment values rules out any general expression of purely individual artistic expression. It is probably there, but it is not a part of the general or popular culture.

Despite the vulgarity present on television, and its acceptance as being part of 'entertainment', there are times in the Philippines, when, like the 'bikini show', things get out of hand and a storm is let loose. Even commercial television programs feel the wrath of both the public and government agencies, if they step over the line. It was the night of March 12th, 2011. One of the most popular variety entertainment programs on Philippine commercial television began, and there was no premonition about the storm that was about to break loose in regards to the content of the show. The show itself is often inane and vulgar. Presumably, Filipinos are used to that, but on this particular night things were judged to have gone too far. A subsequent newspaper article (29) reported: 'The Department of Social Welfare and Development (DSWD) has stepped into the controversy involving a television show . . . .', where a 6-year-old boy '. . . was made to dance in a lewd manner in exchange for P10,000. The DSWD said the incident that aired March 12 on TV5 is clear case of child abuse.'(30) The part of the show in question showed a young boy 'gyrating in a distasteful manner' and the audience and the host 'manifesting no evidence of concern or alarm for the child'. So ran the statement of the DSWD. The view was that the child had been subject to degrading and demeaning treatment. Problematic is the potential for exploitation in these situations. The participants in the show are paid money to perform. Big wads of money are handed out to those who take part and provide the 'entertainment'. The Philippines is an impoverished country, and participants in the show often come from a background of poverty. The young boy was seen to perform and dance like a 'macho dancer'. 'Macho dancing' in the Philippines is sometimes used as a code phrase for male prostitution. All in all, the performance by the young boy, the money given as an inducement, and the reportedly insensitive way that the host and the audience treated the boy, were deemed to have crossed the line in terms of good taste and appropriate treatment of a minor. The producers of the show and the management of the television station subsequently issued an apology. According to them, the boy has performed in the past in school programs and mall contests. Indeed, such "sexy dancing", as it is commonly referred to, is innocently enjoyed by Filipinos. The producers and management of the station expressed "profound regret for any insensitivity on their part, and wish to thank all those who have expressed concern. We are always grateful to be reminded of our obligations to the viewing public. In turn, we hope to make clear that the objective of the show has always been to bring joy and hope to Filipinos . . . .", the statement read.(31) The DSWD also advised that it was going to search for the boy's family, to determine the incident's effect on the child, and to see if the child and his parents required any counseling.(32) Naturally the contemporary modes of communication, the social media networks like Facebook and Twitter, were ablaze with comments and condemnation of the show. As a consequence of all this, the television show in question was removed from the air for a period of two weeks. One hopes that during the respite, those that normally viewed it perhaps picked up a nice book to read or watched a television program of educational value. The show is now back on air. The audience continues to shout and scream incessantly at what might be considered nonsense, the television networks make money from their commercials, and life goes on.

The Philippines is a "strictly Catholic" nation with an estimated 81–85% of the population belonging to this faith. It is reported that Filipinos adhere, can I say, religiously, to the tenets of the Catholic Church and its doctrines. The Philippines is one of the few nations worldwide where there is no divorce law. Pornography is illegal. Churches on a Sunday are crowded with worshippers. The stance of the Roman Catholic Church is clear in regards to homosexuality. It regards homosexuality as a sin and a perversion, an 'unnatural' form of behavior. 'Even if there is a genetic predisposition toward homosexuality (and studies on this point are inconclusive), the behavior remains unnatural because homosexuality is still not part of the natural design of humanity.' Further, 'The Catholic Church opposes homosexual activity because it is intrinsically disordered, an abuse of our human nature. (33) So preaches the Catholic Church. For the enlightened and rational person one would simply refer to the American Psychological Association, which stated, 'The research on homosexuality is very clear. Homosexuality is neither mental illness nor moral depravity. It is simply the way a minority of our population expresses human love and sexuality. Study after study documents the mental health of gay men and lesbians. Studies of judgment, stability, reliability, and social and vocational adaptiveness all show that gay men and lesbians function every bit as well as heterosexuals.' (34) In contradiction to the Church's dogmatic and negative stance on homosexuality, most Filipinos, despite being strongly Catholic, take a rational, enlightened and tolerant view of the matter. They seem fascinated by male homosexuals, who are usually effeminate and feminized in their appearance. This is in contrast to gay males in the West who, in general, seem mostly more masculine. I repeat, in general. The gays in the Philippines seem to congregate occupationally around the hairdressing and beauty salons. They are skilled at applying make-up and can appear very beautiful and feminine. I have a Filipino friend who is gay, and I mean *really* gay. He (she) goes to work to all intents and purposes as a woman, complete with earrings and artificial breasts. This is not that unusual amongst feminized homosexuals in the Philippines. Check your colleagues carefully! Myself and another masculine-looking, straight male friend, met him one day at his work, and then we planned to proceed to another appointment. He offered to take us there on his motorbike. I was laughing so much at the thought of a gay male complete with temporary breasts, a muscled straight Pinoy and a white foreigner whizzing down the street perched on an old motorbike that I begged off the offer deciding to walk instead. The local population would not have raised an eyebrow at such a sight, except maybe to ask themselves: "Why is that foreigner on such an old motorbike?" Foreigners are all rich, you see, and should only be seen traveling in SUVs, or so the thinking. There are numerous gay movie and entertainment stars, and "Miss Gay' pageants abound. Homosexuality seems generally well tolerated, and being gay in the local parlance is 'bakla'. My gay Filipino friend once invited me to a Miss Gay beauty pageant that was to take place at a beach resort. I was not able to attend the actual pageant but went to the resort the next day with my neighbors and a Filipino friend. It was a public holiday, so everyone wanted to get down to the beach, as is customary in the Philippines. My friend and I arrived there at around 9a.m. and it was already crowded. The resort was the typical tropical paradise location that the Philippines offers in such abundance. It was a glorious day, with the sun shining and generating a warmth that perfused one's bones and one's soul. It is difficult not to feel happy on such a day. The white sands of the beach ran in a crescent shape around the outline of the island. The seawater was clear and inviting, and the coconut trees and their foliage provided a gentle movement as visual manifestation of the invigorating tropical breeze. I have previously suffered from episodes of rheumatoid arthritis, at times being incapacitated by joint pain in my feet and hands, but this is the climate which warms my bones and joints and in which I feel most relaxed. I have not had any further significant joint pain since I have been living in the Philippines. Apart from the general public and my neighbors, all of the participants from the Miss Gay contest were there. These were men dressed up as women, with some looking beautiful. Different groups of people sat in various beach cottages around the beach area. The Filipino friend I was with is, like many Filipino men, muscled and masculine, and we had both been working out at the gym regularly so we had nicely defined physiques. We were walking around the resort, catching up with neighbors and friends. We walked near to the beach hut where a group of Miss Gay contestants, friends of my gay friend, were situated. They must have had a blast of a time the night before because they were in high spirits and still consuming alcohol. As my friend and I approached this group of queens they started pointing at us and shouting '*bakla, bakla*', which means '*you're gay, you're gay*'. I just could not stop laughing at this. As the old English saying goes, it was a clear case of 'the pot calling the kettle black.' (The notion that a claim someone is making about others applies equally to themselves.) Or as Shakespeare once wrote as he highlighted the irony of a '. . . raven that chides blackness'. I would have told them this but they would not have understood me, as many such sayings and idioms cannot be translated literally to another language. With my Australian/British accent, they would not have understood me anyway, but then neither would a lot of people in Australia. Especially after I've had a few beers. Presumably, they were just turning the tables and calling out to others what someone would call out to them, especially Filipino children, who like children anywhere, can be malicious in this regard. We met my gay friend a little later and he told me (it is always difficult to know whether to address the effeminate gays as he or she, but they do prefer the feminine form of address be used), that he placed 4th in the Miss Gay contest. He asked me to come over to the beach hut to meet his friends, that is, the ones who had been calling out to us. We begged off from this, knowing that, based on our earlier experience, we were not likely to become engaged in any intelligent or stimulating conversation with this group, who seemed confused about who is actually gay. It was a great day, and everyone had a good time. Presumably amongst this groups of 'gays' there are homosexuals, transsexuals and transvestites, and the full spectrum of sexual diversity. In all its behavioral richness, it would keep a sexologist happy in research for ages. Now there's an interesting job! Despite the strong Catholicism in the Philippines, Manila is often referred to as the gay capital of Asia. While the male homosexual seems to be generally well tolerated in daily Filipino life, is prominent in the arts and entertainment, and can flirt openly with a straight male contestant during a television talent show, the female homosexual, or "tomboy" has a much lower profile and seems to be less accepted in mainstream society. Vice Ganda is an openly gay Filipino entertainer. He has a very funny show which is broadcast on commercial television, and in which he often flirts with his straight guests, much to the delight of the audience and television viewers. His popularity is such that his Facebook site in 2010 was reported to have over one million fans, more than any other Filipino entertainer or public figure.(35) And so we have another contradiction: the Philippines is a strongly catholic nation but homosexuality is widely accepted.

As I write this I am in an isolated province on one of the islands in the geographical center of the Philippines. It is one of the most undeveloped and poorest regions of the country. I am sponsoring two of the children from a family who reside in this region through High School. It is always good to get down here to see them, and to find out how there studies are going. Education is the golden key to the future. Traveling here from the main city on the island afforded a spectacular view of rolling hills, wide-open meadows and land that has been used for agricultural production for millennia. It is a place where horseback is still the regular mode of transport, and the carabao is the beast of burden, the equivalent of the mechanical tractor in more technically advanced regions. I passed on the way a man and a woman who were on horseback, the man attired in the type of cowboy hat that is commonly used in the region, and the woman at his back holding up an umbrella to stave off the penetrating rays of the sun. Agriculture, cattle breeding and fishing are the only significant industries. I traveled here by trail bike. The roads leading to this area are the usual patchwork of good roads, potholed roads and trails covered in dust or mud, depending on whether it has rained or not. It was a magnificent and fun ride. As part of writing a book about the Philippines, I wanted to experience the land and the elements in their rawest form. To experience the punishing rays of the sun, the ferocity and cleansing sensation of the monsoonal rains, the freshness of the coastal wind. Just in a very small measure to capture what the workers on this land here have experienced facing the elements every day of their lives. The life of the villages here is different to the urban centers, and the big cities like Manila or Cebu or Davao. Some areas have no electricity at all; other areas have a local electricity generator, and an electricity supply that runs from 5p.m. to 11p.m. or midnight. There is limited cell phone coverage, and the internet, by any form, be it via landline or wireless transmission is usually not available. The life is so simple, so uncomplicated, and with the strong moral code that has always characterized Filipino behavior. At the *barangay* (local) dances and social events there is segregation of the sexes. Males and females do not sit together socially unless they are romantically committed or betrothed. The taboo is actually on males and females who are not formally committed to each other dancing together. I have had the experience of attending these events and for the foreigner dancing with other men may seem strange at first, but is actually a lot of fun. In the innocent sensual way of the Filipino, and in their never-ending imitation of Western art and popular culture, there is also lot of what is referred to here are "sexy dancing", even with the other men or with brothers. The men will be dancing with the men, and the women with the women, such is the caution one exercises about transgressing the moral code prohibiting loose relationships between male and female. Unlike the city, where one can live in relative anonymity, one can never escape in these places observation by one's neighbors and family, and censure if the strict moral code is transgressed. One's standing in the community will then be damaged and one will feel shame, as will one's family. I find places like this wonderful to escape to. The pressures, noise, and pollution of the major urban centers is gone. There is sporadic civil unrest here, especially at election time, and a very low-grade chronic conflict between armed groups around the island and the police. On this island the police and the local armed groups play a cat and mouse, sometimes deadly, game of sporadic confrontation. It is not clear whether these groups have a purely ideological agenda, and are aligned with communist-inspired revolutionary movements, like the New People's Army, which is still active, or are just criminal gangs. There are probably groupings of both. Where confrontations occur with these groups, and the police deem a more forceful response is needed, the local military move in and they have some serious firepower. Foreigners are not usually specifically targeted by any insurgent groups outside of certain areas of Mindanao. I have felt completely free to move around, for instance on the island on which I reside, as I please, without any incident. Like any other country on this planet one may fall victim to crime, but I do not feel at all threatened, and I always rely on the good advice of locals as to safety issues.

In discussing Filipino culture in general, one has to comment on the Catholic Church and the hold the Church has had over the thinking of Filipinos. This influence appears to have been gradually weakening, and in fact, it is likely that Filipinos visit their Facebook page far more often nowadays than they do their local church. The piousness, and degree of religious devotion of the old days seems to have gone, and one sees the practice of the Novena in the home, for instance, occurring far less frequently.(36) The Philippine national hero, Dr Jose Rizal, was a man of enormous intellect, passion and literary skill. He is revered within the Philippines. He was also a Freemason. He renounced Catholicism, although a debate still rages as to whether or not at the end of his life, just prior to his execution, he reconfirmed his Catholic faith.

My own first experience dealing with the Philippine Catholic Church in a formal capacity was not a positive experience. It occurred in 1981. I met and planned to marry a Filipina and being a British subject, I was not yet a naturalized Australian, required what is referred to as a 'Certificate of No Impediment'. Many others of British nationality wanting to marry a Filipina have had to go through this requirement too. I am a protestant and not part of the Catholic faith, while my future wife was. This required going through a number of bureaucratic hoops which the Catholic put in place in order for a protestant to marry a catholic here in the Catholic Church in the Philippines. One of these was that I sign a document to the effect that any offspring we produced would be raised as a Catholic. I had no problems with this directive. The Catholic schools in Australia provide a very high standard of education. (Our daughter, Jade, a *mestiza*, was subsequently educated in the Catholic School system, and graduated from a private Catholic school, Our Lady of Sion College, in Melbourne. She received a fine education). Visiting the local priest charged with the responsibility of signing the authorization certificate for the marriage to proceed, I was advised to return the following Sunday after the Certificate of No Impediment and other necessary local documents were obtained. I clarified that I would return to his seminary the following Sunday at 4p.m., with all necessary documents, and the priest would then provide the necessary authorization for the ceremony to take place. All seemed in order. That week was a whirlwind of activity. I proceeded to Manila to attend the British embassy to obtain the Certificate of No Impediment and also local arrangements for the marriage proceeded. The Sunday of the following week arrived and, as previously arranged, I proceeded to the seminary in order to present the documents that were required for the priest to issue the necessary authorization. I arrived at the time appointed and, as is usual, was greeted by a young man who was acting as an assistant to the priest. I explained that I was in attendance due to an appointment being made the previous week with the priest in order for a document to be signed by him. The assistant proceeded to the quarters of the priest. He returned shortly thereafter and stated: "Father is not able to see you. He has been swimming this afternoon and he is tired". Being a foreigner and not used to being treated in such a disrespectful fashion, and appalled by the laziness and rudeness of the priest in question, I made it clear that I was there because of an appointment being made with the priest. If there was no other reason than him being tired, then this was unacceptable. I expected the document I needed to be signed, and I would not leave until this had occurred. The assistant returned to the priest's quarters and some five minutes later came back to me, with the signed document that I required. The priest in question did not appear to pass on his regards or wishes, or to perhaps offer a little prayer for the forthcoming marriage. Unbelievable one might say. However, it did happen. Moreover, surprisingly, it is likely that Filipinos, out of deference to the position of the priest, would have accepted such a situation and left without protest. It was my first introduction to the looseness in which appointments are made and kept in the Philippines, and my first introduction to the laziness and arrogance of some of the clergy here.

My fiancée was at that time a civilian employee of the Philippine Air Force, and worked on the Air Force base in Mactan, Cebu. Surprisingly, I found her superiors and other military personnel to be far more supportive in our plans to get married than the local Catholic bureaucracy. Her department commander was a true officer and gentleman. He had previously arranged for me to stay at the staff quarters of an Air force base in Manila, while I was there to make initial enquiries at the British Embassy about the obtaining of the 'Certificate of No Impediment'. In addition, he provided a letter of introduction for me to the staff at the base. He also apologized that it was not possible at that time for me to fly to Manila on an Air Force transport plane, which made regular shuttle trips to Manila. He did everything one could to assist and be supportive. One finds, the longer one stays in the Philippines, that contradictions abound everywhere. And this was another example. I would have expected it to be the Catholic Church rather than the military, which is often maligned, to be the supportive institution, but the opposite was the case. The Filipino traits of kindness and hospitality, and respect for foreigners and visitors, was manifest in my dealings with the military as employers of my fiancée. For the most part these traits were lacking in the members of the Catholic Church whom I had to deal with. Perhaps these human traits were there, but hidden by the rigid doctrines and bureaucracy of the Church.

It is not clear sometimes just how the priest of today can exercise his role and functions in contemporary Philippine society, with its loosening of morals, its preoccupation with all things sensual, and its decline in piousness and in religious observance. I mention my own experience above in 1981, which highlighted for me just how lazy and inconsiderate some of the clergy in the Philippines can be. As for some other priests, it is just not clear at all as to what they are getting up to. The case below came to light in 2010. I do not include the priest's name because I feel that would be insensitive to his family and to those who knew him to do so, due to the questionable circumstances of his death. On 14 April

2010, in Cebu, a 52-year-old priest was found dead inside a motel room. He was alone when found, at approximately 7:00 p.m. in room 426 of the motel, with only his briefs on. Two young women approached the Inn security guard to report that the guest at room 426 had had a heart attack, and the door was ajar. It was reported that they then immediately left. One woman wore pants and t-shirt while another wore shorts and a blouse. They were aged aged between age 23-26 years. The security guard found the priest lying on the bed, partly covered with blanket. No signs of a struggle were evident. The priest checked in to the motel at 5:45 p.m. and, oddly, gave the alias of "Al Villa". He also recorded that he was from Davao City, not Cebu, and paid P535 for an overnight stay. Reportedly, one hour earlier he begged off from attending the reception of a baptism he had administered because he had to rush to an appointment at 6 p.m. His personal driver for 19 years said that the priest was with a sacristan when he dropped them off in SM City to eat "*halo-halo*" (an ice cream and fruit mixed beverage). The priest was ordained on 18 December 1986. It was later reported that he was a frequent guest at the motel. It was also stated that the priest stayed there when his appointment ends late, and does not want to bother the security guards in the rectory. He also slept in the motel when repairs were being done in the rectory or when the air-conditioning unit in the rectory was broken.(37) One is given the impression that the priesthood live a very comfortable existence. This is in contrast to the Filipino masses that exist in abject poverty and have to feed, clothe, educate and care for large numbers of children due to the stance of the Catholic Church on birth control. If there was any association between the priest and the two women who were present at the motel, and some assume that there was, then I make no judgment in regards to the priest. But I would criticize the Catholic Church, who obligate men to maintain the unnatural state of celibacy. A local Cardinal who knew the priest was later interviewed and stated that there were no suspicious circumstances surrounding the priest's death, however, he admitted that many priests have violated their vow of celibacy.(38) Priests are human after all, and this should come as no surprise as to what the cardinal is saying. Especially when one turns on the television and is met with the site of a skimpily-clad female gyrating her pelvis next to the camera. Day after day.

It would be easier to accept the stance of the Catholic Church in regards to birth control and family planning if the church provided full material support to those huge numbers of Filipinos who are born due to its absence. If they said to the mothers and fathers of those burdened in poverty with large families, "It's no problem, we will clothe and feed and educate your children". However, this does not happen. The bearing of even one child is a huge and awesome responsibility. Imagine this responsibility magnified many times over. It is also a huge and awesome responsibility *for the nation*. Despite the Catholic Church doing everything it can in the Philippines to prevent effective birth control, and place men and women in a position of control in regards to how many children they can afford, the majority of the clergy of the Church enjoy a comfortable lifestyle with none of the worries or responsibilities of parenthood. It actually must also be said that not only the Church, but also the ordinary Filipino to some extent reinforces this stance through a "macho" culture. Often the Filipino will consider his macho reputation enhanced if he fathers a large number of children. Yes, even some out of wedlock! Therefore, in all fairness, it must be said that there is a cultural reinforcer of being seen to be manly by having large numbers of children, independent of Catholic Church dogma against birth control. The main person then responsible for the caring of the children falls to the mother and, as the children grow up, then it falls in some part to the older children of the brood. It is typical of the Filipino male to then, on finishing work, to drink with his drinking buddies, and discuss at length what seem to be inconsequential matters with them. It certainly is not a constructive use of time, and the author is amazed at how long the Filipino can continue to talk and to drink in the one session. I commented on this to my friend, a Filipino, and he stated, "Yes, this is the culture here". It is a culture that really needs to change. In further reference to the Pinoy and his "macho" image, the keeping of mistresses is common, and, especially within the higher echelons of society, this occurs frequently and appears to be the norm. "Pinoy macho" is a behavioral trait that is often apparent.

The educational system in the Philippines is modeled on that of America, and the teachers are well trained, highly competent and highly motivated. In spite of their efforts to instill in their charges education as a life-long pursuit there seems to be an abrupt end to learning for most Filipinos when they leave school. The books and reading are neglected, and the male will often spend his time with his drinking buddies, simply drinking and talking. Sadly, the works of Rizal seem to be then forgotten, and intellectual pursuits abandoned. One would attempt to argue that perhaps with the poverty endemic in the Philippines there is little money to spare for books or further education; however, there always seems to be money available for, and always a ready supply, of alcohol. I lived in a provincial town that had a number of stores that sold second-hand books. For those that might say that the Philippines is a poor nation and there is not the money available for adults to buy books then I reject such an assertion completely. It is not consistent with the facts. The cost of buying second-hand or even new books is comparable to that of buying alcohol. It is just the choices that people make. Moreover, for those that might say that it is a foreigner that is making such an assertion, and he should mind his own business, then this too I reject. This is what other Filipinos have stated to me, that they feel annoyed when they see how much drinking and squandering of time by their compatriots goes on.

One sees one of the adverse consequences of poverty and explosive population growth in the street children one encounters when out and about. As a foreigner, or "long nose", one is conspicuous and often approached by street children who ask for money. In the provincial town where I have resided, they will approach one and hold their hands out imploring money. They will address one as "*kuya*" which means in the local language "older brother". I am, at the time of writing this book, 56 years of age, so being called the equivalent of older brother is nice. Sometimes one is called "*tito*" which means uncle. These titles are also used in an honorary capacity when one is "adopted" into local Filipino families. Some venture to use their English, and address older foreigners as "dad". The author will be very unhappy when it gets to the point when he is addressed as "*lolo*", which means grandfather! I like anyone who calls me *"kuya"!* I very rarely give money to the street children. My Filipino companion informed me that these kids would sometimes gamble with the money, or use it to purchase solvents, which they are addicted to and inhale to get high, or to suppress the hunger that they constantly feel. I carry with me a "goodies bag", in which I have a number of food snacks and a drink taped together and give this little package to the kids that ask for something. One has to be careful and be aware of how many children are around, because if there are not enough goodies packs to go around, disputes will occur among the children as to who gets what. This is a heart-wrenching sight, to see these deprived children fighting over limited foodstuffs. They invariably take what is offered with gratitude, and then beat a hasty retreat. I have wondered about this and speculate that it is protective behavior, both to run to a quiet place to devour the food, and instinctive protection in case the doner has some ulterior motive, or some "strings attached" to the gift. I refer here to the disgraceful behavior of foreigners, and locals, who engage in pedophilia. Illustrative of this, and only one example, relates to the case of a 78-year-old Australian man. Philippine police reported that they had arrested the 78-year-old man, and that he was going to be charged with sexually abusing local girls who resided with him. He had allegedly been abusing as many as seven girls who were with him in his house. The man was a long-time resident of an isolated area in Cebu. The punishment for such offences is 25 years in jail, so for this male, if so convicted, he will spend the rest of this life behind bars. (39) This report highlights the dark side of the foreigner presence in the Philippines, where the relationship to the people here is exploitative, and where foreigners can use their wealth and charisma for inappropriate and sinister ends. More recently, individuals and syndicates have begun exploiting modern technologies such as the Internet. There have been cases reported of foreigners setting up enterprises whereby children have been engaged to do sex web-cam shows, which are transmitted over the internet to other countries. Fortunately, the police investigate and prosecute aggressively such enterprises. Pedophilia is a global phenomenon, and there is reportedly a huge global network of males engaged in this practice. Third world countries like the Philippines are vulnerable. Police services internationally work in a collaborative way to stem this menace. The vast majority of foreigners, however, are obviously law-abiding and make a significant contribution to the economy by living in the Philippines.

One of the endearing things about Filipinos is their sense of humor, and in all things, they will find something to laugh at. It is a survival mechanism, and one of the ways their *joy de vivre* is expressed. They have jokes for everything. In regards to their poor sense of time and shoddy appointment keeping, they joke: How do you know you are at a Filipino party? The answer is that you turn up an hour late and there is still no one there. Moreover, when you arrive there is enough food to feed the Philippines. In regards to the chaotic situation of households, and the huge extended families, they joke that someone is always in the kitchen cleaning up. You are not sure if it's the maid or a relative, but you kiss them on the cheek anyway. Filipino houses are unmistakable, because you see a huge fork and spoon on the wall, a framed picture of the Last Supper, a huge Santo Nino, and a barrel man. You can't even get through the door because there's a pile of 50 shoes blocking the way. (It is a common custom to take off one's shoes when entering a Filipino household. Some house-owners will insist the visitor or foreigner not do this, but I always do, viewing their removal as respectful to the house-owner and to local custom. Don't forget to wear nice clean socks each day!) When the party starts, they begin singing "Peelings" on the karaoke. This is a good-natured dig at the difficulty some Filipinos have in articulating an F sound. (The Abakada alphabet of the Tagalog language has no letter F.) Everyone in the Philippines has a nickname (even the President, who happens to be called "Noynoy"), or an initialized contraction of their Christian names. At parties you will invariably be introduced to "JP, JJ, JT, TJ, DJ, AJ, RJ, LJ, Lingling, Bingbing, Tingting, Wengweng, Bongbong, and Dongdong. When the party is in full swing, the men will be watching the Pacquiao fight on the illegal cable boxes on the 70" LCD in the movie room. (In the Philippines electricity and cable TV wires are often illegally split to feed various households and families. This is a particularly dangerous practice when it comes to electrical wiring, and is the cause of numerous fires. The LCD TV is a status symbol.) Most families have at least one

OFW relative, and they joke about the calls often made between the OFW and home. The OFW has obviously been sending money back, to set up the various commonly established businesses in the Philippines.

"*Husband*: hon musta ang tindahan? (Honey, how's the store?)
Wife: dept store na! (It's a department store now.)
Husband: ang tuba-an? (The coconut liquor business?)
Wife:: KTV bar na! (It's a Karoaoke bar now!)
Husband: mga trickad? (And the passenger motor tricycles?)
Wife: taxi na! (We have a taxi now!)
Husband: ang dalawa kong anak? (the two children?)
Wife: LIMA na! (There's five now!)

Spending a lot of their lives using the cell phone Filipinos could not overlook the opportunity to joke about their various cell phone payment methods. They ask, what is the difference between a girlfriend, a call girl and a wife? The answer is: Post paid, Pre paid, Unlimited.

For the Filipino there is no subject that is not taboo from poking fun at. Political jokes are also rife. In addition, the Filipino would know that, just as in any other nation, the problem with political jokes is that they sometimes get elected. In everyday situations in the Philippines there is often the opportunity for humor, even black humor, which Filipinos don't shy away from. I can remember one incident and this relates to the elaborate funerals that are provided for relatives. In Philippine towns and cities often the funerals mourners can be seen, long lines of people with umbrellas up to protect from the tropical sun or rain, following the hearse as it makes its way along the main street of the town. This offers local residents a chance to say goodbye to the deceased. The funeral cars here, the hearses, are often large, old American vehicles that one associates with the Elvis Presley era and Graceland. Those 1960's huge and elaborate gas-guzzling monoliths. I was out walking one day and one of these vehicles passed me buy. It was a huge, white, ornate, American hearse with elaborate coachwork dating from the 1960's. I remember thinking to myself as it passed: "*I wouldn't be seen dead in that*". Filipinos would appreciate that kind of humor.

Filipinos are exceptionally clean people. It is utterly amazing to see from the lowliest village in the province, from a house that is little more than a Nipa Hut, emerge sparkling clean children starting off on their way to school. It is an embarrassment to me to see how some foreigners in comparison, who come from wealthy nations and have the means to travel, appear in contrast so unclean and poorly dressed! Despite the hot temperatures and the lack of money for deodorants that are commonly used in the West, it is very rare to smell body odor in the Philippines. Using the toilets or "CR", Comfort Room, as it is commonly known, can present a challenge. They are often in a dreadful state. Often there is no capacity to flush the cistern, and if water is available, one uses a scoop to flush one's business away. Urine usually is just left to sit there, and often there is not much concern displayed about thorough washing of one's hands after using the toilet. I'm an ex-RN and I get on everyone's nerves by reminding them to wash their hands repeatedly. The best and cleanest public toilets can be found in places like Makati in Manila, and the worst in the rural areas with often little more than an open pit serving as the CR. Filipino men have not the slightest inhibition of urinating in public, whether drunk or not, and can often be seen at the side of the road emptying their bladders. This makes sense when one may be charged a few pesos for using a shopping mall CR. The price increases if one needs to defecate. So the moral of the story for the visiting foreigner is to always use the hotel dunny (Australian slang for CR) before you head out sightseeing for the day.

After eating a meal, which in the Philippines almost always consists of meat in some form, Filipinos have an annoying habit of sucking through their teeth in an attempt to dislodge strands of meat that may be stuck there. They also may use toothpicks and engage in cleaning there teeth, with their mouths fully open. In conjunction with this, there is the intermittent noise of sucking through their teeth. Peanuts are the other food which seem to drive Filipinos to engage in this teeth-sucking behavior. On regular domestic airline flights, to my consternation, peanuts were given out to the passengers, and one had to endure, apart from the usual discomforts of mass transportation, the annoying noise of Pinoys happily engaged in clearing the particles of peanuts stuck between their teeth. For anyone who, like me, suffers from the "4S syndrome"—Selective Sound Sensitivity Syndrome—that is, a syndrome in which certain noises are perceived to be extremely irritating and annoying, this can be a trial.(40) Filipinos are also prone to eating frequent 'snacks' during the day. These snacks take a multitude of forms, from bread and pastries to burgers or corn chips, from eggs to noodles or fried banana. Sometimes, all of those together too. Whatever might be readily available. For those who can afford it, they eat snacks before breakfast and after breakfast and then before lunch and after lunch, indeed throughout the whole day. It can get quite out of hand, reaching the point where you might ask someone happily munching, "Is that your snack?' To which they may reply, "No, it's my snack before I have my snack." An acquaintance of mine once advised me that he only ate one slice of bread for breakfast. Being duly impressed with the self-control and iron will of this individual who denied himself food, I was later disillusioned. He could be seen before and after breakfast eating 'snacks', but these do not seem to be counted in one's 'official' food intake. One can boast as to the simplicity and lightness of one's diet, while at the same time engaging in the consumption of large amounts of calories 'on the side!'

Sociability and gregariousness is characteristic of the Filipino. They are highly sociable and highly hospitable people. They need to frequently have fun, to laugh and celebrate. The karaoke is perennial, and the Filipino loves to sing. When we are discussing here such cultural and behavioral traits, this is what can be referred to as the 'mindset' of Filipinos. It is the same as discussing the mindset of the Germans when we talk about their propensity for preciseness, and the mindset of the Japanese who must be at a meeting *before* it is scheduled to begin. It is no accident that I have mentioned two nations, Germany and Japan, who happen to be two of the most economically prosperous and dynamic nations in history, and it is my contention that such economic success is determined, at least in part, by the mindset of its population. Prior to any further discussion of this point, let us define our terms first. Wikipedia, the internet based encyclopedia, defines the phrase and concept of mindset in the following way: 'In decision theory and general systems theory, a mindset is a set of assumptions, methods or notations held by one or more people or groups of people, which is so established that it creates a powerful incentive within these people or groups to continue to adopt or accept prior behaviors, choices or tools. This phenomenon of cognitive bias is also sometimes described as *mental inertia*, "groupthink" or a "paradigm", and it is often difficult to counteract its effects upon analysis and decision-making processes."(41) Further to this, the phrase 'global mindset' has come into common parlance in business. The Financial Times Lexicon defines this term in the following way: 'In a company with a global mindset, people view cultural and geographic diversity as opportunities to exploit and are prepared to adopt successful practices and good ideas wherever they come from. The twin forces of ideological change and technology revolution are making globalization one of the most important issues facing companies today.'(42) The author was present at a live telecast of the boxing match, between Manny Pacquiao and Shane Mosley in 2011, at a sports hall in a Philippine city. Justifiably proud of this Filipino boxing master the place was jam-packed with Filipinos all eager to see their hero in action. I appeared to be the only foreigner present and the crowd would have, as usual, assumed I was an American—an "*Americano*". Yes, we all look the same! I was seated in the upper rows of the stadium and surveyed below me the mass of people crowded together. One is again struck in such situations, in contrast with the West, with the lack of differences in hair color. All hair on their heads black, all features uniform, whereas in the West people come in all colors! With ginger, blonde, black and 'mousy' colored hair. I must have stuck out like a sore thumb with my white skin and 'long nose'. Despite the boxing match between the two nations, between a Filipino and an American, there was no sense of tension or hostility towards me as a foreigner at all. One of the first things that happened when I sat down was that the Filipinos who were sitting in front of me offered me a drink. "Have a drink, brother", they said as I took my seat. I did not know these people but Filipinos cannot help being hospitable. One encounters such friendliness and hospitality everywhere in the Philippines. Manny Pacquiao won the boxing match that day, again through a faultless display of exceptional skill and natural athletic talent.

This, complemented by a superb trainer, Freddie Roach, who happens to be an American, has led Manny Pacquiao from the depths of childhood poverty to a rich, famous and illustrious boxing career, and election to the House of Representatives of the Philippine government. He displays none of the "shyness" that many other Filipinos have towards foreigners or of learning from foreigners. He has literally fought his way to the top of his career. He instinctively understands that one learn one's craft from whoever it is that has something to teach. He has displayed a ferocious appetite for success, and has pursued his goals with an iron will. In short, Manny Pacquiao, in addition to his extraordinary physical talent, has a **mindset** that is necessary for success.

What then can we conclude from our discussion above? In addition, how can we link these conclusions to the economy of the nation, for instance? Filipinos generally display behaviors, thought processes and a mindset that are not adaptive to the economic conditions of the 21st century. They, in general, have a poorly defined concept of time and of precision, and with a few exceptions, they have not the same degree of hunger for business or the innate business acumen of the Chinese or Japanese or Germans. In addition to this, there is a strong sense of complacency about the current predicament of the Philippines within its population, and no sense of urgency about what needs to be done. It may be easier to call this complacency demoralization, as the nation has been let down time and time again by officials who abuse the trust invested in them by the populace. The Philippine economy will limp along, principally due to the crutch provided by overseas Filipino workers. The remittances they provide are a significant contributor to the Filipino economy, however future overseas labor market demands and conditions may be subject to change, and one should not rely on this source of national income. It is likely that the downward slide of the Filipino economy relative to other economies will continue, unless the brave efforts of certain public officials to introduce a culture of efficiency and business models adopted from overseas is widened. The other critical factor is overseas investment, which is badly needed. Catastrophic natural events, a military coup, or a weakening overseas labor market or the global economy, will weaken and damage the

Filipino economy further. That is unless, of course, the coup leader is a selfless and incorruptible individual who has the capacity to drive the country out of its complacency and change the current mindset. Alternatively, if Filipinos actually adopt the mindset of Manny Pacquiao, showing no fear of confronting the world, of learning from anyone who may have something to offer, of displaying enormous self-discipline and self-confidence, of fighting their way up from the lowest position to the highest, and of meeting foreigners on equal terms without any sense of inferiority, then things might change.

There is hope. There are corporations like the low cost airlines, who operate according to first world standards, and if they can, then so can every other business in the Philippines. There are individuals like Manny Pacquiao, who can become a world champion, and from lowly beginnings become rich and influential and fear no man. There are suburbs like Makati in Manila that are extremely clean and orderly and organized. It will take extraordinary leadership, it will take enormous determination, it will take a fair bit of luck, and it will take the conscious changing of a current mindset that has led to economic decline, and is characterized by complacency, diffuseness of thought, sociability as opposed to a strong work ethic, and courage to face the world as equals. It will, in addition to this, require rational and effective economic planning and, *first and foremost,* appropriate measures to contain population growth. This will require the current government to face down the Catholic Church, and its inappropriate attempts in meddling in the affairs of state. As the Philippine constitution states 'The separation of Church and State is inviolable.' Period. The Philippines must set in place clear and strong boundaries, within political life, between institutions, between the Church and State and between the military and the State. Moreover, it must incorporate values and concepts that are adaptive and necessary to competing in a global economy in the 21st Century.

The economic damage incurred from sustained high population growth is significant, and the environmental damage, directly or indirectly, enormous. The issues of food provision and food security on a national level are yet to be appropriately addressed or remedied, and with the country now a major importer of its staple food, rice, with a growing population the nation is placed in a highly vulnerable situation. Food and energy security, as we will detail in chapter 3, are compromised. As also discussed in the passages above, where families have high numbers of children, those children are predisposed to under-achievement through either limited educational opportunities, cognitive impairment subsequent to the high levels of noise and chaotic environments, or physical and neuronal damage through malnutrition. There also needs to be thought given on a national level about adult role models and what examples and behaviors are needed to display to children, so that they will see and imitate adults engaged in lifelong reading, study, appreciation of the arts, and continuous self-realization.

CHAPTER 2

The Unlucky Country—a land plagued by natural and man-made disasters.

> KEY POINT: In addition to the nation being economically handicapped by its archipelagic form, it is also handicapped by frequent disasters, both man-made and natural.

THE SECOND LARGEST volcanic eruption of the twentieth century took place in the Philippines, on the island of Luzon, and only 90 kilometers northwest of the capital city of Manila. Up to 800 people were killed and 100,000 became homeless following the Mount Pinatubo blast, which climaxed with nine hours of eruption on June 15, 1991. On that day, millions of tons of sulfur dioxide were discharged into the atmosphere. As a consequence, there was a decrease in the temperature worldwide over the next few years.(1) The Mount Pinatubo eruption was a catastrophic event and its effects were felt globally.

To give some background details in regards to Mount Pinatubo, it is part of a chain of composite volcanoes along the Luzon arc on the west coast of the island. Luzon is the largest of the islands of the Philippines. This arc of volcanoes is due to the subduction of the Manila trench to the west. The Mount Pinatubo volcano experienced major eruptions approximately 500, 3000, and 5500 years ago. The word itself, 'Pinatubo', means, 'made to grow' in Tagalog. There is an oral tradition amongst local people suggestive of a folk memory of earlier large eruptions. This ancient legend tells of *Bacobaco* 'the terrible spirit of the sea', who could metamorphose into a huge turtle and who threw fire from his mouth. When being chased by the spirit hunters, *Bacobaco* fled to the mountain and dug a great hole in its summit showering the surrounding land with rock, mud, dust and fire for three days; howling so loudly that the earth shook. The word may also be construed as meaning 'culturing grounds'. An indigenous group of people, the *Aetas*, had lived on the slopes of the volcano and in surrounding areas for several centuries, having fled the lowlands to escape persecution by the Spanish. They were a hunter-gatherer people and they were extremely skilled in surviving in the dense jungles of the area.(2) The events of the 1991 Mount Pinatubo eruption began in July 1990, when a magnitude 7.8 earthquake occurred 100 kilometers northeast of the Pinatubo region, determined to be a result of its reawakening. In mid–March 1991, villagers living in the area began feeling earthquakes, and this prompted vulcanologists to study the mountain. There were approximately 30,000 people living on the flanks of the volcano prior to the disaster. On April 2, small explosions from vents dusted local villages with ash. It was the early signs of a catastrophe about to unfold. The first evacuations of 5,000 people were ordered later that month. Further earthquakes and explosions continued. On June 5, a Level 3 alert was issued for two weeks due to the possibility of a major eruption. Volcanic activity and eruptions are measured on a scale of 1 to 5, with 1 indicating typical background surface activity, to number 5 indicating hazardous large volcanic eruption in progress.(3) The extrusion of a lava dome on June 7 led to the issuance of a Level 5 alert on June 9, indicating an eruption was in progress. An evacuation area 20 kilometers away from the volcano was established, and 25,000 people were evacuated. Clark Air Base was a massive and strategically important U.S military installation located near the volcano. America had placed its forces in the Philippines to allow it to project its power and influence into the Asian region. The 'unsinkable aircraft carrier' that the Philippines represented was about to be shook mightily. And Americans too would be caught up in this demonstration of nature venting its capricious fury. The Clark Air Base had to be evacuated on June 10th. The 18,000 personnel and their families were transported to Subic Bay Naval Station, and most were returned to the United States. On June 12, the danger radius was extended to 30 kilometers from the volcano resulting in the total evacuation of 58,000 people. On June 15, the eruption of Mount Pinatubo began at 1:42 p.m. local time. It lasted for nine hours. There transpired numerous large earthquakes due to the collapse of the summit of Mount Pinatubo and the creation of a caldera. A caldera is a large, usually circular depression, at the summit of a volcano, formed when magma is withdrawn or erupted from a shallow underground magma reservoir. The removal of large volumes of magma may result in loss of structural support for the overlying rock, thereby leading to collapse of the ground and formation of a large depression.(4) The caldera reduced the peak from 1745 meters to 1485 meters high. It is 2.5 kilometers in diameter. Thus, the event had transformed the very shape of the mountain itself. Coincidentally, at the time of the eruption Tropical Storm Yunya was passing 75 kilometers to the northeast of Mount Pinatubo, causing a large amount of rainfall in the region. The ash that was ejected from the volcano mixed with the water vapor in the air to cause a rainfall of fragments of volcanic rock and ash, referred to as tephra, that fell across almost the entire island of Luzon. The greatest thickness of ash deposited, 33 centimeters, occurred approximately 10.5 kilometers southwest of the volcano. There was 10 centimeters of ash covering an area of 2000 square kilometers. Most of the estimated 200 to 800 people who died during the eruption were actually killed by the indirect effect of the weight of the ash collapsing roofs and killing the occupants of the buildings. Had Tropical Storm Yunya not been nearby, the death toll from the volcano would have been much lower. So there occurred on that day a terrible synergistic effect between the volcanic eruption and a passing storm. In addition to the ash, Mount Pinatubo ejected between 15 and 30 million tons of sulfur dioxide gas. Sulfur dioxide mixes with water and oxygen in the atmosphere to become sulfuric acid, which in turn triggers ozone depletion. A total mass of sulfur dioxide (SO_2) of about 17 million tons was ejected. This is the largest volume ever recorded by modern instruments. Over 90% of the material released from the volcano was ejected during the nine hour eruption of June 15. The eruption plume of Mount Pinatubo's various gases and ash reached high into the atmosphere within two hours of the eruption, attaining an altitude of 34 kilometers high and over 400 kilometers wide. This eruption was the largest disturbance of the stratosphere since the eruption of Krakatau in 1883. The aerosol cloud spread around the Earth in a period of two weeks and covered the planet within a year. The stratospheric cloud from the eruption persisted in the atmosphere for three years. During 1992 and 1993, the ozone hole over Antarctica reached an unprecedented size. Satellite measurements of ash and aerosol emissions from Mount Pinatubo confirmed that the eruption had a significant effect on ozone levels in the atmosphere, causing a large increase in the destruction rate of ozone. Ozone levels at mid-latitudes reached their lowest recorded levels, while in the southern hemisphere winter of 1992, the ozone hole over Antarctica reached its largest ever size until then, with the fastest recorded ozone depletion rates being measured. There was an eruption of Mount Hudson in Chile in August 1991, and this also contributed to southern hemisphere ozone destruction. Measurements demonstrated a sharp decrease in ozone levels at the tropopause, which is the boundary between the troposphere and the stratosphere, occurring between in altitude from approximately 8 kilometers at the poles of the Earth to approximately 18 kilometers at the equator, when the aerosol clouds from Pinatubo and Hudson arrived. Again, synergistic effects occurred to worsen the destruction. The cloud from the eruption that was over the Earth had the effect of reducing global temperatures. In 1992 and 1993, the average temperature in the Northern Hemisphere was reduced 0.5 to 0.6°C, and the entire planet was cooled 0.4 to 0.5°C. The maximum reduction in global temperature took place in August 1992 with a reduction of 0.73°C. Such is the precision with which these events can be measured today. The eruption is believed to have influenced such events as 1993 floods along the Mississippi river and the drought in the Sahel region of Africa. The United States experienced its third coldest and third wettest summer in 77 years during 1992. Overall, the cooling effects of the Mount Pinatubo eruption were greater than those of the El Niño that was taking place at the time, or of the greenhouse gas warming of the planet.(5) There were remarkable sunrises and sunsets visible around the globe in the years following the Mount Pinatubo eruption. Glorious and beautiful events of golden color that revealed nothing of the destructive and deadly fury that had led to these displays. Another astronomical event due to the eruption was the altered appearance of lunar eclipses. Normally even at mid-eclipse, the moon is still visible but much dimmed. In the year following the Pinatubo eruption, the moon was hardly visible at all during eclipses, due to much greater absorption of sunlight by dust in the atmosphere. This dreadful eruption even dimmed our view of the glories of the heavens, and hindered astronomical observations.

On top of the enormous environmental and atmospheric damage wrought, the human impact of the disaster is staggering. Further to the up to 800 people who lost their lives, there was almost US$500,000,000, half a billion dollars, in property and economic damage. The economy of central Luzon was significantly disrupted. In 1991, the volcano destroyed 4,979 homes and damaged another 70,257. The following year 3,281 homes were destroyed and 3,137 were damaged. The destruction continued on its malicious path. Damage following the Mount Pinatubo eruption was usually caused by lahars, which are rain-induced torrents of volcanic debris, that killed people and animals and buried homes in the months after the eruption. Additionally, another Mount Pinatubo eruption in August 1992 killed 72 people.(6) The United States military never returned to Clark Air Base, turning over the damaged base to the Philippine government on November 26, 1991. Even today, in 2011, the region continues to rebuild and recover from the disaster.

As with every other event nowadays that is subject to media capture, a video of the Mount Pinatubo eruption and its aftermath has been uploaded to You Tube. You Tube has a comments section, whereby individuals who have watched the video can express views or reactions in regards to the video. The comments were placed using the You Tube member names of individuals, hence their real names are not known, and neither can the authenticity of the accounts be immediately verified. However, their authenticity is taken in good faith, and there is poignancy and an immediacy to the accounts that brings home the emotions felt on that day. A total as at the time of writing (2011) of 278 comments were recorded in response to the video. I include just a few. The comments so listed on You Tube are added verbatim, exactly as they appeared on the website, and they were dated as being made in the year 2010.

'i was 3 years old when pinatubo erupted i remember a little i am in front of a store with my mother and i look up the sky i see dark sky n its raining stone (buga) n ashes im so scared im crying that time my mother run while she carry me . . . the lindol n more is a big bad dreams for me . . . . but tnx god bcoz im stil alive . . . .'

'This has to be the second most scariest moment of my life. I was 7 years old living in a nearby town called Floridablanca Pampanga (only a few Kilometres from Mount Pinatubo). I recall the sky turned dark though it was 10 in the morning. It was like 12 in the midnight. The land was jumping moving up and down (not sideways). It was raining rocks, stones, pebbles, ash anything the volcano can throw out of its crater. I can hear shouting, crying, panic in the streets.'

'this eruption killed over 700 people not just from the eruption itself but from breathing disorders starvation and lahars rip ppl . . . . and destroyed over 200,000 homes this is the worst eruption in history'

'mas malaki ang pinsala samin sa pampanga nung june 15 1991 . . .ang dami nabura, ang dami nalibing ng buhay sa lahar, buti nalng nakasurvive kami ng pamilya ko, sobrang nakakalungkot lang ang mga di nakaligtas,'

Author's note: The writer of this comment above uses the Tagalog language and states: 'The damage was really big in my place in Pampanga, June 15, 1991 . . .a lot of destruction . . .a lot buried alive by the lava . . .good that we in my family survived . . . , I was very sad for those that didn't survive.'

Author's note: The following comment is obviously from the child of a United States serviceman who was caught up in the disaster: '*remember when this happened i was living in Subic and my mom brother and i got evacuated on the Abraham Lincoln and my dad stayed behind then after about 6 months we got to go back but it was never the same i miss Subic sometimes met a ton of friends that i still talk to today.*'

Author's note: Here a comment from a U.S. serviceman: '*wow—hard to believe that will be 20 years ago this June . . . I was an Airman at Clark AB and evacuated to Olongapo City—left a couple of days after the eruption aboard the USS Abraham Lincoln . . .*'

'*I was there for the eruption. Ive never seen anything so scary in my life. We had to evacuate to Subic and i put my wife and eight month old daughter on a ship. My wife and eight month old daughter left on a navy ship and i left a few days later. I never got the chance to say goodbye to many friends and family left behind. I really loved the P.I. They are some the best people i have ever met. always smiling no matter what. I'd really like to go back someday*'

'*i was 9 when this happened one of our apartment gave in due to the heavy ashes on the roof it was crazy . . . and i remember seeing people carrying their dead love ones covered in white sheets . . . i will never forget that!!!*'

'*There were 3 ships in Subic Naval Base when Pinatubo Erupted June 15, 1991, the USNS Kilauea (my first ship), USS Los Angeles, and the USS Rodney M Davis FFG-60 (my last ship, I was on board this ship when it all happened). It was pitch black, couldn't seen anything, only the ships had electricity but we had to shovel ashes all day and all night because the ship was getting heavy due to hard rain at the same time. We were the first ship to take AF/Navy dependents to Cebu*'

'*We moved in Sn. Fdo. Pampanga when I was 10 (1995). I saw Porac and Bacolor. Olongapo was looking better then. But Bacolor and Porac was still worse.U could only see rooftops. There was a Catholic Church where you could almost jump to touch the roof*'

'I saw these too, I was on vacation from the States when this eruption happened. I couldn't understand why it was so dark at 3'0pm. After we were told of the eruption, I volunteered with the DSW to bring food to these places. This was where we passed on our way to one of the barrios, amazingly people were still smiling everywhere. I have seen indigenous people of the Philippines for the first time. It humbled me to see that they needed only few things to live' (7).

The Mount Pinatubo eruption is but one example of the catastrophes that have afflicted the Republic of the Philippines. This nation has topped the list of countries that are most vulnerable to disasters, as stated in a recent study by Brussels-based Center for Research on the Epidemiology of Disasters (CRED). The Philippines topped CRED's list after it experienced 25 disasters in 2009, followed by China with 24.(8) Among these disasters were tropical cyclones Kiko, Pepeng and Ondoy. These cyclonic events claimed hundreds of lives and destroyed property amounting to billions of pesos. The nation was also recently identified by the World Bank as among the countries affected the most by climate change, which means it is more prone to experiencing typhoons, floods, landslides and drought. It was subsequently given a financial grant expected to help in designing strategies to mitigate disaster risks.(9) The above point in regards to climate change is a crucial point in view of the damage that increased weather severity has on the Philippines, and also in view of predictable and adequate rainfall needed to sustain crops and offer food security. We discuss this further in chapter 3 in regards to the issue of energy production for the nation and global warming.

As a result of its geological structure, the country experiences on average 887 earthquakes every year, some of which have proved to be damaging. Out of 220 volcanoes in the archipelago, 22 are classified as active. Other volcanoes, such as Mount Mayon, are even more active, and surrounded by many communities at risk to lahars and other hazards. Lahars is the term used for a volcanic mudflow. It is a mixture of tephra and water, and has the consistency of wet concrete. Luzon is significantly more at risk than areas that are more southern. Mindanao is fortunate, as it is generally free from typhoons. Environmental degradation is also playing a significant role in increasing the incidence of natural disasters. Population growth and poor land–use planning have led to the massive depletion of natural resources and destruction of the environment. (10) An example of this is the March 24, 1996 mine tailing tragedy in Marinduque, which affected 20,700 people. It occurred when 1.6 million cubic meters of copper mine waste spilled into the Boac and other nearby rivers. This was by far the country's worst industrial pollution disaster.(11)

In the wealthier nations of the planet, it is normal to have insurance coverage for pretty much everything. Life insurance, car insurance, travel insurance, unemployment and disability insurance. The list goes on, and it includes some strange insurance risks. Lloyds of London is internationally famous and will insure more or less anything. In the 1940's the executives at 20th Century Fox movie studios had the legs of the actress Betty Grable insured for US$1 million each. The Rock and Roll star Bruce Springsteen in the 1980's insured his gravelly voice for US$6 million. Rod Stewart is reported to have also insured his voice. (12) Whether mundane or exotic, for any insured items a premium is calculated depending on the degree of risk as formulated by an actuary, an insurance risk specialist. In the wealthier nations, high disposable incomes allow the purchasing of such services as insurance. It's big business. In poorer nations such as the Philippines, despite there being significant exposure of the economy to natural disasters, insurance coverage is very low. In the year 2000, the non-life insurance premium total collected was US$458 million, which amounts to a paltry 0.6 percent of GDP. It is estimated that less than 10% of all residential property policies in this nation cover natural perils. The total number of fire policies with endorsements for catastrophic events is estimated at less than 50,000, which appears to be extremely low for a nation of the population of the Philippines. Apart from the lower disposable incomes in this nation being a factor in this, perhaps also psychological issues are at play. *Bahala na!* Come what may! It's fate. *Kapalaran!* We can only speculate, as I know of no formal research conducted by the insurance industry regarding this. In any case, as a result of this low insurance coverage, the cost of natural disasters is largely borne by government and homeowners when disasters strike. While no single factor can explain such a low insurance penetration for natural hazards, the underdeveloped state of the insurance market in this nation, and low demand for insurance products, seem to be key factors. According to a World Bank report,(13) the Philippines non-life insurance market is known to suffer from excessive fragmentation, fierce competition, low capital base, and, as a result, excessive dependence on international reinsurers for claims paying capacity. The market is currently served by 98 domestic and 12 foreign-controlled direct insurance companies. As a result, so states the World Bank report, competition has led to low primary rates in almost all classes, but particularly for natural perils. 'Despite the existence of a regulated earthquake tariff of 0.1% through the bundling of earthquake and fire coverage (with the latter being subject to market competition), local insurers until recently effectively bypassed the earthquake tariff regulation, which led to the under-pricing of earthquake risk.'(14) The cost to the Philippines in direct damage as a result of disasters is enormous. It has been estimated to be PHP15 billion per year with further costs through indirect and secondary impacts. This equates with more that 0.5% of the nation's GDP.(15)

When looking at this issue in general terms, natural disasters are defined by the CRED as events where 10 or more people are killed; 100 people or more are affected; a state of calamity was declared; and there is a call for international assistance. The classification structure that is used for natural disasters are geophysical-like (earthquakes and volcanic eruptions), hydrological like (floods and landslides), meteorological like (typhoons), climatological like (El Niño), and biological like (animal infestation and epidemics).(16) The CRED report, cited above, added that 14 out of the 25 disasters to hit the country last year were classified as meteorological, 9 were hydrological, and 2 were geophysical. The report stated that 11 million Filipinos in almost all parts of the country were badly affected by the typhoons mentioned above. This in turn led to significant depletion of the country's meager calamity funds.(17)

In the Philippines, it is nearly one in ten people that are affected by natural or man-made disasters each year, but many of these victims are left to fend for themselves. Disasters are, as a consequence, seen in the Philippines as a major source of poverty and vulnerability.(18) That same old geophysical caprice that gave the nation an archipelagic form, situated the nation in the "Ring of Fire" of volcanic islands, around the rim of the Pacific Ocean. It also placed this nation in the typhoon belt, resulting in about eight million people, from mainly rural areas, being adversely affected by typhoons. Despite this, it has been estimated that only one-half of those so affected receive any assistance from either government or private aid agencies, and what they do receive is a relatively tiny amount of their normal income. As well as a lack of funds there has also been concern expressed about inefficient aid delivery processes and the wastage of resources. One result of all of this is that the poor risk falling into 'perpetual poverty traps.' Additionally, the Philippines has started to experience the adverse effects of climate change. These include occurrence of more intense typhoons, continuous rainfall which causes flooding, and prolonged drought. SEARCA (Southeast Asian Regional Center for Graduate Study and Research in Agriculture) (2009), reported that to date, climate-related risks account for almost 50% of deaths and about 80% of economic losses in the country. In relation to agriculture, there are four relevant impacts which emerge. They are, an increase in temperature, changes in rainfall, sea level rise, and weather hazards. Poor environmental quality (e.g., poor soil and water management, improper land use, and dilapidated infrastructure) aggravates the adverse impacts of climate change. Greatly influenced therefore is food production and food security.(19)

The above discussion gives a pertinent overview of the situation. Sadly, other calamities occur in the Philippines beyond those already highlighted. Many fires occur and there appear to be a myriad of reasons for these. One example of the various reasons fires can occur is that of arson being employed as a method to rid specific areas of squatters, those large numbers of homeless people that are displaced by disaster or civil unrest or economic hardship. Where the owners may wish to reclaim the land on which squatters have settled, and legal means to move them have failed, or been circumvented, then the squatters shacks and buildings are 'mysteriously' burnt down. To claim the proceeds of fire insurance policies is also another cause of arson cases. Other fires are simply due to negligence and poor safety standards, and others may occur naturally. The Philippines is a country that suffers many lethal lightning strikes. Globally there have been a number of studies done using lightning detection networks located in some countries. There are also satellites in use that have optical detectors designed to recognize lightning flashes. Gracefully orbiting our Earth these sophisticated electronic packages will peer down below and look out for the signs of the electrical fury of the Earth. Our planet and its atmosphere is a colossal electrical and electromagnetic living being. What this means for Filipinos is that certain occupational groups are vulnerable to getting caught up in the gigantic electrical forces of nature. There are disastrous consequences for the ordinary Filipino farmer or fisherman, who is often exposed outdoors, and has to brave the elements in his daily toil to feed himself and his family. The most recent data suggests that there are about 100 flashes of lightning per second globally, of which 80% are in-cloud flashes and 20% are cloud-to-ground flashes. This gives us approximately 20 flashes to the ground per second globally, and therefore 1,728,000 flashes to the ground globally per day. This is how the electrical balance between the Earth's surface and the atmosphere is maintained.(20) The Philippines is frequently affected by electrical storms. This is particularly hazardous for Filipino fishermen and farmers, as mentioned. The World Bank recognizes these events as being significant, due to their frequency and cumulative toll. 'In addition to the large catastrophes that command a considerable humanitarian assistance response from the international community, there are an even larger number of small hazard events that do not register on the global or even national news scene but that consistently wipe out the few assets of the poor, locking them into the poverty cycle.'(21) This includes the disaster of losing a loved one, the breadwinner of the family, for instance, through a natural adverse event. Filipino fishermen and farmers toil daily for a meager wage. They are, during the course of their work, exposed to hazards, such as lightning. The daily death toll from such events do not make the news, but their deaths are cumulative and to each family involved it is a disaster, just the same. Mr. Michael Putly runs an online agency called 'struckbylightning.org' which documents lightning strikes globally, and reports of death and injury.(22) While engaged in research for this book I emailed Mr. Putly to request data in reference to lightning strikes in the Philippines He very kindly sent me the following information from his database as it pertains to the Philippines.(23) These are only the recorded instances, and no doubt represent only a fraction of total. The others occur in isolated regions, or are simply not reported or documented. For the years 2005 to 2010, the database gives a total of 32 reported lightning strikes, and they exemplify the destruction that lightning incurs :

Name (Sex/Age) Date Locale Outcome Location

Father and son fishing, (M/?), Sat, 09/25/2010 Catanduanes, Bicol, Philippines. *Killed fishing.*

Boy killed & father missing (10/M) Fri, 09/24/2010 Gigmoto, Philippines. *Killed fishing.*

3 dead 3 critical (M/?) Wed, 09/08/2010 Ligao City, Philippines. Killed. *Farming. Outside.*

Jovie Tablos (F/42) Fri, 08/13/2010 Laoag City, Philippines. Killed. *Farming field, Outside*

4 duck raisers (M/?) Fri, 07/23/2010 Manila, Philippines. Killed. Cell Phone. *Underground Shelter.*

18 Police Officers (?/?) Tue, 07/13/2010 Sibonga Town, Cebu, Philippines. *Injured outside Police Office.*

3 fishermen (M/16) Thu, 06/24/2010 Manila, Philippines. Killed. *Fishing outside.*

3 fishermen (M/25) Thu, 06/17/2010 Laguna Lake, Rizal, Philippines. Killed *Boat fishing on Water.*

boy (M/16) Sun, 05/30/2010, Philippines. Killed. *Outside taking Shelter under Trees*

5 farmers killed (M/?) Sat, 09/19/2009, Philippines, Killed *Farming*

Sister Elnora Butaslog (F/?) Mon, 10/27/2008 Misamis Oriental, Philippines. Unknown Outcome. *Beach during the storm.*

Father killed, son injured (M/?) Tue, 10/21/2008 Pinamungajan Town, Cebu Philippines *Killed outside.*

Man swimming (M/28) Tue, 10/14/2008 Batangas, Novaliches, Philippines. *Killed in water swimming.*

3 dead 9 injured in 2 incidents (?/?) Fri, 10/03/2008 Manolo Fortich, Bukidon Province, Philippines. Killed. *Farming outside.*

2 killed 1 hurt (F/4) Wed, 09/24/2008 Barangay San Nicolas, Agusan del Sur, Philippines. *Killed outside.*

1 dead 2 injured (M/60) Tue, 09/09/2008 Carmen, North, Cotabato, Philippines. Killed. *Indirect, indoors.*

Muin Assari & Adolfo Mahari injured (M/54) Fri, 08/29/2008 Sibiling Island, Basilan Province, Philippines. Killed. *Boat on water.*

Simon Tolete killed 7 hurt (M/?) Wed, 08/27/2008 Magarao town, Camarines Sur, Philippines. Killed.

Jerome Pangantihon (M/19) Tue, 08/26/2008 EB Magalona, Negros Occidental, Philippines. Killed. *Farming, outside.*

Milagros Baldovia & others (F/62) Sat, 09/22/2007 Davao del Sur, Kiblawan, Philippines. Killed. *Dry laundry. Outside.*

Ediza Manjares & 2 sisters (F/7) Tue, 06/12/2007 Kuyawyaw, Quezon, Philippines. Killed. *Boat on Water.*

Melecio Omac & Jimson Ehorpe (M/44) Sun, 10/15/2006 Pilar Town, Tagbilaran City, Philippines. Killed. *Underground Shelter.*

3 killed (M/?) Mon, 09/18/2006 Tagbilaran city, Bohol, Philippines. Killed Indoors. *Underground shelter.*

Roy Gambola & 2 others (M/24) Sat, 09/09/2006 Sagay, Philippines. Killed *Burnt indoors.*

Edgar Bansil & Jonathan Genese (M/38) Wed, 07/12/2006 Lubao Town, Pampanga, Philippines. Killed. *Farming field outside.*

Reynaldo Magpantay, Village Chief (M/?) Tue, 07/04/2006 Tagkawayan, Quezon, Philippines. Killed. *Cell phone. Outside.*

5 people (?/?) Fri, 10/21/2005 Cebu, Philippines. Killed. *Underground Shelter*

107 in armory (?/?) Mon, 09/12/2005 Camp Bagong Diwa, Taguig, Philippines. Injured *Indirect, indoors.* Military

Rosemarie Purisima (F/9) Fri, 06/03/2005 Asturias, Cebu Philippines Killed Indoors, *Underground Shelter.*

Rose Sumugat & 2 injured (F/18) Wed, 05/18/2005 Bacolod City, Negros Occidental, Philippines *Killed, Burnt. Farming field, outside.*

Of a total of 30 records (recorded cases). A statistical analysis provided by Mr. Putly shows a greater grouping on weekdays which I presume reflects the occupational nature of the cases, rather than weekend recreational outdoor activities.

Sunday: 2 (6.25%)
Monday: 3 (9.38%)
Tuesday: 7 (21.88%)
Wednesday: 7 (21.88%)
Thursday: 2 (6.25%)
Friday: 7 (21.88%)
Saturday: 4 (12.50%)
Unknown: 0 (0.00%)

Lightning takes a steady toll, mainly on those who have to face the elements as part of their daily toil, and we must remember them, in the same way that we remember those killed by typhoons or by drowning.

In addition to the steady toll that lightning takes on Filipino farmers and fishermen, we have also had disastrous fires within this nation. On 18th March, 1996, the deadliest fire ever recorded in the Philippines occurred, and it is referred to as the Ozone Disco Tragedy. It happened when a fire broke out at the jam-packed Ozone Disco in Quezon City, Manila. This catastrophe claimed around 160 lives, mostly teenagers, and is the deadliest fire ever recorded in the Philippines. Before the tragedy, the Ozone Disco was one of the more popular discos in its time, located strategically at the corner of Tomas Morato Extension and Timog Avenue, in front of the Boy Scouts of the Philippines Memorial. The disco was inaugurated in 1991. Its location was previously home to another club called Birdland in the 1980s. It was one of those places that young people would go to. To have fun, to meet friends, to relax, to engage in having a *gimmik*. They felt safe. They were with friends. They were in Manila, that Megacity where all sorts of emergency services and hospitals were available. There was no inkling of the catastrophe about to unfold, and in minutes rob them of their lives. The fire was reported to have started at around 12:30 a.m. at the disk jockey's booth. Survivors recounted that electrical sparks and a series of firecracker-like explosions came from the booth before electricity was cut. The whole disco was then plunged into darkness. At the same time, smoke filled the establishment. At that time around 350 people were inside, mostly students from various schools celebrating their graduation and the end of classes. There were, in addition, 40 club employees. The official capacity of the club was for 35 persons.(24) It could not have happened at a worst time. The fire quickly spread throughout the disco, aided by the flammable materials used in the interiors of the building, such as the decorative egg cartons used in the ceiling, and the acoustic foam insulation. Light fixtures fell from the ceiling as it was consumed by the fire. Moments later, the mezzanine fell, crushing some of the revelers trapped in the innermost part of the disco. Panicking and unable to find a fire exit, many rushed to the narrow corridor leading to the front exit. However, the front doors measured less than two meters wide and swung *inwards*. Detail is critical in many, many situations. To affect rapid exit in an emergency, doors should swing *outwards*. Just such a tiny and seemingly insignificant detail can have such huge consequences. The crowd in their panic pushed at the doors, closing them shut, instead of pulling them open. Panic is something that overtakes a person. People do not think rationally when seized by panic. One will engage in actions that out of desperation appear to be correct, but are in fact counterproductive and compound the tragedy that is unfolding. The situation was compounded by, incredibly, security guards locking the door from outside, thinking that a riot had broken out inside. By the time firefighters were able to open the doors and put out the flames, many had died; in the ensuing stampede to the exit, partygoers were suffocated, trampled, or burned to death. Firefighters discovered numerous bodies, piled-waist high along the narrow corridor behind the doors. These bodies were charred beyond recognition. This forced victim's families to identify the bodies through the personal effects of the victims, such as jewelry. Some bodies were never even identified. These were buried in mass graves. The fire raged in its deadly fury for four hours. It claimed around 160 lives, and it left 310 persons injured. It also caused around PHP15 million worth of damage to property. Investigators stated that faulty or overloaded wiring may have caused the blaze. It spread quickly because the inside walls of the disco were made of combustible soundproofing materials. The site has never been refurbished for commercial use after the fire. An investigation of the incident was immediately ordered by President Fidel V. Ramos. It was discovered that the disco had numerous violations of the National Building Code. This included the lack of fire exits, emergency lights and alarm systems; the narrow door, which swung inwards; and overcrowding. The disco's permit to operate was also found to be dubious, as well as other permits issued by the Quezon City government.(25)

A few days after the tragedy, criminal charges were filed against the owners and operators of the establishment. The charges were later dismissed against some of the accused, however two individuals were found guilty of reckless imprudence resulting in multiple homicide and multiple injuries. Despite being sentenced to four years in prison, it was reported that two posted bail and did not serve any time behind bars. All six were also ordered to pay PHP25 million in damages to the families of the victims of the tragedy, but the company operating the disco had filed for bankruptcy. Therefore, only a portion of the amount was actually paid out. Charges were also filed against twelve officials of the Quezon City government. An organization, called Justice for Ozone Victims Foundation, Inc., (JOVFI) was established. It complained not just of the slow pace of justice but also of being "shortchanged", because of the light sentences meted out by the court.(26)

Filipinos are superstitious and are prone to believe in ghostly events. Due to the horrific nature of the fire at the Ozone Disco, numerous instances of paranormal activity in the area have been reported. Nearby tenants have reportedly seen faint dancing silhouettes as well as disco music coming from the venue in the evening. Reportedly, the site has also been visited several times by the Spirit Questors, a Filipino psychic organization at the request of the JOVFI. The fire is still mentioned today, and on searching for references to it on the internet the author found the following posting, on a Singaporean website dedicated to documenting supernatural events and ghost stories.(27) I emailed the website administrators to request permission to reproduce the story in its entirety, and this was granted.(28) The name of the Filipino posting the story is not given. It reads verbatim:

'In March 18, 1996, at around 4pm local time, the night club or as it is commonly referred to in the Philippines as "disco", the Ozone Disco caught fire. It happened in Quezon City, Manila. I had to mention the location to point out that it happened in a metropolitan area where, supposedly, such matters would have been avoided or at least dealt with accordingly in a quick manner. You can just imagine it being in the nation's capital where police and fire service members are within a call away as opposed to it being in a rural area where it would take quite a while for response to reach their destination. Now I was still in the Philippines when this happened, I was 11 years old and I am 24 now and living abroad. This was a first in the Philippines and it is said to be the worst club fire in the world. More than 160 people died and about 92 others were injured. This incident shook the entire Metro Manila and up to this day, families and friends and simply everyone who knew about this incident still have not coped with the sadness and grief of such a tragic event. As for those of you who are wondering how it happened, well, there are a number of reasons but I think THE most popular and widely accepted FACT was that the "doors open inward rather than out". If you ask anybody, they will tell you exactly that. When the fire broke out, nobody noticed, when the BLAZE grew that is the only time people realized that there was a fire. It being popular at that time, people would flock to it. It became a symbol of social status and this made it even more popular with the younger generation of that time. That being said, the place was packed and when the blaze grew, people panicked and they all rushed to the ONLY door (see? there's another reason, just one door and no fire exit) and just imagine, the door opens inward. Even if they tried, nobody could open the doors. Push? how? there was no room. The location of the fated Ozone Disco or simply "Ozone" to most people, is now desolate up to this year of 2009. Now here is where my story begins. Soon after the incident, the sight of burnt corpses made headlines. May it be TV or newspaper (internet wasn't mainstream at the time) people would only find the horrible accident that occurred there. It had been the news of the year. People would talk about it and could not come to accept how a sad and tragic event could happen. The Ozone disco became a thing of interest, and as you may have already guessed, a great number of "hauntings" have been reported in the area. This happened a couple of years after the incident. Me and my friend were in a jeepney (public transportation, look it up) at around 9pm on our way to our other friend's house. Our jeep passes by that route and we would always look out the window at the now desolate place where the Ozone once stood. It was just me and my friend, the driver then told us "You boys keep looking at that place and you just might find something that'll scare the wits out of you!" I then turned to look and sitting next to the driver was a man with his head turned at 180 degrees looking at me! I could stop yelling curses, luckily the jeep had to slow down for an intersection and i jumped out with my friend pacing after me. The place was filled with local bars (not discos) so there were lights so I was a bit (0.001%) relieved but could not brush the horror out of my shaking self. My friend then asked me "what's wrong?" I told him "for pete's sake did you not see it?" He said "saw what?" I interjected "That man on the jeep!!" My friend stopped looking at me with one eye brow raised. He knew (I did to, sorta) that it was just me, him and the driver in the jeep. Think that was the end of that? I really had to be a bother that night and had to ask my friend to accompany me home (to which he kept questioning my manhood). Upon arriving home, I told him he could stay, but he's not one who believes in such "supernatural" things so he refused and left. I was sitting in the couch or "sofa" still feeling my heart go a mile a minute, my mom was still awake chopping vegetables for tomorrow. My uncle, who was a taxi driver, came home. He went to get a drink from the fridge and then sat down with me in the living room. We started chatting. As much as I hated to bring up anything about the Ozone disco, unfortunately he, my uncle said "that [Ozone] disco, sure is sad isn't it?" I just said a quick and apathetic "yeah". He went on to say "I mean it somehow affects [taxi[business" I said nothing. "I went by the Ozone but did not stop there, a few buildings from it I picked up my last customers for the night before heading home. Then, an old man on a rusty old bicycle started to follow me, he seems too old to be able to catch up, but somehow, he does not want to stop following me. I tried to drive a little faster but my passengers told me not to as they were not in a hurry, to me it sounded like easy cash, I can get a high fare just by going slow. The old man, still in view in my rearview mirror is gaining on me. I came to a red light and had to stop, (around 12 midnight, stoplights in the Philippines take longer to change) the old man, got off his bike, and started walking towards us, he finally stood by my window and knocked two gentle knocks. I promptly, annoyed as I was, turn down the window and asked "There a problem?" and he began to talk in a slow and cracky voice "I noticed you have been driving round the block, are you lost?" I told him "no, my customers are joy-riding". Told man scratched his chin for a second, my uncle told me and he seemed satisfied enough "But I did notice, your two passengers don't seem to have any heads" said the old man as he picked up his bike and went off. My uncle stopped there and went to get some sleep. Ozone is not of this world.'

For the families of the victims and those, who like the writer of the web post above, were caught up in the negative energy of the event and alleged haunting, it is a disaster and a tragedy that will never go away. Events seem to happen in clusters, and spooky events are no exception. The phenomenon is what C.G. Jung referred to as 'synchronicity'(29) At the time of writing this book I had been thinking about the text for this chapter, and had already completed documenting the above ghost story in regards to reports of headless passengers in a taxi. On taking a break from the toils of writing I turned on the television and on cable TV an episode of an American detective series was playing. The title of the episode was displayed at the top corner of the screen. It read, 'The headless woman'.

The potential for accident or disaster is ever-present, in all nations. I have been to events within the Philippines where event planning and event safety planning appear to be minimal to non-existent. Even after the salient lessons of such disasters as the Ozone Disco fire. Filipinos live on the edge. Once in a provincial city I attended an event that was held at the local stadium. Food traders and local restauranters had erected tents and temporary structures around the arena to serve those attending the event. A band was scheduled to play at the event, and electrical wiring that connected power points with amplifiers lay strewn across the wet concrete floor, which people had to walk over. The arena, when the event started, was jam-packed with people. My companion and I inched our way through the crowd to try to get a seat, or to stand in a position to afford a view of the events. There were no Marshalls at the entrances to the stadium area, to provide crowd control or perform a security check. I was carrying my "goodies bag", which is a sports bag with packets of foods and drinks for any of the poor local kids who extend their hand towards me, "*Kuya?*", imploring food or a gift. The local mayor and other dignitaries were attending the event. Anyone could have easily carried a firearm or a bomb into the stadium, in a bag like the one I had. There are plenty of terrorist groups and crazed individuals who would engage in such acts. Where was the security and where were the risk-management and risk-reduction measures that should have been in place? After the event, my companion and I went to eat at one of the local temporarily erected eateries at the stadium. After the meal, I wanted to use the CR and we asked where the CR was. I was invited to go through to the back area of the tent. Assuming that by passing through the kitchen area I would reach a CR, I proceeded through but on reaching the back kitchen area, I was told by a kitchen employee, in the local language, to just urinate in the corner of the kitchen! Food scraps and seafood shells lay everywhere on the floor. Feeling decidedly queasy in the stomach I left the eatery area, paying particular attention to avoid the electrical wiring that was on the floor. Fortunately, there were no bombings at the event, no electrocutions and no mass outbreaks of food poisoning, but the potential for these incidents was there. Filipinos live close to the edge. I have seen them texting while riding a motorbike, and incidentally, picking their nose while riding a motorbike! I have also seen Filipinos attempt to repair electrical equipment while the device is still plugged in to the live mains, and I have seen them refueling a motorcycle while happily puffing away on a cigarette. '*Bahala na!*' Come what may!

Not surprisingly, due to the number of islands that constitute the Philippines and the proximity to water that the population has it should come as no surprise that drowning occurs frequently. It is the second leading cause of death among children aged one to fourteen years in the country, and therefore outnumbering deaths from serious diseases such as tuberculosis, malnutrition, cancer and meningitis. Almost 2,000 children die yearly from drowning and 35.6 percent of all drowning victims are children up to 14 years of age. More severe flash flooding is now reported in the Philippines and surveys have shown that 10% to 12% of drowning fatalities happen during flash floods. Boys are twice more likely to die from drowning as girls of the same age. 10% of all drowning deaths in the Philippines relate to maritime disasters. Not surprisingly, it is the nation's unique geographical and climatic conditions that pose an increased risk of drowning.(30)

To alleviate poverty, the Philippines has to overcome external and internal challenges. On the external side, it must cope with fluctuations in global markets on which it depends heavily. On the internal side, it needs to win back the confidence of investors in order to raise the currently low volume of investment that is necessary for the country's development. I mention the other factors and other changes that need to be made in detail in chapters 3 and 6. Volcanic eruptions, flashfloods, landslides, typhoons, oil spills and fires. The Philippines suffers the full spectrum of natural and man-made disasters, at enormous cost to the economy, and resulting in great suffering for the population. The ancient elements of Earth, Water, Air and Fire appear to be at their angriest in this archipelago. In addition to calamitous events of immediate impact, is the inexorable damage that is occurring through environmental degradation in the Philippines, secondary to certain forms of energy production, unregulated industrial processes and the environmental burden of an exploding population. All of these events claim lives, damage the nation's infrastructure, displace countless numbers of people and provide a constant drain on resources. They are a constant challenge in terms of management and effective disaster-response intervention. In one regard the Philippines is unlucky, it cannot prevent typhoons or earthquakes or other such events, but some disasters have been due to negligence, poor attention to detail, and poor adherence to safety standards. Even the simplest of measures could prevent or reduce the impact or severity of them. Bombs go off in the Philippines but bags are not checked at public events, like the one I attended. Some disasters can clearly be avoided with foresight, prudence, attention to detail, and adherence to safety regulations currently in place.

Such events such as typhoons have been worsening in severity and the cause for that is global warming, due to human industrial and energy-production activity. As has been said, there are some things one cannot change and there are some things one can change. The Philippines must identify, control and eliminate those causes of man-made disasters, and work to lessen the production of CO_2 as a by-product of its energy sector. In addition, should we include, in any discussion about disasters, the political disasters that have so adversely affected this nation, and contributed to its downward economic spiral? I think we should, because they are likely to have done more economic damage than all of the others. I include here such political disasters as the latter days of the Marcos regime, when all of the idealism and vigor and hope of the early days were gone. The regime sank into an inefficient, self-absorbed and corrupt clique of the elite who were busily engaged in enriching themselves. The assassination of Benigno "Ninoy" Aquino was another unmitigated political disaster. The numerous military coups, and the meddling in the affairs of state by the Catholic Church, are an on-going political disaster. In addition, the continued poor governance, nepotism and murder of Filipino journalists are other aspects of the disaster that this country is living every day. All of this takes a huge toll on the economy of the nation, its democratic principals and structures, and its international reputation as a good place to live and to do business. Like the Ozone Disco tragedy these events will always come back to haunt the nation, in one form or another.

CHAPTER 3

Economic Prosperity—a fading dream for the Philippine nation?

KEY POINTS: the Philippines has slipped badly in terms of economic performance, in relation to the other nations of Asia. The reasons for this are multi-factorial.

IN 1960 THE Philippines was reported to be the second wealthiest nation in East Asia, next only to Japan.(1) How things have changed! On October 26, 2010, the President of the Republic of the Philippines, President Benigno Aquino III, left the Philippines to complete a state visit to the Republic of Vietnam. One of the goals of the trip was to '. . . learn about Vietnam's rice production method. Like many of the Philippines' neighbor states in South East Asia, Vietnam benefited from the training by the International Rice Research Institute based in Laguna. Vietnam exports rice to the Philippines.'(2) The President's trip to Vietnam and the desire to learn about 'Vietnam's rice production method' is another sobering reminder of just how the Philippine economy, and its capabilities in such areas as rice production, have declined. When we are discussing rice, we are discussing the staple food of the nation. Like crude oil, it is an essential item and like oil, it now has to be imported in large amounts. Rice is the staple food of the Philippines and 90% of the nation's farmers are engaged in growing it. Rice is also a political commodity in this nation, and any shortages could cause civil unrest. It also puts the country at risk. Because of the global economic crisis, the country almost ran out of supplies in 2008. (3)(4) And now huge amounts of it have to be imported. In 2011 the Philippines's National Food Authority, announced it planned to import an additional 300,000 metric tons of rice. This was required in order to ensure enough rice was stockpiled, in case of typhoon damage to harvests. In the last three years, the total rice output of the Philippines was only 10 million tonnes on average, while the country consumed 13 million tonnes. That other essential item for transport and industry, oil, has proved itself a burden on the nation's balance of payments figures. In 2010 the oil import bill surged by 40% to $9.96 billion dollars.(5) This was the result of higher crude oil prices. Higher global market prices of crude oil raised the country's oil import bill by 40 percent to $9.96 billion in 2010, from the previous year's $7.11 billion, according to data from the Department of Energy (DoE). Similarly, the cost of imported finished products rose by 22.8 percent to $4.597 billion, at an average cost of $84.946 per barrel. With regard to where the imported oil comes from, the Middle East, not surprisingly, is still the major source of imported crude oil, supplying 80.6 percent (54.23 Million Barrels) of the total crude mix. Malaysia, Indonesia and Brunei supplied a combined 11.6 percent (7.81 Million Barrels). The remaining 7.7 percent came from that other oil giant, Russia. The country's total crude and petroleum products inventory as of the end of 2010 was 13.821 Million Barrels, and this inventory is enough to meet the country's requirements for 46 days.(6) The oil production capacity of the Philippines is limited. It averaged just over 25,000 barrels per day (bbl/d) during the first nine months of 2006. Between 1996 and 2000, it had no oil production at all. During the last several years, production has increased, primarily due to the development of new offshore deepwater oil deposits. The increased production volume is still very modest, however, in relation to the country's need.(7) The Philippines then is dependant upon the importation of its staple food, and on the importation of the lifeblood of any economy, that is, oil. With the necessary importation of these essential items, the nation has left itself vulnerable to external variations in supply and pricing, which can adversely affect the economy. One of the key questions that every nation must face, is that of energy security. Few people know this but the Philippines was some years ago on the verge of being a nuclear power. In a desperate attempt to lessen the nation's dependence on oil, the Philippines built in the 1970's a nuclear reactor. Located in Bataan, the nuclear power station has never produced a single watt of power. It is an interesting story and a lesson in high ambition but poor planning. It is nearly 30 years since the construction of the Bataan nuclear power plant commenced. The costly project was never completed, and Filipino taxpayers are reportedly still paying US$155,000 a day in interest on the loans for the project. Although its planned capability was to produce 621 Megawatts of electrical power, it has never produced any electrical energy at all. Not a spark of electricity has been produced, and its equipment stands lifeless. During the oil shock of the 1970's, when the oil producing nations of the Middle East increased by a large amount the price for oil, and realized its use as a political weapon, many nations began scrambling to find alternative energy sources. Ferdinand Marcos, the President of the Philippines at that time, authorized the construction of the plant in order to lessen the nation's reliance on imported oil. From 1976 to 1984 work proceeded on this costly white elephant, and in the end left a bill that was as cool as the nuclear reactor itself, US$2.3 billion. It is located 97 kilometers north of Manila, and has always been controversial. After the overthrow of Marcos, it was inspected by a team of international inspectors who deemed the plant as being too unsafe to operate. One can understand the anxiety of the inspectors, who discovered that it was built near major geological fault lines, and near Mount Pinatubo volcano, which was dormant though at that time. Following the overthrow of Ferdinand Marcos the government of his successor, Corazon Aquino, banned the use of nuclear power. This was subsequently enshrined in the Philippine Constitution. Tipping the decision against the power plant was the Chernobyl disaster in the Ukraine just after she came to power. Subsequent to the decision, in 2011 we have had the Fukushima nuclear power plant disaster in Japan, which occurred for precisely the same reasons that the nuclear inspectors and Corazon Aquino feared—an earthquake. There have been plans to convert the plant into a non-nuclear power station, however this will reportedly be too expensive. The debt repayments for this plant are the nation's single biggest financial obligation.(8) The power station is still being maintained and there is provision for guided tours of the plant for those so interested. At least in this way a little revenue is produced, and it provides educational benefits in regards to teaching about nuclear issues. Because the plant never commenced operation there is no danger of radiation, and all parts of the plant are accessible.(9) The high electricity rates in this nation disadvantage the country economically, and imported coal and oil are expensive.(10) It would be easy to criticize the initial decision of Marcos in hindsight, but it is important to remember in this instance that the Philippines was being faced with oil prices that were rising astronomically. Further, the nation faced a complete reliance on this essential resource being delivered by other nations. It was a logical and appropriate step to consider alternative sources of power, to reduce the nation's power costs, and to ensure energy security. The only problem was that things went wrong with the planning and the execution of the project, and that the inherent dangers of operating a nuclear power plant in an earthquake-prone country became evident with the occurrence of disasters elsewhere. While engaged in writing this chapter a brownout occurred in the Philippine town in which I was residing. 'Brown-outs', as they are referred to in the Philippines, are common, and are due principally to the poor infrastructure relating to the electricity supply system. Also, it's common for supply lines to be illegally tapped with wiring to supply houses that do not wish to pay for their electricity, or do not have the means to do so. This hazardous practice places a greater demand on the supply grid, and provides no revenue to assist maintenance or upgrading of the generation or supply system. The power lines are aboveground and therefore prone to catastrophic damage in typhoons. Most businesses of any significant size use back-up generators to protect against these frequent 'brown-outs''—which incidentally in Australia or the United Kingdom are referred to as 'black-outs''. Domestic electricity rates in the Philippines are the highest in the world. I know this from personal experience. When renting an apartment in a regional town in the Bicol region, I paid in March of 2011 PHP575—for my monthly electricity bill. I do not use air-conditioning, and the only electrical items are those of a small household. While using exactly the same appliances, in exactly the same way, the electricity bill had risen by September to PHP960-. The Philippines holds the unenviable record of having the highest residential power rates not only in Asia, but also in the entire world. Officials of the Energy Regulatory Commission (ERC) and the Power Sector Assets and Liabilities Management Corp. (PSALM) admitted this in 2011. The energy officials said the Philippines has overtaken Japan as the country that charges the highest electricity rate on residential users. This was during the course of a hearing by the House Energy Committee on the high cost of electricity in the country. (11)

As reported above, the brief shift in the direction of nuclear power in the Philippines came to a costly end, the only enduring legacy is the continuing financial cost of the nuclear plant. The Philippines, in line with other nations. uses coal as an energy source for the generation of electricity, but this is judged by such organizations as Greenpeace as having significant negative consequences. I cite a Greenpeace article to highlight the other dimensions of unsustainable population growth, and the cost of attempting to meet the energy needs of more and more millions of people, with energy sources that are damaging to one's health and the environment. Filipinos are living in the 21st Century and demand all of the associated energy-hungry appliances and processes that are available to a consumer society. My next-door neighbor has air-conditioning, and he told me that his baby starts to cry when it is turned off. Apparently, the baby will not settle to sleep without it. Our neighbor accepts this, and keeps the air conditioning on. Filipinos have lived for centuries without air-conditioning but are now increasingly becoming reliant on its use. This has financial and environmental consequences that we must take stock of. The issue of energy production and energy security is critical for the Philippines, and we must examine it in detail. We must also consider the environmental issues that are raised in regards to energy production, as they are going to have a significant impact on the nation, its prosperity, and its quality of life.

Greenpeace has reported on the operation of coal-fired power plants in the Philippines and the environmental consequences and dangers. According to Greenpeace, ash samples taken from a 735 Megawatt coal-fired power plant in the Philippines were found to contain hazardous substances such as arsenic, mercury and lead.(12) The burning of coal is one of the leading contributors to climate change because it emits 80% more carbon per unit of energy than gas, and 29% more than oil. The Philippines is a nation that, like many others, is going to be adversely affected by climate change. Not only the release of carbon has significant damaging consequences, but also the release of the substances such as mercury and arsenic will have adverse human health effects. The Greenpeace article states that in a study completed by the European Commission (EC) in 2003, on different types of power generation, it was coal-fired power plants that registered the highest external cost. In comparison to this, renewable energy sources such as wind power exhibited the lowest external cost. Also known as externalities, external costs arise when the economic or social activities of, say, a power station, have an impact on a set of people, and when that impact is not fully accounted, or compensated for, by the power plant. Thus, a power station that generates sulfur dioxide or mercury emissions, causing damage to human health, imposes an external cost. Environmental costs are thus "externalized" because, although they are real costs to members of society, the owner of the power station is not taking them into account when making decisions related to its economic activities. Such factors as climate change, reduction in life expectancy, health morbidity as with respiratory diseases or cancer, the adverse impact on buildings such as steel or paint corrosion, and damage to the ecosystem. These must be included in the overall cost calculations of using such power sources. The external cost generated by coal-fired power stations was calculated to be massive. The calculations by Greenpeace yielded for the year 2003 an external cost of between PHP19.3 billion to an astronomical PHP67.9 billion as it applies to the Philippines (based on power generation of 14,517 Gigawatt hours).(13) The Philippines has nine coal-fired power plants.(14) When someone states that coal is 'cheap' these figures, the external costs, and the inevitable consequences of the use of a fuel that is toxic, and a contributor to climate change, are not taken into account. The Philippines is listed at number 32 on a list of the top 50 countries with the highest CO2 emitting power sectors. It is reported to emit 35,900,000 tons of CO2 annually. At number 1 on the list is the king of the energy and resource wasting nations of history, the USA, with a staggering 2,790,000,000 tons of CO2 per year produced. Carbon emissions impose a huge cost on society by threatening the basic elements of life, such as access to water, food production, health and the environment. Economists have elsewhere estimated these "social costs", which are referred to as "external costs" in the Greenpeace article I cited, at anywhere from US$8 per ton to as high as US$100 per ton of CO2.(15)

The biggest environmental threat facing the planet today is considered to be climate change, and the burning of coal, as I have mentioned, is one of the biggest culprits in provoking this change. What sort of consequences do we see because of climate change? We can anticipate an increased severity in hurricanes, as a consequence of the rise in sea temperatures, for example. Moreover, which country is going to be right in the firing line for any increase in hurricane severity? Yes, the Philippines. Hurricanes and typhoons, by the way, are simply different names for tropical cyclones. The common term of use in the Philippines is typhoon. Therefore, I will use that term here. The nation is already adversely affected by typhoons. An increased severity of these, plus an increasing population, equates with greater potential for death and destruction. We are looking down the road to more disasters, and these are partially human-induced due to global warming, through having an economic and energy producing system that is based on carbon. These are the global adverse effects, which are likely to impact in greater measure on this nation. For local communities it is the local adverse health effects of burning coal, in the production of energy, that also have to be contended with. Human induced climate change *is* underway. With this, the Philippines is in a precarious position, and highly vulnerable. It is with great shame that I have to state that the nation that I am a citizen of, Australia, is per capita one of the biggest carbon emission producers on the planet. Fortunately, the Australian government has recognized this, and while I engaged in writing this book carbon tax legislation has been introduced in Australia to discourage the burning of fossil fuel, and steer the nation towards clean, renewable energy. There is no lack of evidence that human–induced climate change is underway. The Greenpeace article I earlier noted cites research by the National Center for Atmospheric Research in Colorado, which found widespread drying occurred over much of the world including Asia, and identified rising global temperatures as the major factor for increased drought. Crop yields may drop by 10% for every 1 degree centigrade of rise in temperature.(16)

The Philippines encourages tourism, viewing it rightly as a valuable source of revenue for local communities, businesses and the government. One of the attractions for tourists is the natural beauty of the nation, of its land and its seas. The nation has one of the most diverse ecosystems on the planet. It is home to 488 of the known 500 coral species worldwide. And over a third of the 2,300 identified fish species in the Philippines are reef-associated.(17) But this is all at risk. Coral bleaching is the loss of color from corals under stressful environmental conditions. High water temperature has been the major cause of coral bleaching events worldwide in recent decades. In 1998 and again in 2002, major bleaching events in inshore reef waters of the Great Barrier Reef, in Australia, raised concerns about the health of the reef. With predictions that temperatures will continue to rise as a result of global climate change, the future of tropical coral reefs is causing concern worldwide. (18) Corals tend to die in great numbers immediately following coral bleaching events. Unrestrained global warming will be catastrophic for marine ecosystems worldwide, and the Philippines again is in a situation of particular vulnerability. The land and the seas that are required to support the exploding population of these islands, and to support critical revenue sources such as tourism, are at serious risk of marked degradation. In addition, global warming is increasing the ferocity of typhoons. These are very serious matters indeed.

Coal plants have been identified as one of the largest sources of mercury emissions. Mercury is a substance so toxic that all it takes is .002 pounds of mercury accumulated over a year to contaminate a 10 hectare lake to the point where fish caught are deemed unfit for human consumption. A typical 100-MW coal plant has been estimated to emit at least 25 pounds of mercury a year. (19) There is an old English saying, and that is, "As mad as a hatter". It refers to someone who is behaving bizarrely, or as if insane. Its origins come from the fact that the substance mercury used to be used in the 1800's for the production of felt hats. Due to continual occupational exposure to the toxic fumes of mercury, which is a neurotoxin, the hatter suffered psychiatric disturbance in the form of a psychosis, or in lay terms, madness. It caused other symptom too, such as trembling (known as 'hatters' shakes'), loss of coordination, slurred speech, loosening of teeth, memory loss, depression, irritability and anxiety; a collection of symptoms called 'The Mad Hatter Syndrome.' So it is a particularly toxic substance. It can, in significant amounts, cause death in exposed adults, and can cause severe brain damage in the developing fetus.(20) This frightening true story is not over. When this substance enters water, and it can do this directly or via deposition from the air. it is transformed into methyl mercury. This is a more toxic form of the substance and it accumulates in fish, and then the humans that eat the fish. This particularly nasty toxin, produced by the process of burning coal to supply this nation's energy needs, has a deposition rate of over 900 kilometers. Even at low concentrations, there is strong evidence of fetal neurotoxicity. The Greenpeace report cites studies by the US National Academy of Sciences which in 2005 reported that exposure to mercury emitted by coal fire power stations 'causes lifelong loss of intelligence in hundreds of thousands of babies born each year.'(21)

A World Wide Fund for Nature-Philippines (WWF-Philippines) study called 'PowerSwitch' stated that the country can '. . . . in the next 10 years . . . raise the share of indigenous renewables in the power mix to 50 percent.' It also noted that in 2009, 29 percent of the Philippines' power came from coal. Citing the Department of Energy's latest forecast, the WWF stated that by 2012, a full 50 percent of the country's power will be taken from coal. (22) But there is good news. And it is from no less an authoritative source than the World Bank, which stated, 'The Philippines is one of the leaders in East Asia and the

Pacific (EAP) region to utilize its indigenous renewable resources in power generation . . . . '. Further, 'The government must continue to give priority for renewable energy, which currently provides 30 percent of power supply in the country. The Philippines has also adopted its milestone Renewable Energy Act of 2008 which intends to activate renewable energy development by creating an attractive market for energy generation.'(23)

I cited in Chapter 1 studies reporting cognitive impairment in children where high levels of noise are pervasive. And here we have another adverse factor, this one on a physiological level, regarding the potential for the intellectual impairment of Filipino children. That is, the production of a neurotoxin, mercury, as a by-product of energy production in the Philippines. The full potential of children, their intelligence, their cognitive skills, and their physical and mental development, can only be realized in environments that are healthy and free from adverse factors. These issues relate directly to the health of the nation and the intellectual performance of children, who are the future of the Philippines. The Philippine government needs to listen to organizations such as Greenpeace and accept the recommendations that are offered in their report.(24) The children of this nation, the land which we inhabit, and the seas which we depend on for food, are critical resources. They are all suffering damage and impaired functioning due to factors that are, in essence, preventable. The report written by Greenpeace which I cite above was dated 2005, but of course, the facts relating to such issues as mercury pollution remain pertinent. The report stated the following 'Greenpeace is calling for 10% of our power to come from the sun, wind and modern biomass power by 2010.'(25) It is now 2011, and I followed-up on this recommendation that was made by Greenpeace, to see what the current state of play was in regards to any government progress. In 2009, 29 percent of the Philippines' power came from coal, but there seems to have been clear progress made in regards to renewable energy, with it accounting for 27.2 percent of the total primary energy mix. If one includes natural gas, the Philippines green power generation stands at 55.1 percent.(26) Natural gas is, of course, not a renewable source of energy, but it is a far better alternative to coal and may serve as a bridge to a totally renewable energy future. The problem has been, of course, that due to the exploding population in the Philippines, the expansion of electrification to all areas of the country, and the ever-present hunger of a massive consumer society with all of its electronic wonders, the nation is for ever playing catch-up in terms of providing energy. But top marks to the Philippine government for steering the energy sector on the road to renewable energy. This must continue. For the future, there is no other rational choice.

The environmental and economic costs to sustain a rapidly growing population are enormous, and yet the Philippines has failed to restrain and plan its population. The economy of the Philippines is further disadvantaged as a result. The largest and most powerful lobby group for the prevention of any measures to limit population growth, and allow effective birth control, has been the Catholic Church of the Philippines. In contrast to Western nations, the Catholic Church exerts a powerful influence over the thinking and behavior of the masses, and also of Government. The Philippine Constitution makes clear, 'the separation of Church and State is inviolable'. This sentence is clear and unambiguous. The Church is not the elected government, it has no role in the formulation of governmental policy, except as part of a consultation process, and it should not at any point exert or attempt to exert political influence, that would prejudice the passing and enactment of effective legislation. Particularly legislation that empowers individuals to choose and plan their own lives and that of their children, and affords them the human right of effective birth control. In discussing economic issues and the economic performance of the Philippines, it is critical that the Philippines consider and control its demographics. The Philippines must limit its population growth, and realize that it is the population numbers and the demographics that will determine the fate of your nation, as much as anything else. In the introduction, I stated that this book has been titled the 'The Unlucky Country' as this nation is, in so many ways, the antithesis to the nation of Australia. Population is another such factor that is antithetical between these two nations. In the 1960's Australia's population was considered so low that the phrase 'populate or perish' was promulgated. Australia is a huge land mass. Roughly equivalent in size to the United States of America, it has a population of only 23 million people, whereas the USA has 300 million. The total land mass of the Philippines would fit snugly into Australia's mainland area of 7,659,861 square kilometers 25.5 times over, yet Australia has approximately only one fifth of the population of the Philippines. The Philippines has a total land mass of 300,000 square kilometers. Like every nation, it has finite resources, natural as well as economic. The Australian politician, Peter Costello, was the Treasurer of the John Howard Government that so transformed the economic face of Australia. While in office, he once made a highly significant assertion, that is: "Population is destiny". He was not only referring to Australia, and to its predicament in regards to a relatively low population, and one that demographically is aging. He would have been also referring to any nation. The aging or 'graying' of the population refers to the fact that there is now in Australia a higher percentage of individuals who are aged and in retirement. These individuals are not employed, do not therefore contribute to the tax base that is needed for infrastructure and health care services for example, and they themselves require increasing amounts of increasingly costly health care, and aged pensions. They may also be engineers, doctors, nurses, IT specialists, teachers and other specialist occupational groups that may be essential for the functioning of an advanced industrialized economy, but have now retired. This leaves large gaps in the manpower profile of the nation. To be politically correct, the last term I used should be 'person power', that is, gender neutral. Australia, in order to fill shortages in its military ranks, will now allow women to engage in frontline combat roles. There is no reason why this should not occur. It has been happening in Israel, for instance, since the mid-1990's. The budgetary ramifications of such factors as the 'graying' of the population, in relation to the payment of aged pensions, are so serious that the Australian government has now lifted the aged pension age from 65 to 67 year of age. The solution for Australia, in contrast to the Philippines, has been to accept large numbers of young immigrants, among them of course Filipino OFWs into its workforce. The Philippines exports workers, Australia imports them.

In 2011, the government of President Aquino introduced the Reproductive Health Bill. Top marks to the Philippine government in regards to this. The Government is taking its role seriously in terms of its responsibility for setting the demographic parameters of the nation, and therefore its future economic performance and capacity to feed, clothe and educate its children. The issue of family planning and population control is central to the future of the Philippines and its economic success. UNFPA, the United Nations Population Fund, is an international development agency that promotes the right of every woman, man and child to enjoy a life of health and equal opportunity. UNFPA, in its own words, 'supports countries in using population data for policies and programs to reduce poverty and to ensure that every pregnancy is wanted, every birth is safe, every young person is free of HIV/AIDS, and every girl and woman is treated with dignity and respect.'(27) Can anyone ever argue against such sentiments? These are very noble and desirable objectives. In regards to the economy of a nation, family planning programs create conditions that enable women to enter the labor force and families to devote more resources to each child, thereby improving family nutrition, education levels and living standards. Slower population growth in nations such as the Philippines cuts the cost of social services as fewer women die in childbirth; and demand eases for water, food, education, health care, housing, transportation and jobs. In this nation, high population growth is outpacing economic progress. Family planning is a powerful tool in combating poverty. However, universal access to family planning it is not yet a reality, certainly not among the poorest. A study of 48 countries estimated that the proportion of people living in poverty would have fallen by a third if the birth rate had fallen by five per 1,000 people in the 1980s. Just to maintain existing conditions, countries with rapidly growing populations must double the number of teachers, equipment and classrooms every 20 to 25 years. Researchers estimate that universal access to family planning could save the lives of about 175,000 women each year globally. Increasing birth intervals to three years could also prevent the deaths of 1.8 million children under 5.(28) Having fewer, healthier children can reduce the economic burden on poor families and allow them to invest more in each child's care and schooling, helping to break the cycle of poverty. As women become more educated, they participate more in the labor market. Spaced births and fewer pregnancies improve child survival. Depending on the services offered, each dollar spent on voluntary family planning can save governments up to US$31 in health care, water, education, housing, and sewers. Being able to manage their fertility empowers women in other areas of their lives. (A frightening thought for some Filipino macho males perhaps!) It really does all sound so sensible. And further, a global cost-benefit analysis found that spending US$3.9 billion on contraceptives for women in the most needy of developing countries could prevent 52 million unintended pregnancies and 22 million abortions, and save on health care costs.(29) This very important fact should be noted by the Catholic Church, who purportedly base their opposition to contraception in the Philippines on the notion that birth control leads to abortion being practiced. Effective birth control can *prevent* abortions. There is no one who finds abortion more abhorrent than I do, but abhorrence to abortion should not prevent individuals obtaining their human right to family planning. And the key would be to prevent fertilization occurring in the first place, if the intention is not to become pregnant. Thus preventing individuals engaging in abortion as a consequence of an unwanted pregnancy. The Catholic Church allows the natural rhythm method as a form of birth control, but this method is very unreliable. There is an old joke, "What do you call people who use the rhythm method? Answer, "Parents!" The Roman Catholic Church is a male-dominated, male power-based, ultra-right wing, conservative, intolerant, self-interested and fossilized organization. Alright, I admit it, apart from that it's OK. Women have no power in the hierarchy of the Catholic Church. It is clearly failing women on the whole issue of family planning. To leave women disempowered is of no consequence to the hierarchy and male power brokers of the Catholic Church. They believe in the disempowerment and lower status of women. Breed, produce babies, suffer adverse health consequences, but don't have any control or choice in any of this. A female Pope? A gay Pope? Now, that would be a day to rejoice for equal rights. How about a black, lesbian, female Pope? Why not? An insult to the Church? There is no greater insult than preventing every individual on this planet with choice, with empowerment, with good health, and the right of every child to be wanted, and to be properly fed, clothed, educated and cared for. The Roman Catholic Church should start to think more about human rights and equality, and less about dogma. I do not have any sympathy or respect for some of the fat cat bishops and prelates of the Catholic Church. Those people are well fed and well looked after, unlike the millions of children that are born into poverty each year. These are the children that have to run around in rags and dig for something to sell at garbage tips. I know that there must be good, caring, humble, progressive and truly spiritual men in the ranks of the bishops and prelates of the Church. And I would say to them, you really ought to be fomenting revolution in your ranks, and in the power structures of the Church, because if there is one institution that would benefit from, and is overdue for, revolution it is the Catholic Church, globally and in the Philippines.

We already know that the Philippines, in terms of key economic and social indicators, was ahead of Indonesia, Thailand and Vietnam 40 years ago. The nation has now fallen behind and that trend is likely to continue. The difference with these other nations mentioned above is that they carried out successful population management programs. As a result, all three are now enjoying the dividends of effective family planning. That is, rapid economic growth, decreasing poverty, and a better quality of life. There is a very important principle that has been stated, in relation to nations that are populous and in poverty and this is 'Fertility Fall Precedes Economic Growth'. Indonesia is perhaps the clearest case of the causal relationship of population management to economic growth and poverty reduction. A low population growth rate translates into a higher gross domestic product (GDP) per capita, and this translates into higher incomes, higher savings, and higher investments. Effective population management interacted with economic growth to trigger a virtuous circle that made a central contribution to reducing the percentage of the Indonesian population living in poverty, from 40 per cent in the late seventies, to around 11 per cent in the mid-nineties. That translates to an overall reduction of almost 75 per cent in two decades. For those who have studied this issue they state that a key factor is national leadership. Former President Suharto of Indonesia has been credited with having had the vision for Indonesia in this regard, and thirty years ago thought about this issue and provided the high-level political will. Today, the demographic mix and profile is coming together. Indonesia is said to be on the threshold of its "window of opportunity," with a "dependency ratio", that is, the ratio of people aged 0–14 and aged 65 and above, compared to the working age population of 15 to 64 years, moving from 51.9% in 2005 to 48.8% in 2010 to 44.7 in 2020 to 44.0% in 2030. The entry of this new cohort into the labor force has coincided with the unfolding of a new, sustained boom in the Indonesian economy. This has seen Indonesia grow by 4.9 per cent during the lowest point of the current global economic crisis in 2009, even as other economies were plunged into recession. For Indonesia, its debt burden has been reduced, its credit rating has been upgraded, and most importantly, and in contrast to the Philippines, it has a rapidly growing middle class. This is a key point and of critical importance. Further, Indonesia has become of great interest to local and foreign investors.(30)

The same as occurred in Indonesia in regards to family planning should have occurred in the Philippines. Sadly, as mentioned above, the Philippine Catholic Church has resisted at every opportunity to assist with effective control of population growth. As stated above, the government of President Benigno Aquino III has attempted to put in place a rational birth control program, and has attempted to pass legislation in this regard. The Bill is referred to as the Human Reproduction Bill. The Catholic Church of the Philippines has gone to ludicrous lengths to oppose this Bill, and has openly threatened the President of the nation, who happens to be a Catholic, with excommunication. An article that appeared in a Philippine newspaper reported that, 'The president of the Catholic Bishops' Conference of the Philippines (CBCP) on Wednesday reminded President Aquino III that (those) providing contraceptives to poor couples who opt for artificial birth control face excommunication from the church. Speaking on the church-run Radio Veritas, . . . the current CBCP president, said that even Mr. Aquino may be covered by excommunication. Mr. Aquino, a practicing Catholic, has stood by his position that Filipino couples who choose to use artificial contraceptives should be allowed to do so. When asked if Aquino might be excommunicated if he insists that government should distribute artificial contraceptives, the Bishop said: "That is a possibility . . . . Right now, it is a proximate possibility."(31) Excommunication is the highest punishment for erring members, for those who assault the Pope or are involved in abortion. Catholic groups state that some artificial contraceptives are abortifacients. The Bishop who was quoted above, according to the article, said he has talked to bishops in Mindanao and the Visayas and they were supportive of calls by lay Catholic groups to hold protests against the government's plan to distribute artificial contraceptives. The Bishop whose views were aired in the article, reiterated the Church's opposition to the passage of the reproductive health bill, which has been re-filed in Congress. The article states, "We have been consistent with our position that we are against it. Because if the reason is the population problem connected to poverty alleviation, I don't (think population increase) is a problem. (That) is not an issue."(32) He further stated in the article that pharmaceutical companies and laboratories will be the ones who will benefit, "because they are the ones supplying the pills and other contraceptive devices."(33) The Bishop has got that bit right. Pharmaceutical companies obviously will benefit. However, so will Filipinos and the Philippine nation, by being unburdened from exploding and unsustainable population growth, and all of its associated economic and environmental costs.

The issue of out of control population growth, and the issue of the deterioration in the Philippine economy are linked. Out of control population growth, and an absence of effective family planning and birth control equates, in countries like the Philippines, with sustained poverty and economic underachievement. I have studied the situation that the Philippines finds itself in. My analysis leads me to the conclusion, that without effective birth control and family planning within this nation, and other measures such as the retainment of engineers, scientists and technicians, what is going to happen is that the garbage dumps are going to get bigger and bigger, and the number of poverty-stricken children scavenging on them is also going to grow bigger and bigger. There is not going to be any way to break out of this cycle of poverty. Failure to act will allow other nations, who have got there act together on this and other issues, to race ahead economically. The Philippines cannot "take off" economically, for the reasons I have outlined in this book. Excessive population growth is a critical factor, and is as important as the other factors, one being the drastic shortage of research and development scientists and engineers to fuel any growth in science or knowledge based industries. The current government of the Philippines needs to press ahead with its plan to introduce effective family planning programs for the populace. The 1987 Constitution of the Philippines declares: 'The separation of Church and State shall be inviolable.' (Article II, Section 6). The Catholic Church has no mandate under the Constitution of the Republic to involve itself in the affairs of state. President Aquino must face down the bishops. There is too much at stake for the nation and those in poverty to do otherwise.

In today's world, global competitiveness is the reality and every nation is forced to compete with other nations. The Darwinian principle of 'survival of the fittest' applies in the economic area of global trade. In the 21st century everything occurs so much faster, so many economic processes occur in 'real time'. The world is now a purely capitalistic economic system. This means that competitiveness has increased, and requires the continuous necessity to become more efficient and more productive. The lifeblood of the capitalistic economic system is, of course, monetary capital and the availability of money for investment and economic growth. Second to that necessity is the need for oil. Oil is the lifeblood of the world's industrial and transport system. It is a finite resource, and inevitably, the world is going to in the future have to shift to other energy sources to fuel economic processes and growth. There has evolved in the last 20 years another essential requirement to the current global capitalistic system, an essential that has become embedded in the economic processes and the very psyche of mankind, and that is the internet or World Wide Web. So many processes related to economic activity, trade, and the free flow of money and information depend upon it that it has become an indispensable requirement of everyday life. The internet is now an essential infrastructure requirement of every advanced economy worldwide. The facilitation of economic activity, the provision of goods and services, and the requirement for economic growth necessitates an effective infrastructure system. By this, we mean good roads and transport systems, good postal services, good telecommunications systems, and a national high-speed internet system. I mentioned in Chapter 1 that I had made the journey from the Bicol region to Manila by sea and road. To engage in such a journey is a good way to see and observe the state of that critical area of infrastructure, that being roads and bridges. I was actually shocked to see and experience the poor state of what is referred to as the national highway leading from Pilar to Manila. The roads and bridges infrastructure of the Philippines is in a poor state indeed and significant investment in this area is needed. One must also be cognizant of the need for recurring funding for these infrastructure projects, and this is an additional but necessary burden to the economy. However, the reality is that there is no possible way to create a modern, dynamic and efficient economy without their being the full spectrum of supporting infrastructures in place. In the West new business models have been introduced that utilize the internet as a tool of commerce. I refer to such business models as eBay. In the West, to engage in such a model of commerce one would simply order the goods over the internet from the EBay seller and the articles would be posted out in the public mail system. In countries like Australia or the US there is a very low risk of the goods not arriving. However, in the Philippines, we have a significant problem. Searching the internet for references to mail theft in the Philippines the following 'Yahoo! Answers' internet site was illustrative in regards to the question: 'Is there a foreign mail theft problem in the Philippines.'(34) There were 9 answers posted, all of them negative and highly critical of the Philippine public mail system. The question was so posted in February 2011 and I give here the responses, recorded verbatim, below:

Question posted: '*Is there a foreign mail theft problem in the Philippines?*

Is it reasonable and safe to do a mail order business from the Philippines? Is there a significant inbound and outbound foreign mail theft problem in the Philippines?

Do the Philippine Customs usually charge import duty on the valued inbound mail received into the Philippines?'

The 'Best Answer' that was chosen by voters on the site was:

'Mail theft is a huge problem in the Philippines. Especially anything coming in with a foreign address.

Customs crocodiles are even worse, charging anything they please and feel they can get away with.

Doing a mail order business in the Philippines is a really bad idea unless your dealing with high value items that are worth using a courier service like fedex and even then the customs crocodiles will kill you in duties.'

Other comments listed included: *'The only reliable way to receive mail is through a courier.'* And, *'There is no 'foreign' mail theft problem . . . . IT IS ALL DONE BY THE FILIPINO POSTAL WORKERS.'* And, *'BIG BIG problem. I suggest that you find another business.'* And, *'What you mean foreign mail. Even local mail.'* And, *'The postal office will never admit it. Just look at the proliferation of courier services all over the country. That should answer your question.'* And, *'Mail order BUSINESS? Only if you can afford to use special couriers like LBC . . . . to get it on the plane'*

To verify individually these posts on the 'Yahoo Answers' site is not possible, however the responses are illustrative, and reflect what everyone who is in the Philippines knows, and anyone who has sent mail regularly from overseas knows, that is: the regular Philippine mail service is unreliable and theft and pilferage are massive problems. It is also reflective of the *reputation* of the Philippines in terms of its capacity to transact business internally and externally. The comments above fit in entirely with my own experience. What an unreliable and inefficient mail system means, in practical terms, is that anyone wishing to start a trading business is reliant on the private courier services with associated higher costs. This can cripple a small business. Goods and services business models, such as eBay, rely on the effective and reliable transfer of goods, usually by the public postal system. Where the mail system cannot deliver, and this phrase is here meant literally, then small businesses suffers as a result, and ordinary Filipino citizens who are trying to start a trading business via the internet are put at significant disadvantage.

Another issue that has been present as a factor in hindering economic growth and investment is that of intellectual piracy. The Philippines is on the US blacklist of nations tolerating intellectual piracy. A newspaper article in 2011 reported that the Philippines is taking measures in order to be removed from the list.(35) One of these was the crushing of PHP350 million worth of counterfeit goods on 'World Anti-Counterfeiting Day.' But this was just a very small fraction of the amount of counterfeit goods in circulation. Every form of consumer goods is at risk of being counterfeited. The issue is important, as the government believes more investors will come to the country if intellectual piracy and counterfeiting is eliminated. However, despite this being a huge problem there are reports that progress is being made by the Philippines and other trading partners, in enacting significant legislation protecting intellectual property. In 2007 a study was conducted into software piracy rates and the Philippines was stated to have a software piracy rate of 69%. (36) In 2004 an article appeared which stated that Intellectual piracy was robbing the Philippines of potential investments in software development. The author of the study found a 'high negative correlation' between investments in software development, and Information Technology (IT) in general, and estimates of intellectual property thefts for the four years to December 2002.(37) IT investments quadrupled from a year earlier in 2000 when the piracy rate posted a seven percentage-point decline to 70% in 1999, according to the study. 'Similarly, investments in 2001 climbed by 38.2% when piracy rates dropped by nine percentage points in 2000.' For 2004, the data indicated 61% of all software used in the Philippines was pirated, down from 70% in 1999. 'On the other hand, the investment level decreased in 2002, when the Philippines posted a higher piracy rate in 2001 of 63 percent.'(38) Philippine exports of IT software and services reached $US186 million in 2002, when the industry's contribution to the country's gross domestic product was less than 1%. Philippine software exports were expected to reach almost $1 billion by 2010, more than twice the $423 million earned in 2007. The industry was enjoying an annual growth rate of 30%. Software services account for nine percent of the total business processes outsourced to the Philippines. This is in contrast to Call Centers, which account for 74 percent. It was further reported the local software industry, however, continues to suffer from the loss of IT-skilled graduates, including programmers, who leave for better-paying jobs overseas. (39) So we have in the Philippines clearly a problem with piracy. In the waters of the nation with piracy of the seas, and in its markets with counterfeit goods and intellectual and software piracy. The government has recognized the damage these practices can do to the economy, and has been taking measures to stem their proliferation.

Now let us discuss the thorny subject of corruption in the Philippines. There are various forms of corruption, and they include bribery, extortion, cronyism, nepotism, patronage, graft and embezzlement. All of these forms are practiced in the Philippines. It is a global problem, but is worse in some countries than others. Worldwide, bribery alone is estimated to involve over 1 trillion US dollars annually.(40) 'Corruption also generates economic distortions in the public sector by diverting public investment into capital projects where bribes and kickbacks are more plentiful. Officials may increase the technical complexity of public sector projects to conceal or pave the way for such dealings, thus further distorting investment. Corruption also lowers compliance with construction, environmental, or other regulations, reduces the quality of government services and infrastructure, and increases budgetary pressures on government.'(41) This was one of the reasons the Corazon Aquino government was so wary of the Marcos Bataan Nuclear Power Plant project. The construction of the plant was felt to be likely riddled with corrupt processes, and the possible compromising of building regulations, due to the "skimming off" of money or materials for designated areas of the plant. So this kind of corruption is almost always blamed for the ills that beset the Philippine economy and is cited in explaining why the country is so economically underdeveloped. In 2010 the Philippines was placed 134th on a list of

178 nations that constituted the Corruption Perception Index.(42) That's a bad score. The country that was perceived to have the least corruption was Denmark, which came in at number 1 with a score of 9.3 out of 10. The score for the Philippines was 2.4 out of 10. Somalia came in last, and is the country judged to be the most corrupt, with a score of 1.1.(43) It is no secret that corruption is rife in the Philippines. But is this necessarily a bad thing, and does it explain all of the country's ills? In regards to a nuclear power plant or other such major building project, then clearly corruption is a very bad thing. Money being "skimmed off" leads to sub-standard construction and the potential for disaster. Beyond this, does corruption, in the form of bribery for instance, hinder economic efficiency or does it improve economic efficiency? It may do this by allowing bribed officials to circumvent a plodding bureaucracy, and thus facilitate rapid action and rapid outcomes, improving thereby the efficiency of the economy. The one obvious and massive drawback that corruption does have is on the tax base of the economy. Central governments rely on tax collection to fund health and education services for example, and to build and maintain the infrastructure of the nation. Let us look at other nations to see what their experience has been. Let us look at one nation that is an undoubted economic success story, an economic "miracle". It is a nation that has displayed phenomenal economic growth rates. And surprise, surprise, that nation also has very high levels of corruption. The nation I am referring to is India. It is a huge land with a huge population. The nation also has 415 living languages. It is blessed with a contiguous land mass; it is not geographically fragmented like the Philippines, which suffers in hidden ways due to this. India is a Federal Constitutional Republic; it has 28 states and 7 union territories. The Indian economy is the ninth largest in the world by measures of nominal GDP. Here is the interesting part. Despite having phenomenal economic growth rates, and a burgeoning middle class, it was listed in 2010 as number 84th on Transparency International's Corruption Index.(44) Corruption in India is perceived to have increased significantly, with one report estimating the illegal capital flows since independence to be US$462 billion(45) But in India the growth in corruption and economic growth have taken place hand in hand. This is not to say that one would actually

encourage corruption. However, without it in the Philippines, it is likely that the bureaucratic hurdles that so beset the nation would be far bigger than they are now. When one, in the Philippines, goes 'under the table' to obtain a service, that is, pay the official involved an unofficial payment for accelerating the process, matters occur extremely quickly. The requested service occurs or the necessary documents appear, or what needs to be "arranged", is arranged quickly. The payer of the bribe is satisfied with this, and the official is satisfied too, because on top of his wages, he receives extra money. However, that money will not be directly taxed. The intended economic process that the payee of the bribe is involved in speeds along. If the unofficially received money, the bribe money, is circulated within the local economy, it remains a stimulus, facilitating further economic transactions. The bribed official has hit pay dirt and he heads down to the local mall to get a nice haircut, buys some Filipino produced groceries and drinks, and then gives his wife a share, who spends it at the beauty salon. That is all keeping locals in employment. It's actually just the same as if the person paying the bribe had instead used the money themselves to get a nice haircut, buy some Filipino groceries, and, well you get the gist of my argument by now. There is in the Philippines a Goods and Services Tax (GST) of 12%, so any use of that money to purchase goods and services in the open market is caught by the Government, if the trader is compliant with the provisions of the GST. Then a proportion will fall into the Government coffers. This should fund infrastructure, health, and educational services. The problem is, of course, that the corruption does not stop at the local level and involve relatively small sums. It also disadvantages those individuals who cannot afford to pay "under the table." The poor are disadvantaged, unless of course, they happen to be the person receiving the bribe. At top government levels, corruption happens too, and it can take a more pernicious form, as in the Marcos era, for example. The money that Marcos and his cronies embezzled was mostly salted away in US and Swiss bank accounts. It's not just Marcos. He just happened to get the most publicity. What he and his cronies did was only the tip of the iceberg and what we know about publicly. For decades capital has been hemorrhaging from the Philippines, in illicit ways There is likely vast sums flowing out from the Philippine economy every day, day in and day out, making its way to overseas bank accounts. That money is therefore not circulating in the Philippine economy, and provides no local economic stimulus. The corrupt go on their shuttle trips to the US to spend all that money on US goods and services and real estate. Therefore, the money is effectively lost to this nation. There is an old Filipino joke, "What is the difference between corruption in the USA, and corruption in the Philippines?" Answer, "In the USA the corrupt go to jail, while in the Philippines the corrupt go to the USA." Corruption, in any form, is considered by most economists as a distinct disadvantage, and indicative of, and perpetuating, weak governance and low tax efficiency.(46) Embezzlement is the act of dishonestly appropriating or secreting assets by one or more individuals to whom such assets have been entrusted.(47) When practiced by a select few, when the amounts are extremely large, and when the money is taken out of circulation, or not used for investment in the host country, it is damaging to the economy. On the other hand, when corruption is democratized, that is, is widespread, and the money stays within the local economy it may lubricate growth because it efficiently bypasses the inefficiencies of government or other bureaucracies.(48) So let us be clear. Corruption is not necessarily a hindrance to economic growth. It depends on the form it takes. And neither is having a dictatorship as a form of government necessarily bad. It simply depends on the form it takes, as we shall see when we discuss the nation of Singapore later. Stashing ill-gotten gains overseas is detrimental to the economy. Money in circulation locally, whether tainted or not through bribery and corruption, stimulates the economy.

The issue of the "necessity", when one wishes to obtain rapid outcomes, to engage in bribery, is pertinent to the Philippines. A report has stated that this nation has a 'cumbersome bureaucracy'. It is run by close to 1.5 million civil servants and is structurally challenged by weak mechanisms for planning, agenda-setting, and policy-making. There is a poor performance management and measurement system. It is an overly large bureaucracy, however it is riddled with gaps, overlaps, and duplication of functions, activities, and jurisdiction at all levels. There is a reported overemphasis on rules and procedures instead of directing resources towards the realization of intended outcomes and impacts. It is a highly politicized bureaucracy, with a lack of managerial and technical competencies; and it is characterized by wrong mindsets, attitudes, and corporate culture.(49) Apart from that, it's OK! So there are enormous inefficiencies within government departments due to the above shortcomings. I have had the opportunity to observe such processes at first hand. I observed a Filipino friend undergo the operation of starting-up a business in his hometown in the Philippines. The business permit was acquired via the local City Hall. This is the Mayor's Business Permit, as it is referred to. The process involved the business being subject to scrutiny by local government departments, for example the fire department, and the health department. This process proceeded uneventfully and appeared to be handled efficiently. However, the whole process stopped there. Following issuance of the permit there was no other support or information or guidance received from the local or central government to assist anyone starting a business. Noting this I did go to the local City Hall, without the knowledge of my friend, to make a request to the mayor that a letter of encouragement be given to this budding businessperson, my friend. My letter was passed on to another official by the administrative staff of the Mayor, and I chased this person up to discuss this issue, asking, as I had in my letter, that letters of encouragement be sent out to individuals who are starting a business. I was advised that a letter could be sent out, but one never arrived. I did expect that perhaps my friend would be invited to join a local business group, or be given some materials on how to successfully grow one's business, and perhaps information on who could provide assistance and mentorship if needed. However, nothing of this nature was forthcoming. It got even worse when he applied for his Bureau of Internal Revenue, or business tax number. We went to the local BIR office. Just as an aside, a woman was sitting in front of us in the queue. While waiting with my friend I heard repeatedly the cluck, cluck, cluck, of a chicken's cackling coming from where the woman in front of us was sitting. I kept thinking to myself, that woman has a funny cell phone text alert; it's the sound of a chicken cackling. However, I couldn't work out why she didn't check her phone to read her text while she was sitting there. She later got up to leave and when she turned to face us, I noticed that she in fact was actually carrying a chicken in a plastic bag. I can only presume that the business she had started, and was present to register with the Tax Office for, had something to do with chickens. The jokes we could create from this episode are legion. How about, "I was at the BIR office and I was going to register, but I chickened out". Or, "Guys, get down to the BIR, there's chicks there!." It provided a light moment in the otherwise dull time of waiting. It was our turn next and the clerk who dealt with our enquiry completed an entry in the computer system. It took a few minutes. He then gave my friend a Bureau form that he had to sign. My friend was then told that it had to be faxed to the BIR head office in Manila. The clerk advised my friend that a fax service was available in town and he should avail himself of this. I found it astonishing that it was left to the individual to expend the expense and trouble and time of having to fax a BIR document externally from the BIR office in which we had just visited. The government should be encouraging tax compliance by making it as easy as possible to register a business. We left the office and went to a local courier shop that had a fax service. The sales assistant tried to fax the form but to no avail, the lines were constantly engaged. She enquired as to where the document was being faxed to, and when told it was the BIR in Manila, she shook her head and told my friend, in the local language, the English equivalent of, "You have a snowball in hell's chance of getting any forms faxed through to the BIR." This was in the year 2011. Why didn't the local BIR office take the form and fax it themselves using dedicated fax lines to the central office? Alternatively, even better, why did they not have a simple, inexpensive document scanning machine, to scan the signed form of my friend and then e-mail it to the BIR head office in Manila as an attachment? Simple, efficient, quick and inexpensive. But sadly not available.

One encounters these inefficiencies, hurdles and figurative brick walls wherever one is in the Philippines. The author once attended the offices of a government agency in Manila. This particular agency had what they referred to as a 'one-stop-shop' to allow anyone who was attending to complete an application process for the particular service offered, in one go. Or so it was stated. I spoke to one of the staff who outlined the application process. She then gave me some forms, one of which was the main application form. I stated to her that I would like to get started on the process and complete the form straight away. She advised me that I couldn't do that as it had to have the information completed in typewritten form! Oddly, they did not have a typewriter there and available for anyone to use, and neither did they offer to have the document completed via a word processor and then printed out to be signed. Despite my advising that I was only visiting Manila and would not have the immediate opportunity to lodge the form again, she reiterated that that was the policy of the agency. The clear and common sense answer to this inefficient service was readily available, a typewriter or someone to transcribe the form there and then, but the agency that I speak of did not provide it, or assist further. I had no choice but to leave with the form. One-Stop-Shop? Hardly. When I reported above on the comments made in a report about the Philippine government bureaucracy, to the effect, 'There is a reported overemphasis on rules and procedures instead of directing resources towards the realization of intended outcomes and impacts', I know exactly what is meant. The same agency engaged in the usual Filipino obsession with American dollars, requesting that certain payments and deposits be made in that form of currency. There is a big world out there and there are many different currencies, with some now worth a lot more than the Greenback, which continues to lose value. While we are in the Philippines, why don't we just transact in the good old local currency that is legal tender? That is, the Philippine Peso.

The other often-cited reason as to why the Philippines is in an impoverished state is that the political system is dysfunctional. Like corruption, this cannot of itself explain poverty in the Philippines, as there are other nations who have become extremely prosperous while being ruled by political systems that are less than democratic. Singapore, as we have mentioned, is one example. Singapore, in contrast to the Philippines, has experienced extraordinary success in regards to its economic development. In the 1950's and 1960's, like many other nations of the time, it was an economic backwater. Lazing its days away, like the titled British expatriates who sipped their drinks at Raffles

Hotel, it lived a genteel existence in the steady flows of the global economic currents of the time. It is a tiny nation, situated on an island off the southern tip of Malaysia. Its population resided mostly in slums or houseboats.(50) It lived this sedate existence until 1965 when a man of remarkable capability and vision came to power after Singapore's independence from the United Kingdom. Prime Minister Lee Kuan Yew ascended to power and transformed the nation in a way that is simply astonishing. Born in 1923, Lee became the first Prime Minister of Singapore in 1959. He is widely credited as the architect behind Singapore's remarkable transformation from third-world country to first in just under a generation. In 1990, he stepped down as Prime Minister, but continued to wield significant influence on government decisions as a cabinet member, first as Senior Minister and later as Minister Mentor. Despite repeated clarifications that he only holds an advisory position, Lee is still believed to hold sway over many executive decisions. So this former Prime Minister of the nation, and those he placed around him in key positions, developed a vision. And they paid scrupulous attention to every detail, every variable and every demographic factor in setting Singapore on the road to economic success. Following his rise to power, over the next twenty years the Singapore economy grew eightfold. The government also had at its disposal a population eager to work, and a population mindset where consensus was easily achieved. The government had no problem ruling this nation. It was geographically small, and contiguous in morphology, and the people of this land felt comfortable living in a culture of clear boundaries and predictable outcomes. The nation runs like the proverbial Swiss watch.(51) I have been to Singapore and one is always astonished by the breathtaking efficiency of its economic processes. Singapore has maneuvered itself into being a central economic hub of the region. Its airport is spectacular, like a city in itself. How does one keep a place like it clean? Imagine all that dusting! But it is spotlessly clean, and runs, as does everything else in Singapore, like clockwork. For a very small nation, Singapore thought big, and succeeded big. Singapore is now a first-world nation. It did for a time, I was told by a Singaporean some years ago, try to avoid becoming so recognized, as the nation would then lose certain advantages available to it with a third world status, but it couldn't resist the huge tide of its own economic prosperity and had to become so recognized as a first world state. Adjusting for cost of living differences, Singapore's GDP per capita was ranked 3rd globally by the International Monetary Fund in 2010. It would be very hard to find evidence of homelessness or poverty in Singapore, although an official figure of 0.3% is given. Jobs are freely available and there is a strong work ethic. Deciding that they were breeding too fast to allow sustainable economic development, the Lee Kuan Yew government set up free family planning clinics and tied a number of incentives to having small families. Alongside this, there was an education campaign to communicate with the populace, and explain the reasons for what they were doing. Workers in Singapore contribute a proportion of their earnings to a savings fund, what we would call in Australia a superannuation fund. Employers match the contribution of the employee, and because the money cannot be accessed until the age of 55, there is a huge pot of gold for the government to invest in national infrastructure, housing and government services. Southeast Asia has developed considerably over the past half-century, but Singapore has leaped even further ahead of her much larger and well-endowed neighbors, including the Philippines. It is testament to the combined effort of all Singaporeans, under the erstwhile stewardship of Lee and his team, that the country now stands as an oasis of prosperity, orderliness and efficiency. It is almost as an oddity in contrast to the region.(52) The majority of Singaporeans own their own apartments. They live a very orderly life, with jaywalking, spitting, and anti-social behavior banned. Chewing Gum was not allowed to be sold. There is the State lottery but little other gambling. And trafficking in drugs equates with the death penalty. Reportedly, Singapore University scholars have called the nation a "meritocratic, elitist, Confucianist, bureaucratic state".(53) You can always rely on academics to find a contrary negative postulation. It sounds like they're a bit grumpy, but everyone else in Singapore is happy. It is a stunningly successful "meritocratic, elitist, Confucianist, bureaucratic state". It is a nation that has used the capitalistic system in a thoroughly pragmatic way, but is at heart socialist and has ensured a relatively equal distribution of wealth. All of the money going through the government coffers seems to trickle down to the masses. More power to anyone else who wants to use the same model of government. Even if it is a dictatorship.

So the contrast between Singapore and the Philippines is very marked indeed. Singapore is a tiny island; it is only 637.5 square kilometers in size. There have been land reclamation projects, and reportedly, it may grow in size to a princely 800 square kilometers by 2030. By contrast, Cebu, to mention just one island of the Philippines, is 4,468 square kilometers in size. Singapore in 2010 had a GDP (Gross Domestic Product) of US$234.0 Billion. The Philippines had a GDP of US$188.7 Billion.(54) Singapore has about one twenty-fifth the population as that of the Philippines. Singapore could fit into the Philippine total land mass 470 times over. Singapore is dwarfed in comparison to the Philippines by every measure including its resources, its population, and its land area, and yet Singapore economically outperforms the Philippines by an incredible margin. The most commonly accepted method of determining the wealth of countries, and comparing generalized differences in living standards as a whole between nations, is to use GDP on a Purchasing Power Parity (PPP) basis in current International Dollars.(54) International Dollars are a hypothetical unit of currency. You cannot actually possess or exchange an International Dollar, the unit is simply used for making economic calculations. Economists are very fond of the hypothetical, and engaging in conjecture, but make no mistake about it, the wealth that Singapore generates is real. Gross Domestic Product (GDP) represents the strength, or output, of a country's economy. The measure that most economists prefer is GDP (PPP), that is, GDP based on Purchasing Power Parity per capita. GDP (PPP) per capita compares generalized differences in living standards overall between nations. PPP takes into account the relative cost of living and the inflation rates of countries, rather than using just currency exchange rates, which may distort the real differences in income.(55) In a list of the wealthiest nations Singapore listed 4th out of 182 nations with a GDP based on PPP of $52,840 International Dollars. The Philippines was placed at 127th on the same list, with a GDP based on PPP of $3,604 International Dollars for the year 2010.(56) Let us imagine someone who had seen both these countries, Singapore and the Philippines, twenty years ago, and then fell into a coma. By a medical miracle, that person emerges from their coma in 2011, and again visited Singapore and again visited the Philippines. There is only one logical and rational question that he could pose to the Philippines after seeing the contrast in the two nations. That is, "What the hell have you been doing?"

The evidence for the comparative slide in regards to the Philippines trading and economic position is apparent by other measures. Including those on a day-to-day, experiential level. My very first experience of the Philippines was a trip to Cebu in 1981. Coming from Australia, the exchange rate at that time was approximately PHP20 to the Australian dollar. At the time of writing this book, in 2011, the exchange rate is now approximately PHP45 to the Australian dollar. Over the intervening years, using the exchange rate as an indicator of relative economic strength between the two nations, one can conclude that the Australian economy has become more than twice as strong as it was, in comparison to the Philippine economy. This is a great advantage to the foreigner, as it allows one in the Philippines to live so well, if one's retirement income or income source is in such currencies as the Australian dollar. For the Philippines, its fortunes are reversed, and its economic decline continues. Australia has indeed shown consistent economic growth and is now a trillion dollar economy. With a population of only 22 million people, it has utilized its resources very cleverly in order to propel its economic growth. The great economic dynamos in the Asian and South Asian region of the last decade, that is China and India, have bought Australian resources to help fuel their economic growth. Australia cleverly placed itself in the slipstream of the startling economic dynamism of these nations. Australia has not only worked hard it, it has also worked *smart*. The last 15 years of economic policy in Australia have been critical in maneuvering this huge nation into the slipstream of global economic growth. At the helm of this huge economic and resource-rich vessel during this critical period were two politicians of note, John Howard, the Prime Minister, and his Treasurer, Peter Costello. These two men were capable and astute politicians, along the lines of Lee Kuan Yew of Singapore. However, in Australia they operated within a purely democratic framework. Their administration has passed, but their political legacy has lived on. Australia is not crippled by significant corruption, and the machinery of government and political processes work very efficiently. Australians are not prone to thoughts of civil unrest or revolt. That is only likely to occur if the 'footy' or any other sports were cancelled on a Saturday afternoon. They have enjoyed a very stable history and have many factors working in their favor. For good reason has Australia been referred to as 'The Lucky Country.' But lucky or not, it has still had to think hard and to work hard to set itself on the road to sustained economic prosperity.

The political process, by contrast, within the Philippines, is dysfunctional. We have made the distinction between good and bad corruption, and there is good and bad political dysfunction. Singapore did not function as a democracy in the truest sense. It was actually a dictatorship, a dysfunctional democracy. However, this helped Singapore. It was the right leadership, the right skills, and the right vision. In the Philippines, there are the *structures* of a democratic nation in place, but *in practice,* the nation does not function as a true democracy. It may do in parts of the nation, but in other parts, you will find fiefdoms and warlords. Same nation, different world. We will discuss this further in Chapter 5. Due to the close association and high positive correlation in the Philippines between wealth, family and politics one could say that the Philippines is in some ways more of a monarchy than a democracy. Political power can be gained as something akin to a hereditary right. For me personally it does not matter in what way a nation is ruled. You can have the purest, most democratic nation in the world, and it may be home to huge numbers of people in poverty. Or you could have a dictatorship that functioned extremely well, and was benevolent and smart and disciplined, and it managed to drive the economy skillfully to the benefit of all. With poverty afflicting only a tiny minority. Just like Singapore. I know what I would prefer. Democracy is just a word, how people live is the important thing.

In the United Kingdom in the 1970's, we saw the rise to power of an extraordinary female politician, who exerted not only enormous influence over her country, but also globally. She was Prime Minister of the United Kingdom from 1979 to 1990. In her alliance with Ronald Reagan, for instance, they carried the mantle in the fight against communism. This politician, named Margaret Thatcher, was fond of relating to others that her father was an ordinary British shopkeeper, and that she was born in the small apartment above the small grocery shop where he traded. Her parents used to go on vacation separately, so that there was always someone there to care for the shop. It was definitely a working class existence. More about her later, because her politics and her style provides an interesting story. Within the Philippines, it is unthinkable that people from such "ordinary" backgrounds could ever become president. There may be a few exceptions to this, and one exception may turn out to be someone like the current world boxing champion and senator, Manny Pacquiao. Such is his story, and his mindset, that he will be mentioned also later in the book. However, for the most part, it is only the elite families and the wealthy that have the means to engage in politics Filipino-style. The Philippine population, who are admittedly at times coerced to vote for a certain politician, and this occurs frequently in local or regional politics, are also hopelessly "star struck", and are attracted to those with the charismatic trappings of wealth, or a showbiz connection. What happens in this regard in the Philippines also happens in other third-world countries. In these ways, the linkages and high correlation between politics and wealth become evident. The Philippines has a relatively high level of wealth inequality, compared with most of its regional neighbors. In 2003, the richest 20% of the Philippine families received more than half of the national income; while the poorest 20% accounted for only one twentieth.(57) Again the ugly head of past poor governance in the 1970's raises its head. It transpired that a good deal of the foreign debt of the Philippines consisted of loans that financed projects of political cronies of the then president. Most of the projects failed, and because the loans were coursed through Government financial institutions, they were eventually assumed by the Government.(58) What this means in practical and simple terms is that the money ended up in private pockets. However, the repayment of the loan was assumed by the nation and therefore indirectly by the populace. Those Filipinos that engaged in this embezzlement took off to the States, bought real estate there, and likely hired blonde prostitutes that they drove around in their silver Mercedes. Or perhaps it was a black BMW. The blondes were a nice change from the Filipina mistresses they kept at home. It was a nice lifestyle away from the prying eyes back home in the Philippines. The tab was picked up by the Philippine government and thereby the Philippine populace. Keep paying those taxes, folks, your money is needed! The mindset of these embezzlers was strictly old boy network and Pinoy macho. They didn't miss a trick, and neither did the hookers. Everyone was happy, except the masses at home that had to accept their fate. The Church taught them how to be pious, humble and accept suffering. The ruling elite mouthed the same sentiments for the sake of public image, but their allegiance was to the Swiss bank accounts and the do-as-you-please lifestyle. For the Catholic Church the allegiance was to Rome, or more correctly, to the Vatican. As long as the Pope is happy, and Catholic dogma is rigidly adhered to, then it's all dandy. The Roman Catholic Church still wields enormous influence over the majority Catholic population and to a large degree over government policy.(59) In 2011 some Bishops were being driven around in brand-new SUV's that they had petitioned from the Government. More money wasted. A nice drive out, whiz past the populace, a little wave and a sign of the Cross here and there, have a swim, then back to the air-conditioned rectory. None of the responsibilities and worries of raising a family in poverty. The same as in 1981, when I had my first negative experience with the Church. The assistant would have said, "Father, there is someone here who has an appointment that was made to get a document signed." The response I got was "Father is not able to see you. He has been swimming and he's tired." In the same situation, the Filipino would accept this. Just like the vomit that was on the bus that was going to Manila. Put your hand over your nose and mouth. Accept it. Pretend it's not there. Be uncomfortable. Suffer. Not me. The priest and his assistant got the same response, as did the driver of the bus, which was, this is unacceptable. I got the document signed, and the vomit was cleaned up on the bus. However, I should not have had to do that. I should not have been placed in that position. I have a sister-in-law who is a nun in the Philippine Order of Poor Clare Sisters. I have visited her at her convent. She lives under the most simple of conditions.

It is a life of sacrifice, charity, and self-denial. She is a beautiful person and there are few people that I love and respect more. There are people in the Church that I respect and admire. However, some Churchmen are lazy, pompous and inconsiderate. In addition, as regards their interference in the affairs of state, there is only one thing I would say. "Butt out." (Butt out is an English phrasal verb meaning 'stay out of other people's business.') Leave the affairs of state and the formulation of national policy, including the decision of whether to have a national family planning and birth control program, to the Government and its representatives. Give your opinion; you have a right to do that. Then read the Philippine Constitution to remind yourself of its provisions. However, don't interfere and threaten the President of the day. This chapter is principally focused on economic issues. What has this to do with the economics of the Philippines? The answer is, everything! We need to get *everything* right, including population planning and control, and standards of service. How many foreign tourists are going to come back to this country if they have to travel in buses where there is vomit on the floor? It starts here with common sense attitudes, not necessarily the complexities of macroeconomic theory.

There is another issue that should generate great concern, another negative economic indicator within the Philippines, and that is the shrinking of the middle class. This issue has huge economic as well as political ramifications. It was during the economic boom years of the Ramos administration that many Filipinos, who had been part of the OFW Diaspora, returned to the nation. The economic boom created optimism that perhaps at last the Philippines was on the road to prosperity. Sadly, this growth and optimism was not sustained. The Family Income and Expenditures Survey (FIES) is conducted by the government every three years,(60) The average family income in 2000 was reported to have grown by 17.3-percent from 1997. But adjusted for inflation, the average family's real income actually fell by 3.9 percent. The methodology of the Survey is to divide the population into deciles, or 10 levels, depending on their income. The FIES shows that the net incomes of the top two deciles of the Philippine population grew by an average of 18.5 percent, while the net incomes of the bottom five deciles fell an average of 55 percent. The middle three deciles saw incomes grow by about 12 percent since 1997. These figures demonstrate that while the overall economic pie is getting smaller, the upper 20 percent are getting a larger share, and the lower 50 percent are getting a smaller share. As the gap between the upper and lower classes grows, the middle is literally caught in between. The upper middle class has seen modest growth in its real income, but the median to lower middle class is falling and becoming poorer, implying that the middle class is getting smaller, both in numbers and influence.(61) Another important indicator relating to the shrinkage of the middle class is the migration of students from private schools to public schools. Figures from the Department of Education show a slow but steady decline in private school enrollment over the decades. In school year 1967-68, 59.5 percent of high school students were enrolled in private schools, while 40.5 percent went to public schools. This trend has slowly but surely reversed itself over the past 32 years. By school year 1999-2000, at least 75.9 percent of high school students were going to public schools and only 24.1 percent were in private schools.(62) So the middle classes are shrinking all the time, and the poor are getting poorer and the rich richer. This is not the demographic and economic profile that we want. The article that I sourced this information from reported that a survey had been done by an independent agency, and when asked if a democratic form of government were suitable for the development of Philippine society, 84 percent or those Filipinos questioned agreed. But when asked if it were *not* important for a government to be democratic as long as it did a "good job," 79 percent agreed. The article closes by giving a quotation from one of those middle class Filipinos who are still left in the country, expressing his disenchantment with the political process. "What we need in this country is a strong man."(63)

Filipinos are ambivalent about those who govern them. On the one hand, they seek democracy and equality, but on the other hand recognize that perhaps some problems will not be solved until "a strong man" is in power. Revealing too is the statement "a strong *man*". Presumably, this infers that a woman could just never do the job! As we have seen, there are many countries that have benefited from a benevolent dictator, like

Singapore. The perennial problem is: because a dictator holds all of the power, there are effectively no mechanisms in place to ensure that the dictator remains benevolent! There are many examples of dictators who were not benevolent, but whipped their countries into shape. Stalin was one such man, and his authority and brutality drove the fast-paced industrialization of the Soviet Union and laid the foundations for its emergence as a Superpower. He did this while murdering countless individuals with the same heartless efficiency and fervor that he drove the industrialization of his nation. "When you make an omelet, you have to crack a few eggs." Stalin was a monster. His methods and his style of dictatorship are never acceptable.

Without any doubt, Manila provides the centralization of economic power within the Philippines. Visiting this Mega city one is struck by construction activity going on everywhere, by the clogged roads and toll ways, and by the large number of those monsters of the roads and environment, the SUV. It is the most densely populated city on the planet. Manila, because of its wealth and its Mega city status, plays host to the international jet setters, and people who are famous because they are famous. In August of 2011, Paris Hilton jetted in to Manila. Apparently, she lost two cell phones during the flight, or maybe just after. If the mystery is ever solved please let me know. It's important. But at least I know now why she didn't call me. Paris was asked when she got here what she thought about the Philippines. She said that she loved the food. Wow! That's deep. Her fans would have gone into ecstasy over that comment. When you are a part of the Hilton family, and on top of that paid megabucks for just being famous, you don't have much to worry about. I just wonder how the women's magazines that you find in the West, with their usual sensationalistic journalism, wove her comments into a juicy story. Maybe, "Paris suffers terrible heartache in the States after being separated from Filipino food." If she's eaten too many spicy Filipino dishes make that "terrible heartburn." I'll have to race out to get my copy of the magazine. I feel like wasting some money on nonsense. If I give the impression of being just a tad cynical, I can only say, "You've got that right." It just annoys me that people can get paid squillions, (squillions is a hypothetical figure. It means both 'a hell of a lot', and "far too much."), for doing what amounts to nothing. We can talk about her, because she's not someone who will read my book. Can you blame her, we might ask. We've just been through some heavy economic stuff in this chapter, so we need to lighten up for a minute. Paris was here in the Philippines at the invitation of a company operating a beach club. The managing director gushed that the company "put our absolute trust in Paris' abilities to fully-integrate a superior lifestyle that cannot be found elsewhere in the country."(64) That's for sure. She was also going to be opening her signature luxury brand at a shopping mall too. Luxury brands have a big, big market in the Philippines. Like, maybe 0.00002% of the population may be able to afford them. She'd be better off opening the store in the USA. That's where all the Filipinos with money shop. She'll bump into everyone she sees in Manila. Twitter and Facebook will be alight, with teenage girls from Brazil, to Japan to Australia in raptures over Paris' latest utterances in Manila. The writers at the silly women's and teenage girl's magazines in Brazil, Japan and Australia will be working furiously and asking, "What kind of a story can we make out of this?" In Melbourne, Australia, groups of teenage girls, who should be doing their homework assignments, will be standing in circles, clutching their hands to their chests and screaming loudly. They've been following the internet postings about Ms. Hilton's travels. "Oh, my God,", says one, "Did you hear what Paris said in Manila. Like, this is, like, just sooo cool. Like, oh my God . . . . she said . . . ." The others will stare at their companion with wide open eyes, in anticipation of what the girl with the special knowledge about their idol is going to say. With the excitement increasing every second, one of them asks, "Well, what *did* she say?" The reply is, "Oh, my God, this is just sooo cool, she said, like, this is awesome, she said she loves the food." The others will be in a frenzy. Even the male friends that hang out with them, the nice boys who could never take to rugby, and prefer spending time with the girls talking about the stories in teenage girl's magazines, will be ecstatic. They'll all agree. "That is just sooo cool, it's just, like, amazing that someone can say that. We love you, Paris." Celebrities and people who are famous because they are famous, but we don't know why they're famous, are coming to Manila. That's great. Now, has anyone found Paris Hilton's cell phones? *Tama na*! (That's enough!) We've had a giggle, we'd better press on. To be serious about this, and I am now being serious, it is excellent that Paris Hilton and others like her, and any foreign tourist or celebrity, are coming to the Philippines. A new beach resort is being built; Ms. Hilton is promoting it. This is good for the Philippines. Every tourist comes here with money to spend. That means jobs created here. That is good for the economy and the nation, as long as that money remains circulating within this economy, it will be a stimulus. So, joking aside, tourism is good for the Philippines, and more people should visit and retire here. More power to anyone who is making that happen. We love you, Paris. I'll just have to put up with the silly stories in those silly women's magazines.

In this nation, there are numerous instances of politicians engaging in ruthless practices in order to gain political office. Some regions of the Philippines are run along the lines of a fiefdom. Almost everything is under their control. It's not wise for journalists or authors to investigate too deeply, or to issue open comment in certain areas of local Philippine politics. The survival rate of those so engaged is not likely to be favorable. This is a sad fact. As stated previously, many Filipino journalists have been murdered. Due to the geographic fragmentation of the Philippines, the central government exerts a weak influence in certain regions, and it's left to the local political families or clans to fight it out amongst themselves for political office and the reins of power. Like a transmitter beaming out its electromagnetic waves, the strength of the political and cultural signals from the political offices of Manila diminishes over distance. The outlying areas of the archipelago, receive not only attenuated electromagnetic waves from the Manila media, but attenuated signals and influence in regards to political and cultural influence and control. The southernmost regions of the Archipelago have strong Muslim cultural and political influences, and there is on-going conflict with the central government in regards to control over these areas. The Philippines is not unique in this regard, with another Asian country, Thailand, being in the same situation.

Within Australia, and other remarkable economies such as Singapore, effective government policy formulation and enactment has been a prominent feature of its success story. Just like the shape, or morphology of a nation, demographics can be said to determine its fate. Economies such as Australia and Singapore have planned, analyzed, and projected all the factors relating to economic growth and sustainability. That is precisely why they have been so economically successful. Government policy and intervention occurs on the basis of rational analysis. This is critical and essential to economic growth. Please note and I emphasize here, when formulating rational economic policy there is no place for religious doctrine or dogma. A nation is either a secular state or it is not. Australia and Singapore are secular states. Further to their capacity to engage in rational economic analysis, the above-mentioned nations have enacted policy in a clear and unambiguous manner. They have achieved a solid reputation as a place to do business, and when things do go wrong, they will investigate and prosecute aggressively any such cases without fear or favor. Business processes in nations such as Singapore and Australia are for the most part transparent, and certainly in regards to Australia the concept of 'conflict of interest' is a widely held concept and is expected to be practiced rigorously by politicians. Here it is so defined, in a way that is self-evident: 'A conflict of interest is a situation in which an individual has competing interests or loyalties.'(65) It's such a simple concept but Filipinos have never understood or accepted it. A conflict of interest can exist in several kinds of situations. It can exist with a public official whose personal interests conflict with his or her professional duties. Or with an employee who works for one company but who may have personal interests that are in competition with his or her employment. It could occur with a person who has a position of authority in one organization that conflicts with his or her interests in another organization, or with a person who has conflicting responsibilities. Examples of these would include situations where the employee's personal business resulted in a conflict of interest with his other business responsibilities. In legal matters, where a judge had a conflict of interest because he had a personal relationship with one of the parties in the lawsuit. The responsible judge, one displaying good ethics, would remove himself from the case. He or she would recognize that they could not make a fully objective and unbiased judgment where they had a direct interest into the outcome of the case. A board member of a corporation, recognizing a conflict of interest, would sign a conflict of interest agreement after disclosing his affiliation with one of the company's suppliers. More generally, conflicts of interest can be defined as any situation in which an individual or corporation (either private or governmental) is in a position to exploit a professional or official capacity in some way for their personal or corporate benefit. The Philippines, as we all know, has a long history of the total disregard for conflict of interest principles and guidelines. This is why governance has in general been so poor, and the efficiency of the government, and of the economy, so seriously disadvantaged. Filipinos, and Filipinos in political office, will tend to put family interests first. Even before those of the nation. In some situations a spouse, child, or other close relative may be employed (or applies for employment) by the family member, or goods or services are purchased from such a relative or a firm controlled by a relative. For this reason, many employment applications ask if one is related to a current employee. If this is the case, the relative could then remove themselves from any hiring decisions. Abuse of this type of conflict of interest is called *nepotism*.(66) During many presidencies in the Philippines nepotism has abounded. It occurs in many other nations too, but in some nations, in Australia for example, is taboo. It is not tolerated in Australian society. It is not part of the political culture. So, the concept of 'conflict of interest' is extremely weak in the Philippines. The Filipino mindset is extended family orientated to the extent that when one gains political or economic power or wealth, the family has to be included in this. We mentioned all of this in chapter 1, when we discussed the issue of the degree of individuation of the Filipino. This is one issue, one cultural trait, and one practice that is a distinct disadvantage for the economy of the nation. It hinders the efficiency of the economy because effective decision-making is crippled, and individuals are placed in position of authority purely based on family ties or friendship, rather than an objective appraisal in regards to aptitude and qualifications for the job. Goods and services may be contracted for government or national use purely based on one particular supplier being a family member or a crony. The said goods and services may be unsuitable for the task at hand or overpriced. Often they are both. Nepotism and ignoring conflict of interest guidelines are a poison for the economy and a poison for transparent and effective governance. There always comes a day of reckoning. And it is the Filipino citizen that in the end suffers the consequences of all of this.

Previously mentioned was the fact that we live in a purely capitalistic world. Although pure capitalism is now global, it comes in various forms and in regards to the Philippines the type of capitalism practiced has been named as 'crony capitalism'. This term describes a capitalist economy where success in business depends on close relationships between business people and government officials. It may manifest by favoritism in the distribution of legal permits, government grants, special tax breaks, and other preferential treatment to selected individuals. Crony capitalism is believed to arise when political cronyism spills over into the business world; self-serving friendships and family ties between businesspersons and the government influence the economy and society to the extent that it corrupts public-serving economic and political ideals. When we mentioned earlier in the chapter, the man who awoke from his coma, and the question he would ask, that is, "What the hell have you been doing?" The answer that he would have gotten is likely to have been' "We have been doing what we have always done."

Herein lies the problem. Everything in the Philippines is done to maintain the *status quo*; there has been no real change. For those in power, the ruling elite, the Catholic Church, the rich and the opportunistic who make money along the way, the *status quo* is desirable and any change is perceived as a threat. For the other nations of Asia, and the entrenched interests in this country, keeping things as they are is just dandy. For the other nations of Asia, it is they that will get the investment dollars and the multinational electronics factories. The Philippines will never, on present trends, present any real direct competitive threat to these nations. And it is certainly never going to present any military threat. As I have mentioned before, the other nations of Asia will view the Philippines as a useful market for the export of their products, so there is some degree of self-interest by these nations in having a healthy, dynamic, consumer-oriented society here, but pre-dominance in the region by the Philippines is never going to occur. Not on present trends. The issue of the *status quo* is pertinent and presents one of the lessons of the extraordinary events of EDSA and the Philippine People Power revolution. For a short time *true* democracy reigned. Power actually came *from the people,* and the person holding the nominative reigns of power, Marcos, was toppled. This tidal wave of democratic power, the heady intoxication of those days, slowly ebbed and the elite and the same old Filipino complacency, or call it demoralization, set in again. Placed in office after the rule of Marcos was a President who was incorruptible, and who had the highest of ethical standards. This was Corazon Aquino, and she had every intention of changing the established order. The elite and those skilled in exercising political power, and those who possessed wealth, or were smart and ruthless enough to accumulate it, re-gathered the threads of power back again and weaved them into the ropes that now bind the populace. Again. The Filipino journalists, who justifiably call to account those in power, still get murdered, the poor get poorer, the karaokes and the gambling dens continue to allow the squandering of time and the wasting of money, and the rich and corrupt continue on their shuttle trips to the USA. At the very least, it's all predictable.

Within the Philippines, there has been a paucity of effective economic planning, and when it comes to one of the most important demographic factors of a nation, its population, there has been a significant failure to properly plan and limit population growth. When discussing population factors in regards to the economic strength and growth of a nation there is more to consider than purely the sheer numbers of people. In addition, one must also consider the issue of the professional and academic classes within a society, and how they shape the fate of a nation. The professional classes within the Philippines are motivated to go overseas to work or to live due to higher wages, better living conditions and for further career advancement or educational achievement. Doctors, nurses, teachers, academics and scientists, for example, will earn far more overseas than they would within the Philippines. Within the health sector, this "brain drain" is of significant disadvantage to the health system of the Philippines. More will be said about this crucial point in the following chapter.

Without putting too fine a point on it one must state clearly that in terms of business acumen, the 'Tiger economies' of Asia display a much greater sense of business acumen as compared to the Philippines. Filipinos are very motivated and interested to start businesses but a lot of them are, business-wise, naive. As a foreigner, they will frequently ask you if you have plans "to start a business", or as OFW's (Overseas Filipino Workers) they will plan to use the money they earn as capital to set up a business when they return home. Commonly enterprises are commenced on the basis of fads, or of thoughts that it will generate significant income. Internet cafes are an example of this and are to be found everywhere, the market is saturated with this type of enterprise. A friend of the author, who lives in Manila, and aged in his 30's, is working for a telecommunications company there. He stated he had plans to leave this job and use some capital that he had saved for a business. He planned to set up this business in the village in which he was born, and where his family currently still resided. The place in question is known to me, and it is an impoverished village in one of the poorest regions of the country. The principal income is from fishing or from agriculture, it has no option to allow connection to the internet, its community electricity supply is only from 5p.m. to midnight daily, and it has otherwise poor infrastructure. The amount of money in circulation at any one time is minimal and the residents would be prone to seeking goods or services on credit. In short, any reasonable chance of a prosperous business is unlikely and the individual in question would have been likely to lose his capital outlay. One could say, of course, "why stop anyone investing in such regions, they need the investment so badly?" But such sentiments do not preclude the need for a proper business plan, research on consumer demand in regards to the goods or services offered, a vision of what the business is to achieve, and if it, above all, has a realistic chance of surviving and growing. Certainly, there should be small business investment in these regions, but who shoulders the risks involved? There are businesses and corporations within the Philippines that are very dynamic and efficient and use best-practice business methods, but this it is not uniform or universal.

Australia has shown consistent economic growth and is now a trillion dollar economy, as per its GDP. With a population of only 22 million people, it has utilized its resources very cleverly in order to propel economic growth. The great economic dynamos in the Asian region in the last decade, that is China and India, have utilized Australian resources to help fuel their growth. Australia cleverly placed itself in the slipstream of the incredible economic growth of China and India. Within Australia, and other remarkable economies such as Singapore, central planning has been a prominent feature of its success story. Demographics can be said to determine the fate of a nation, and economies such as Australia and Singapore have planned, analyzed, and projected all the factors relating to economic growth and sustainability. With the Philippines, there has been a paucity of effective economic planning, and when it comes to one of the most important demographic factors of a nation, its population, there has been a significant failure to properly plan and limit population growth. The excessive growth of a population not only puts enormous strain on families and government, who have to provide the necessary resources to educate, clothe and feed the booming population, but a critical factor that must also be considered is energy consumption by the populace. Energy consumption across the globe has grown astronomically within the last 20 years. Within the Philippines, in order to attempt to keep pace with these demands, various sources of energy must be used and coal-fired power plants are being built and used. This has significant environmental consequences as we have discussed above.

I have previously, on a voluntary basis, assisted a Filipino acquaintance in starting a business. I am a retired R.N., and have a superannuation pension from Australia. The registration for his business, to legally register the name and obtain a business permit was relatively straightforward. The DTI, the Philippine Department of Trade and Industry, allows on-line registration of a business name, however, and this was in 2011, if one is outside of Manila one can only use online, to pay for the transaction, a payment system that is linked to one of the Philippine telecommunication companies. Only one. An individual has to have an account linked with this specific telecommunication company in order to utilize this payment system. There is no option for credit card payment, or other generic payment method. Fortunately, there was a DTI office local to us, and we were able to register the business name there. The process at the office proceeded efficiently. While engaged in writing this book, I knew that helping voluntarily would give me a real insight into how business at the grass-roots level is done in the Philippines. I did not want to simply rely on statistics, or discuss matters not directly related to my experience. So I have been involved in sending text messages and attempting to communicate with individuals involved in business, to set up appointments, to talk business, to do business, on behalf of my acquaintance. However, often this was an exercise in frustration. As mentioned before, the Philippines is the foremost nation in the world for texting, but there is not much of it that seems to be meaningful in any way. Again, without the need for statistical data, everyday experiences within the Philippines can highlight the problems that are occurring here. There is little of the real hunger for business, and to do business, that exists in other countries such as Hong Kong or Singapore or Taiwan, these Asian 'Tiger Economies' that have performed economic miracles. The term I use here, 'economic miracles' is actually a misnomer. These nations have succeeded economically not due to any miracle but to sheer hard work, extraordinary capacity to work smartly, to copy other successful products or services unashamedly, and to work as if it was the sole meaning of their lives. These 'Tiger Economies' have a huge hunger for business and a huge drive to succeed and to compete in the world marketplace. They are not intimidated by foreigners. They unashamedly use the ideas and techniques of others. They are extraordinarily organized in the way they work. Sadly, too often the author's experience of seeing business in action in the Philippines has been a negative one. There are individuals and there are businesses in the Philippines that work extraordinarily hard, and smart, and are highly motivated and organized. They employ business practices that are on a par with first world nations. However, sadly too there are those who do not exhibit any real hunger to do business, do not keep appointments or are late, would rather be drinking and singing karaoke, and seem to have to make a huge effort to open the business in the morning due to a hangover from the night before. And it's not a Friday or Saturday night, when one would reasonably expect a night out after a hard week at work. In addition to my direct experience of this, there are the objective data tables and rankings, and nations are judged as to the ease of doing business within them. Economies are ranked on their ease of doing business from 1-183.(67) A high ranking on the ease of doing business index means the regulatory environment is more conducive to the starting and operation of a local firm. Being at number 1 on the table would mean that that nation is the easiest out of all those listed in which to conduct business. This index averages the country's percentile rankings on nine topics, made up of a variety of indicators, giving equal weight to each topic. The rankings for all economies are benchmarked to June 2010. The Philippines ranked at 148th out of 183 nations.(68) That's a bad score for the Philippines. To put it bluntly, nations like Singapore and the other 'Tiger Economies' of Asia have overtaken the Philippines in terms of economic prosperity, due to the fact that they have planned better, worked harder, worked smarter, and more readily welcomed and facilitated business than the Philippines. The business acumen, and the hunger to make profits, is huge in economies such as Singapore, and they do everything with an economic efficiency that is breathtaking. The Philippines *can* do far better, and *should* do better, in terms of its economic performance. If it wants to lift its people out of poverty, it *has* to do better.

However, things could be worse. I always attempt to obtain a sense of balance in everything that is discussed. To end this chapter I am going to discuss the fate of a nation that has really messed things up badly. The Philippines has managed to limp along, but some nations just fall into one big, total economic mess. This should also serve as a warning to this, or any other, nation. It is often assumed that nations will continue on a path to economic prosperity. That despite setbacks and difficulties along the way, a nation will achieve on-going economic growth, the only uncertainty being the rate of growth. In fact, nothing could be further from the truth. Let's take, for example, the nation of Zimbabwe.

It was formally one of the richest and most prosperous countries on the African continent, but now poverty and unemployment are both endemic, driven by the shrinking economy and hyper-inflation.(69) Both unemployment and poverty rates run near 80%. The Zimbabwe Dollar (ZWD) was the official unit of currency, but has now been abandoned. Hyperinflation made it impossible to keep printing the bank notes that were necessary to purchase goods and services. The country now uses other currencies such as the US dollar, British Pound, the Euro and the South African Rand. Most general laborers in 2006 were paid under ZWD 200 Billion (US 60c) per month. Yes, that's right, 200 Billion Zimbabwe dollars per month. However, this astronomical wage may only have bought a loaf of bread and a few soft drinks. In 1998, the annual inflation rate was estimated at 32%, which is extremely high to a normal economy. Ten years later, in 2008 the annual inflation rate was estimated at an unbelievable rate of 11,200,000%. In November 2008 the prices doubled every 1.3 days and unofficial statistics estimated for Zimbabwe an inflation rate of more than 500,000,000,000,000,000%. Another economic source gave the rate as 516 quintillion per cent. That is, 516,000,000,000,000,000,000%(70) In order to keep up with the need for money, the national bank introduced new banknotes of ZWD50 billion, ZWD100 billion, and ZWD100 trillion.(71) Having a ZWD$100,000,000,000,000 banknote may seem an awful lot, but it in fact was worth next to nothing, and even then lost further value the longer one held it. These figures are truly representative of the economy of a nation in meltdown. Like the last stages of a dying star, when the outer layers of the heavenly body collapse inwards, the economy of the nation is imploding. Zimbabwe escaped this catastrophic cycle of hyperinflation by abandoning its currency. The only previous example of such rates was the Weimar Republic of Germany between 1921 and 1923. At that time a wheelbarrow full of German banknotes was needed to buy a loaf of bread in the morning, and the price of the bread would have increased by the afternoon! Relative to these economic disasters the Philippines has a very healthy inflation rate by comparison. In 2010, it was 3.8%, this rate having been reduced from the 9.3% inflation rate in 2008. It is expected to remain at 4% for the period 2013 to 2016.(72) The inflation rate is one of the key indicators in regards to a healthy economy, and the Philippines has worked hard to get this right. This is good economic management. On the darker side, there is the 'Failed States Index' of the United States based think-tank Fund for Peace. Typically, the term 'Failed State', as used here, means that the state has been rendered ineffective. It is not able to enforce its laws uniformly because of excessively high crime rates, extreme political corruption, an impenetrable and ineffective bureaucracy, judicial ineffectiveness, military interference in politics, and cultural situations in which traditional leaders wield more power than the state over a certain area. Some states have these adverse factors to varying degrees, the Philippines certainly has, and the Failed State is one that is judged to have these adverse factors operating to the point where its citizenry do not receive proper protection under the law, or do not receive adequate health care or education, and/or there is a scarcity of food. Effective economic management, planning and oversight is largely absent in the Failed State, and there are poor standards of governance, transparency and accountability. In 2011, the Philippines was ranked at number 51 out of a total of 177 nations, with the nation being ranked at number 1 as being that most critical and judged as a Failed State. The Philippines has thus been placed in the 'Warning' section of the table of Failed States. Those from place 35 to 1 are on 'Alert' and are at most risk of political and economic collapse. Nations that are placed between 166 to 177 are not at risk and their political and economic systems judged 'Sustainable'.(73) Things could be worse, but there is absolutely no room for complacency. The Philippines is on warning. It needs to lift its economic game or there is a possibility that the fate of Zimbabwe awaits it. There is *never* room for complacency.

Chapter 4

The Overseas Filipino Worker— a hero of the Philippines.

KEY POINTS: The Philippines has exported its workforce for decades. This has led to significant economic repercussions, both positive and negative. This issue can be discussed on both an economic level, and a human level.

THE STORY OF the Overseas Filipino Worker, (OFW) or Global Filipino, cries out to be told. In any book about the Philippines these heroes, the Overseas Filipino Workers, must be mentioned. Theirs is a story of success and failure, of death and mistreatment, of separation and loss, and above all of great sacrifice. The individuals who make up the overseas Filipino workforce are transported to lands and cultures that are totally alien to them, and at times dangerous. They are separated from their beloved families and often isolated from the mainstream of their host nation. They sometimes reside in isolated compounds, are sometimes offered money as an inducement to give up their Christian religious faith, and are exploited and abused. But they will tolerate all of this due to the mystical bond they have with their families, and the overwhelming drive to support them materially. The average

Filipino sees a grim future in regards to their own nation. They are demoralized and dispirited by the corruption within the Philippines and the dysfunctional political system. Frustrated by poverty and a lack of opportunity, they dream of going overseas, of earning money to support their families, of advancing their careers, of receiving good wages for their toils and work, commensurate with the qualifications they have earned.

The huge economic plus for the Philippines in this arrangement is that the money these heroes remit to their families, and thus their nation, has a huge positive impact on its finances. The Filipino is selfless and will send back home the majority of the money they earn. This money is to support the family, to educate and clothe and feed their children, and help their parents or brothers and sisters. It is also used to realize their dreams, of owning a house and lot, of starting a business, of in the future becoming free to earn money in their homeland with their family, to become a success and earn the esteem and approbation of their families and fellow countrymen. The downside of this phenomenon, of the Overseas Filipino Worker, is that it is in part the professional groups that leave the country to seek success and fortune overseas, the doctors, nurses, engineers and technicians. The very professionals that in any other country would make up the middle class, and are needed here to build the nation and contribute to the wealth and prosperity of the Philippines, and its health and educational system. In terms of numbers, around 8.6 million to 11 million Overseas Filipinos Workers is the estimated count worldwide, or about 11% of the total population of the Philippines. Remittances sent by OFWs to the Philippines contribute to the country's economy, with a value of more than US$10 billion in 2005. This makes the country the fourth largest recipient of remittances with India, China, and Mexico on top of the list. OFW remittances represent 13.5% of the country's GDP, the largest in proportion to the domestic economy among the four countries.(1) The amount of US$10 billion that was remitted in 2005 has steadily grown, and in 2009 about US$17.35 billion in remittances was sent to the Philippines by overseas Filipinos.

Focusing on specific occupational groups within the OFW population, a report recently highlighted the exodus of science and technology workers from the nation. Entitled 'Pinoy S&T workers leaving in droves' the article stated that the number of science and technology (S&T) workers leaving the Philippines for overseas jobs rose by 148%, from 9,877 in 1998 to 24,502 in 2009, a scenario that does not bode well for the country's research and development sector.(2) The highest outflow occurred from 2000 to 2001 when the number rose 59 percent from 11,186 to 17,756.(3) The study is a grim demonstration of how the outflow of S&T professionals will affect the research and development sector of the Philippines. This is a loss to this country, which needs skilled scientific and technical workers to properly address research and development needs. In 2009 the numbers reached a high of 24,502, and this was the highest for any year, except for the period of 2001 to 2003, in which a decrease of 31.06% was evident. It is assumed that this reduction in emigration was due to the brief improvement in the Philippine economy at that time.(4) Nurses and midwives are the professional group who emigrate most. Engineers came in second. Then other health professionals such as medical doctors, dentists, veterinarians, and pharmacists. A 2002 UNESCO (United Nations Educational Scientific and Cultural Organization) study determined that the number of Research Scientists and Engineers (RSE) stood at 48 per 1,000,000 Filipinos. This is significantly below UNESCO's recommendation of the 340 per 1,000,000 needed for economic development. Further researching this, in order to find more contemporary data, I did locate a reference to a 2009 UNESCO report. That gave a figure of 125 per 1,000,000 population. This would indicate that there has been an improvement over the years from 2002 to 2009, but still far short of the 340 per 1,000,000 needed.(5) The lack of RSE's weighs down a country's ability to achieve economic growth, as not enough technology-based investors are attracted to the country, due to the lack of high-level scientific and engineering manpower. The 2010–2011 Global Competitiveness Report by the World Economic Forum ranked the Philippines at 96 out of 139 nations in terms of availability of scientists and engineers, with the nation doing best ranked at number 1. Here we have a sobering set of statistics, and an indicator as to just how poorly the Philippines is faring in terms of having the skilled human resources to effect economic and technical progress. The other factor that needs to be considered is the amount of money spent by the government on Research and Development, (R&D). In 2009, the Philippines spent a paltry US$123 million, or only 0.1% of GDP on R&D. Malaysia, by contrast, spent US$1.06 billion, or 0.64 of GDP. The Philippines invests one fifth as much as Malaysia on R&D.(6) The Philippines is currently incapable of participating to any significant degree in, or profiting from, the science, knowledge and information based world economy, because huge numbers of its scientists, researchers and technicians have gone overseas. Further to this, R&D spending is far too low.

Beyond the science and technology sectors, OFWs are contributing to all sectors of the global economy. The numbers of Filipinos so engaged is staggering. For instance, the Philippines supplies approximately a third of the 1.5 million commercial seafarers worldwide. Filipino mariners sent home a record US$2.5bn for the first nine months of 2009. As with other OFWs, their lives are filled with danger. From November 1998 to 2001, the International Transport Workers Federation (ITF Philippines Branch) recorded 367 casualties among Filipino seafarers, 66% of whom fell ill or met accidents, with 34% dying as a result of sunk ships, explosions and other mishaps. By the time it closed its Manila office in 2002, cases had almost doubled.(7) In regards to this huge group of seafarers, continued employment opportunities are under a cloud. It has been reported that Filipinos are losing their competitiveness in today's demand-driven global labor market. In the last few years, international ships have begun recruiting more seafarers from China and Eastern Europe. These mariners are relatively at par with Filipinos in terms of skills, but will accept lower wages. The Philippines is just one of many countries that supply labor. The demand for Filipino mariners used to experience double-digit growth rates in the 1980's, but that is reportedly now on a downward trend. The Chinese have been very strong in such areas in the last two years.(8) As always, there are other nations willing to supply goods, services and a workforce at cheaper rates. The competitiveness of nations on the global market is fierce and there is never any room for complacency. The global economy, and the competing nations therein, operate according to the principles of evolutionary survival, that is, only the fastest, the smartest, the most efficient, the strongest and the most adaptable, will survive and win. Piracy in the waters surrounding the Philippines will be mentioned in chapter 5, but also on the high seas Filipinos seamen find themselves victim to this global phenomenon. Somali pirates have kidnapped 470 Filipinos since 2006, and are still holding at least 74 aboard six ships. The Philippines has ordered its seafarers, who make up a third of the world's commercial sailors, to go through anti-piracy training before they will be allowed to board ships.(9)

Filipinos constitute such a major global workforce that most foreigners in their own nations have come into contact with them at one time or another. The very first experience of Filipinos that I had was when I commenced my psychiatric nursing training in a large public hospital in England, the United Kingdom, in 1973. The British health system was seriously understaffed and required overseas workers to fill its staff numbers, especially for the nursing profession. The staffing shortfall actually continues to this day, and many Filipino nurses still emigrate to the UK. In order to fill this gap in skilled manpower individuals were recruited from the former British colonies and from nations such as the Philippines, who provided educated, English-speaking and hard-working people. I was the only nursing student of British background in my training class of 13 students, the others having been recruited from overseas, including the Philippines. The training hospital, which was called Fairfield Hospital, was surrounded by the lush green fields of England, and by local villages with their quaint thatched cottages and the timeless, hum-drum life of the English hamlet. For some Filipinos, who arrived during the summer months of England, for the first time in their lives they would have witnessed the changing of the seasons, the leaves on the trees turning to golden brown as Autumn arrived, and the chill in the air as the months inexorably progressed towards Christmas. And then for the first time they would have seen snow, this substance for which, due to their homeland being tropical, there is no word for in their native language. This 'frozen rain", the magical crystalline snowflake, that falls from the sky and magically turns to water as it thaws. At night, lying in bed after a hard day working on the hospital wards, the OFW would have snuggled under the blankets, trying to block out the bone-gnawing cold and damp of the English winter. They would have pined for their families, thought about the sweethearts they had left at home, and dreamed of the tropical warmth of their homeland bathing their bodies and relieving their aching bones. They would have, in their dreamy, half-asleep state, imagined that they were next to their beloved mama or papa. Suddenly, they would awaken as they were dreamily taking the hand of their mother and touching the back of the hand to their forehead in the Filipino gesture of honor to one's elders. For a few glorious seconds they were back home surrounded by the warmth of their beloved parents and family.

The next day they would have written home about their new experiences in this strange land, where people get really annoyed if you jump ahead in the queue, where there are rules and regulations for everything, and where you can never be late. They would have been the objects of envy of those compatriots they left behind in the Philippines, and they slowly and inexorably would have adapted to the way of life and the culture of their new environment. For the Filipinos so recruited to this nurse training program it was a wonderful opportunity to earn money and obtain professional qualifications overseas. They were paid a wage that was exactly comparable to any British person doing the same work, they were treated very well, and lived with full equality under the laws of the land. For each individual their lives and stories are different. For some, their fate was to become married to a local, to work and live their lives within England and to send money, all of the time, back to their parents and brothers and sisters in the Philippines. This was a duty, an honor and a compulsion for the Filipino. Never would they forget their families. This mystical bond was always present, no matter how far away they were. Some used this opportunity, of being in England, to study part-time while doing their nursing training, to become an engineer or computer programmer. These professions seemed, within the Filipino mind, to hold more kudos than a nursing qualification, or for the at times macho Filipino, a more "manly" profession than being a male nurse. For some it was a great success story, and most went on to graduate as registered or enrolled nurses, and to pursue a career that paid, in comparison to wages paid for the same work in the Philippines, a veritable fortune.

Filipinos were very well regarded by the employing health service. They were hard-working and law-abiding, spotlessly clean and respectful. They were loved by their non-Filipino colleagues for their industriousness, their fun approach to life, and for their gregariousness. They fitted in easily to the environment in which they found themselves, and adapted well. This adaptability of the Filipino has time and time again been the key to their success. And Filipinos seemed to work better in a structured environment, where the organization and its structures were already in place. Exceptions to the frequent success stories were of course to be found. I remember one incident relating to a Filipina, a first-year student nurse. Some months into her training there occurred an inspection of her room in the nursing quarters where she lived. No doubt someone had become suspicious of her behavior and tipped-off the authorities. Her room was stuffed full of National Health property. It transpired that this individual was stealing from the wards on which she worked everything that she could lay her hands on. Bed sheets, medicines, crockery, cutlery, tea bags, packets of biscuits, stationary and anything else that was not nailed down was being stolen by her, and progressively sent back by her in boxes to her relatives in the Philippines. She was of course dismissed from the National Health Service and left to an ignominious fate of returning to her homeland in disgrace. It is not known to me what became of her, but her sense of entitlement, and lack of scruples, befitted more the attitude of a dictator in a third-world country who claims everything within it for their own, rather than the attributes of a nurse. But her behavior was an exception, and the majority of Filipinos were excellent employees and made an enormous and positive contribution to the British National Health Service. Not only was the material environment, and all of its riches in comparison to the Philippines, an overwhelming temptation for many, but also the more loose relationships and more relaxed sexual mores that existed in England a great temptation for many Filipino men. Away from the strict moral codes of their homeland, they were now in an environment where relationships and sexual encounters were much less formal, where sex was more openly discussed, and where contraception was easily available. They were free to do more or less as they pleased, without fear of censure from their parents or families. A lot of the men "played the field" and formed transitory relationships with local women. In the Philippines, due to genetic and racial factors almost all Filipinos are born with black hair and dark features. In the West by contrast Filipinos are presented with an amazing diversity of color of hair and eyes, and blonde women have always been seen as particularly attractive by Filipino men. They also decorated their rooms with pictures from *Playboy* and *Penthouse* magazines, no doubt in celebration of the new-found libration from the strict moral codes of the Philippines, and with pictures of David Cassidy who was the Justin Bieber of the early 1970's. How do I know the bit about the *Penthouse* magazines? Alright, I admit it. I probably borrowed a few copies of the magazines now and again. I'll probably get an email now from 'TJ' Mendoza, a Filipino, from Basingstoke, England. 'Hey, give me my Penthouse mag back. You know the one, 1975, edition 4. You said you only wanted to read the serious articles in it over a few days.' Sorry TJ, it's in the mail, minus the pictures. That's payback for the damned noise you made on that stereo system of yours, while I was rostered on night duty and trying to sleep during the day. Joke only. David Cassidy, whom I mentioned earlier, was the quintessential *'pogi'* (handsome) Caucasian that Filipinos, even the men, found so fascinating. He had a band called 'The Partridge Family', and a television show that was the typical corny American fare of the time. The Filipino males were also fixated on buying elaborate stereo systems, and the more flashing lights and noise amplification their stereo equipment had, then so much the better. It was all a typical clinical case of stereo system envy, rather than penis envy, and they seemed to compete with each other as to who had the biggest and loudest stereo system. For the other nationalities living in the nursing residence this was no fun, as true to form the Filipino would play their stereo system at high volume anytime of the day or night. Fortunately, karaoke hadn't been invented then, so the British population was spared the off-key renditions of *'Dahil sayo'* ('Because of you') that would have otherwise been sung, day and night. It was for them paradise to be living in a place where such items as stereo systems could easily be purchased, even after sending back money to their family, and having such freedom to do more or less as they pleased.

For the local English villagers the presence of Filipinos, these exotic oriental creatures, was a pleasant curiosity. The Filipino man and woman is a beautiful creature. Dark-skinned, eternally cheerful and with radiant smiles, they could brighten the gloomiest English winters' day. The local men found the Filipinas, with their dark skin and almond eyes, their beauty and deportment, extremely alluring. Like the advertisements for the chocolate bar 'Turkish Delight', that played on television in England at the time, the women were "full of Eastern Promise". Just how far this promise went depended upon the morals of the particular Filipina in question, but some of them formed relationships with local men and became pregnant after whirlwind romances. It's likely that for most of them pregnancy was considered a good outcome, and at times they would "forget" to take their contraceptive pill, as a pregnancy afforded a tie and a likely marriage to a local man and thus the freedom to stay within the advanced industrialized nation of England, and its lifestyle and wealth. And the security and knowledge that they could always support their family back home.

In contrast to the relatively easy and problem-free existence of the Filipino in the United Kingdom, where OFW's were in an environment that shared common values and customs, and the Christian religious faith, the experience for the OFW in the middle eastern countries appears to be much harder and more problematic. A recent report by one of the Filipino welfare organizations, Migrante, stated that seven to ten overseas Filipino workers (OFWs) are abused or maltreated every day on average in the Middle East. It called on the Philippine government to thoroughly review the labor export program. Also reported was a "sudden surge" in the number of abused OFWs in other countries including Sudan, Libya and other African nations. Further reported was the issue of complaints of labor malpractices being no longer reported as individual cases but in groups. Among these cases were the 200 OFW nurses in Jeddah, 17 distressed and stranded caregivers in Riyadh, and the more than 20 trailer drivers in Dammam, all in Saudi Arabia. These individuals were allegedly the victims of labor malpractices. Migrante is also requesting that the government stop the local economies dependency on OFW remittances, stating that this was being used as a milking cow by government officials, and to introduce genuine economic reform measures that will help stop the forced migration of Filipinos who have no work in the Philippines.(10)

Historically, the term OCW, or Overseas Contract Worker, was used to describe what we refer to now as the OFW. The term reflected the temporary and contractual employment status. The workers' social and physical mobility was restricted by the terms of their contract. Because of the growing profile of overseas work, and of the sense of transience implied by OCW the term has fallen out of favor in both government and media use. OFW has become the preferred acronym. It was the administration of Ferdinand E. Marcos who conceived this employment opportunity program.(11) It was introduced as a 'temporary' measure, to reduce unemployment and prop-up the declining economy. It was a reflexive act that down the track would have significant repercussions for the economy and the nation. The Labor Code of 1974 formalized the Philippine labor migration program, and had as its main goal the promotion of overseas contract work. This would allow the government to reap the economic benefits of lower unemployment and workers' financial remittances. In 1982, the Central Bank, Ministry of Foreign Affairs, and Ministry of Labor and Employment made the remittance of 50 to 70 percent of workers' salaries mandatory through Executive Order 857. Sanctions such as the non-renewal of passports or disapproval of new contracts were imposed on those who did not comply. The government of the day, not surprisingly, had to abandon Executive Order 857 as it was so unpopular. Other voluntary incentives were introduced such as the 'Suwerte sa Bangko' (Lucky in the Bank) program, the Balikbayan (Return to Country) program, and the Overseas Workers Welfare Administration (OWWA) remittance assistance program. According to figures released by the Filipino House of Representatives Committee on Overseas Foreign Workers, some 700 workers, mostly women, die each year following maltreatment by their employers. On average 40

OFWs arrive home in coffins each week, according to an anonymous source at Ninoy Aquino International Airport.(12)

The OFW is not only vulnerable to mistreatment and abuse but also of falling victim to catastrophic illness while working overseas. For one unfortunate OFW in Dubai a PHP2.4 million hospital bill was racked up when he suffered a brain hemorrhage and was in a coma for three months. A Mr. Castro, who was aged 46, worked as a painter, and was admitted to Cedars Jebel Ali International Hospital on May 12 after he suffered an intra-cranial hemorrhage. He received life-saving neurosurgical intervention after he was wheeled into the hospital. Gulf News said he was immediately transferred to another private hospital, in Sharjah, to undergo a decompression craniotomy, and evacuation of the hemorrhage. He was kept in the internal care unit on artificial ventilation. His insurance company paid for the emergency treatment, but they would not pay for the treatment at the Sharjah hospital, as they did not have a contract with that facility. He was transferred back to Cedars. His wife was in the Philippines, and stated it was "impossible" for her to pay the hospital bills. Mr. Castro used to send his wife and family between PHP12,000 and PHP13,000 per month. His full rehabilitation may take many months, or years. The Philippine consulate in Dubai said at the time that they would facilitate his repatriation if he is a member of the Overseas Workers Welfare Administration (OWWA). Fortunately in this case the individual concerned was, through a magnanimous gesture by the hospital, spared the astronomical costs of the intensive and specialized care he required.(13)

Sadly too, OFWs are not invulnerable to being the victim of, reportedly, crimes of passion while overseas. As the following case illustrates. It was reported on 13th August, 2011 that Malaysian Police had arrested two suspects in the killing of a Filipina maid. The district police officer in charge stated 'a love triangle' appeared to have led to the killing of the Filipina, who was not immediately identified in the report. It was believed that both men were in a relationship with her and then resorted to killing her because they were jealous. According to the news report police also seized various items including an iPad tablet stolen from the maid's employers' home. It all sounds a bit odd, and if items had been stolen from the maid's employers' home then it was not simply a case of a crime of passion. However, police stated that they had "wrapped up" their investigation with the arrest of the two suspects. Sometimes, so far from home, events that occur are never fully explained or documented, and local officials in the country concerned may not always rigorously investigate such crimes.(14)

The personal characteristics of the OFW will be as varied as any large group of people. There are those that will prove to be mature and sensible, those that are naive, some are calculating and greedy, others are good-hearted and completely innocent, and some that are immature and cope poorly with stress or separation from their families. As per records of the Philippine Drug Enforcement Agency (PDEA), there are 630 Filipinos languishing in various jails in Asia, the United States, and in the Middle East.(15) There has recently come to public attention the alarming number of OFW's being charged, and some executed, while acting as "drug mules" for drugs syndicates. These syndicates apparently even use the internet to recruit drug mules, and prey on desperate Filipinos seeking work overseas. 75 Filipinos are currently on death row in China, and 35 have been sentenced to life imprisonment, 68 with fixed-term sentences and 27 have cases pending in court.(16) OFWs have been employed as drug couriers for notorious, high-profile international syndicates. In China, drug trafficking of 50 grams or more of illegal drugs is punishable by 15 years in prison, life imprisonment or death, while in Muslim countries, under the Shariah Law, drug trafficking is punishable by death. Some engage in these acts fully aware of what they are doing. There can be no other conclusion than this, as they have swallowed the drugs sealed in plastic, hidden drugs in their underwear, or had them surgically inserted into their genital areas. Others are duped and unsuspectingly carry illegal drugs to the country of their destination. This can happen by being paid to deliver packages, or goods that contain the drugs. One Filipina alleged when arrested that she had been paid to deliver an electric fan. She allegedly had no knowledge that this was packed with drugs. Based on profiles compiled by the PDEA, OFWs charged with drug trafficking generally come from impoverished backgrounds. The PDEA said international drug rings have a preference for young professionals or office workers with presentable personalities because they are less likely to be suspected. Two thirds of those arrested are women, men make up a smaller proportion of those engaging in such activities, this presumably due to the assumption that women drug mules would not raise as much suspicion as men, and are therefore specifically targeted for recruitment. The US State Department has already raised the alarm in its 2010 International Narcotics Control Strategy Report (INCSR). The illegal drug trade in the Philippines has evolved into a billion-dollar industry, valued at over US$8.4 billion (about PHP368.2 billion) a year. The Department of Foreign Affairs said among the cases was that of a Filipina who was arrested at the Guarulhos International Airport by Brazilian Federal Police for possessing five kilos of cocaine contained in 15 bags hidden in her luggage with false bottoms. Based on reports from the Philippine embassy, the DFA said the Filipina told investigators that she bought the bags in the middle of a Sao Paolo street, and intended to sell them in the Philippines.

OFWs go through the whole spectrum of human experience, and for some theirs is a lucky and fortuitous story of becoming rich, in unexpected ways. It is important to include a story such as this to highlight the positive side of the OFW experience. In August 2011 the Daily Telegraph, a British newspaper, reported that a Filipina maid inherited $4 million from employer. The devoted maid had given 20 years of service to her late employer at his Singapore home. She has now applied for permanent residency status in Singapore, but that her new-found wealth had not changed her lifestyle. She refused to be named in public for fear of possible threats to her life in the impoverished Philippines, where wealthy people have been kidnapped for ransom and some killed by their abductors, the article reported. Her windfall, including cash and a luxury apartment near the Orchard Road shopping precinct, came from the estate of her employer who was a medical doctor and philanthropist, and who died in 2010. The maid had also taken care of the doctor's late mother, and was told that she would be a beneficiary of her employer's will when it was drawn up in 2008. Nearly

200,000 foreign maids, mostly from the Philippines and Indonesia, work in affluent Singapore.(17)

Returning to the dark side of the experience of the OFW we find the following reports of a practice reported to be common throughout the Arabian peninsula.(18) That is, a system of servitude where thousands of young women from countries such as the Philippines become virtual slaves for prosperous Arab families. The women are recruited by "employment agents" and transported to Middle Eastern countries. The jobs offered to them sound good, as does the pay. For a female from an impoverished land like the Philippines, to earn the equivalent of US$100 to US$150 a month, over a period of two years or so, is an exciting prospect and a way to help their family. But there is always a catch. Once there, deductions are taken from their pay for the employment agent's fees and for their airfare. Their passports are then confiscated. And the reality of their day to day work becomes apparent. From dawn to midnight, seven days a week, they have to work. They are fed poorly, are beaten and abused, and can even suffer rape. Some are murdered. Despite this it is unusual for charges to successfully brought against their employers.(19) The numbers are staggering. More than 500,000 domestic helpers from Asian countries work in Kuwait, for instance. Within the strict Islamic countries of the Middle East, the Filipino is seen as an Infidel and an outsider. Often too they are regarded as potential prostitutes. There is a multi-million dollar business of trafficking women, and this thrives upon deceiving, or convincing, unsuspecting women and families about the rewards of overseas work. For those that end up as domestic workers, they are often treated as second-class citizens, and for the domestic worker the maid in an Arabic household can even be regarded as chattel. The stories of abuse are horrific. The restriction on their human rights is significant. They will be induced to give up their Christian religion and convert to Islam. Should disaster or death befall them, it will be at times for mysterious reasons, or for reasons not able to be clarified. No one, apart from the diplomatic mission of the country of the worker concerned, cares much. And they are hampered in any independent investigation they may wish to undertake. For those countries in the Middle East who employ

Filipino workers they know that there is very little that the Philippines can do. The Philippines is a third world impoverished country without any significant global political or economic leverage. It is in a position of weakness, knowing that it cannot employ these OFW's within the Philippine domestic market, and the nation is dependant on the huge amounts of money remitted by OFWs. If in the very unlikely event that the Philippines withdrew their OFWs from a Middle Eastern country the workforce would immediately be replaced by willing workers from Bangladesh or Indonesia or Pakistan. One of the cheapest commodities on the world market today is human labor, and impoverished nations such as the Philippines provide a ready supply of workers. But that supply could be undercut by other nations, as was previously mentioned when we were discussing OFW seafarers. We will now examine the mentality, and the religious and cultural factors, that contribute to the experience of the Filipina OFW being subject to sexual abuse, rape or sexual harassment in the Middle East and other parts of the world. There are some preachers in the Muslim world who call for the reinstitution of sex-slavery. Traditionally, in Muslim and Arabic culture, if the slave were a woman, the master was permitted to have sexual connection with her as a concubine. Sharia law permits the sexual enslavement of infidel women. Fortunately, neither Egypt or Kuwait formally permits this, but it is still part of the mindset of traditional, radical Islamic preaching. The article that I sourced my information from states in part, 'In Gulf countries, while sex-slavery may not be formally recognized, the dirty little secret there is that impoverished and desperate women from places like the Philippines are often hired as "servants," effectively performing the functions of sex-slaves.'(20) This is part of what is referred to as the 'Sharia-induced worldview'(21). Reportedly in Pakistan, a non-Arab, but Muslim nation, where Christians make up less than 2% of the population, at least 700 Christian women are abducted annually.(22) It is stated that most of the women raped in Pakistan come from the Christian minority. Those that are victims of the crime of rape receive very little help from the police.(23) Such atrocities are not confined to Pakistan; even in Europe, a Pakistani man recently raped a Norwegian woman, informing her that "he had the right to do exactly as he wanted to a woman."(24) Such is the mindset of some Muslim men, as a result of cultural conditioning. It is within this culture that defenseless and innocent Filipino women are placed, with little or no protection. It would be wrong to portray this mistreatment of Filipinas as only occurring in the Middle East, or in nations that are culturally and religiously different to the Philippines and the West. Sexual harassment occurs globally. However, in the Middle Eastern countries there is little support given to the woman and very little protection is usually offered. Grass-roots Filipino welfare and support groups do a superb job in helping who they can in whatever way they can, and governmental support is also sometimes necessary and effective, as in the case of then-President Gloria Arroyo's intervention in the pardoning of a maid under sentence of death. A Filipino maid in Kuwait was charged with killing her seven-year-old ward, and the attempted murder of two other children of her employer. She had allegedly slit the throat of the seven-year-old boy and his 13-year-old brother. She allegedly also stabbed the eldest sister. A trial court convicted her in July 2007. Her lawyer said she was "temporarily insane" because of her employer's alleged mistreatment of her.(25) The guilty verdict was subsequently upheld by Kuwait's Court of Appeals. The Emir of Kuwait was required to confirm the ruling within two months. The "*tanazul*", or the act of forgiveness on the part of the victims' family as part of Sharia law, remained a remedy open for the Philippine government. It is available as a legal remedy in such cases. The Philippine government had provided all forms of assistance to help her family, and hired the best defense lawyers in Kuwait to help this OFW overcome the verdict. After intercession by the then-President of the Philippines, Gloria Arroyo, the ruler of Kuwait pardoned this Filipino maid and she was allowed to return home to her family. Former President Arroyo had traveled to Kuwait in 2007 to plea for the life of another maid on death row, whose murder conviction was also commuted to life in prison. And so it goes on. Nightmares being lived every day by OFWs and their families.

Filipina women are often desperate to leave their homeland and to find happiness and prosperity overseas. The only other way of doing this, apart from becoming an OFW, is to marry a foreign citizen. Filipinas marrying foreigners is also part of the story of the Diaspora of Filipinos worldwide. American, Australian, European and Canadian men are favored by these women. It has been referred to, disparagingly, as the 'Mail Order Bride' business. They meet online, using all of the contemporary technologies that are available to connect people worldwide and to foster romance. Their fate can be just as sad, just as fortuitous, or just as dangerous as that of the OFW. Although the focus earlier was on the mistreatment of Filipinos as OFWs in the Middle East and other Islamic nations, it is incorrect to assume that countries that are considered safe, and have a Christian religious cultural template, offer complete security for the Filipina. There have been many instances of Filipinas suffering mistreatment and even murder at the hands of foreign husbands. Some have been killed for insurance money, the husband having taken out life insurance policies on the unsuspecting Filipina. Again, in order to provide a completely balanced view we do find cases of Filipinas murdering their foreign husbands, and for exactly the same motivation that is behind Filipinas being murdered. Evil can be found anywhere and in the heart of any human regardless of their race or culture. A Baptist minister from the United Kingdom married a Filipina who was 39 years his junior. He was murdered by hit men allegedly hired by the bride. The pastor was 62 years of age and was battered to death, his body set on fire and then dumped in a swamp in the Philippines, only 21 days after he left the UK for a new life with his young wife. A police chief on the island of Mindanao said the pastor's 23-year-old bride confessed to detectives that she paid two hit men £350 (British Pounds) (approximately PHP23,000) to have him murdered. During police interrogation she alleged that she had arranged his murder out of anger and hatred as he had mistreated her. The pastor was a father of two children and had divorced his first wife. He met his new bride while working in Mindanao as a missionary. Police suspect that the accused was having an affair with the driver of the couple. The death penalty is now abolished in the Philippines. It was on the statute books but not used in recent years. The accused now faces the prospect of life in jail.(26)

Despite all of the hardships and dangers that they face, OFWs should take comfort from the views of "The Purpose Driven Life" book author

Rick Warren. He visited the Philippines in 2006 and hailed OFWs as modern day "Josephs". Apparently, the reason for OFWs is that they are being placed in strategic places to provide blessings to other nations. By using the biblical Joseph as an example, who from slavery rose up to be a VIP (Very Important Person) at the side of the Pharaoh, he feels OFWs may have a role as that of missionaries. I ask the reader to forgive me as I can feel my cynicism growing as I relate this story. The OFW purpose, according to Mr. Warren, as he is quoted in the newspaper article, is that they are placed in the homes of the most influential people in the world in the form of missionaries. According to the newspaper article source I use, he recounted the story but he did not include any specific names or places to identify the actual persons involved. The story was about a Filipino baker, who was offered the doubling of his salary by the King of an Islamic nation, if the baker converted to Islam.(27) Often Muslims do attempt, through monetary inducement, to convert Christian Filipinos to Islam. I just find it strange to think that the King of a Muslim nation would go out of his way to talk to a lowly Filipino baker. Is this story apocryphal? Anyway, according to the story, the Filipino refused to convert to Islam and instead expressed his love for Jesus Christ. Despite declining to convert to Islam, the wages of the baker were still doubled by the King. Mr. Warren's organization does a lot of very good work. The California-based Saddleback Church has more than 300 community outreach people touching base with prisoners, persons with HIV/AIDS, single parents, addicts and homeless people. I have the greatest admiration for Mr. Warren and the work that he does. But in my view the work of the OFW, and their experience, is not a pat biblical analogue. The King of a Muslim nation is likely to be totally isolated from any of the lowly workers of his palace, or his Kingdom, especially foreign workers. And if he came in contact with them, would expect only servitude and not have the slightest interest in what they have to say. Filipinos are often treated with utter contempt in Muslim countries. In some very conservative Muslim nations, if an OFW expressed any purpose or intent to be a missionary, or showed any intention of engaging in Christian proselytizing, they may not be employed there for long. There are many good people and many good Muslims in the Middle East, but they have no intention of listening to, or getting involved with Christianity. OFWs are one thing, missionaries are another. My own view is that these roles don't mix. For the majority of OFWs it takes all of their energy to work and to stay alive. We can all be inspired by the type of story that Mr. Warren tells, however the analogy with the Bible and the story of Joseph holds only in so far as the slavery is concerned. There is no rising through the ranks to take the reigns of the Kingdom. Based on my knowledge about the OFW experience, an OFW is likely to be sent on the first plane back to the Philippines if they start to preach about Christ in a Middle Eastern Muslim nation. I was so fascinated by this story that Mr. Warren gave, about the King and the baker, I tried to obtain more information. I wanted to find out who exactly the characters in the story were. I went to his website, but could not find any way, via his personal website, to contact him by email. I then went to the website of his organization, Saddleback Church, and sent a request for further information about the story, via the online request form and via the email address given. 'Dear Sir/Ms., I am currently engaged in writing a book about the Philippines, part of which will detail the experience of Filipino Overseas Foreign Workers (OFWs). Mr. Warren came to the Philippines some years ago and spoke of the purpose for OFWs. He gave the story of a Muslim King who attempted to convert a Filipino baker to Islam. The baker refused to be converted and the King nonetheless doubled his salary. I would like to use the story in my book. I would be most grateful if you would supply further details in regards to this story, sources and the names of individuals and countries concerned. Thank-you. Yours sincerely, Duncan McKenzie.' I await a reply.

The Philippines, as we have seen, loses many of its high-quality professionals to overseas jobs. The lure is the salaries and professional advancement that is available in foreign lands. While I was living in the Philippines, I made the acquaintance of a teacher who was employed locally in a primary school. She and her fiancé became very good friends, and her story is illustrative of the professionals that live and work in the Philippines, but who the nation is at risk of losing. She speaks flawless English and she grew up in a Filipino household where reading, in English, was encouraged. This household culture of reading and academic interests was a spur to her academic progress. Recently, at the school where she teaches, her classroom required renovation. In addition to the high demands and constant dedication of teaching young children, teachers like her often have the extra responsibilities of finding funds to ensure that facilities and equipment are available for their pupils. Anyone who has done any teaching would be aware of the huge demands and responsibilities that are involved. She is also studying part-time to obtain another degree and further her career. Her salary, in the year 2011, was PHP15,000—per month, or PHP180,000—per year. A comparable position in one overseas country that often has a shortage of teachers, that is Australia, is illustrative. An entry level teacher, (after a 4 year training course to degree status) employed in Australia would receive a salary of approximately AUD56, 000—per year, or the equivalent of PHP2,400,000—at the peso-dollar exchange rate in 2011.(28) That is, the salary for teaching in Australia would be over two million pesos annually. And that is at entry level. A Primary School Principal would earn $136,000 per year.(29) That is the equivalent of PHP5,848,000. It is therefore hardly surprising that professionals wish to go overseas. Fortunately for the country, for the moment at least, my friend remains here teaching. But that lure of overseas work is ever-present.

Before closing this chapter on OFWs we must discuss another manpower and labor issue in regards to the Philippine nation. This relates to the huge internal migration that takes place within the country, essentially driven by the poor in the regional areas of the Philippines, where subsistence farming or fishing may be the only livelihood, moving to the cities and urban areas to find employment, or better-paying work. There is in addition to this, the problem and suffering of persons and families displaced by civil conflict and disaster. A person so affected by civil conflict or disaster is referred to as an Internally Displaced Persons (IDP). They are defined in the following manner, 'Internally displaced persons are persons or groups of persons who have been forced or obliged to flee or to leave their homes or places of habitual residence, in particular as a result of or in order to avoid the effects of armed conflict, situations of generalized violence, violations of human rights or natural or human-made disasters, and who have not crossed an internationally recognized State border.'(30) The other group are, as we mentioned above, those who move internally for purely economic reasons. There are many individuals who seek a better life, employment and higher wages in the urban areas of this nation, and will leave their families for this. They will often find themselves, rather than living the urban dream of a prosperous and care-free life, working in restaurants as waiters for a wage that, by regional standards is good, but the extra earned is offset by the higher prices of everything in the urban areas. For Mega cities, like Manila, which is the most densely populated city on the planet, good-quality, low-priced accommodation for these workers is not readily available, and they may find themselves sharing a room in a shabby boarding house or living in the squatter's areas that can be found around the city. The money that they earn is of course divided between themselves and their families back in the provinces. It is all a matter of scale, in regards to this economic necessity of working elsewhere to help the family. Those from the poor and undeveloped regional areas, where agriculture and fishing may provide the only employment, feel that they are earning a veritable fortune working in the cities, for what in relative terms is still a lowly wage. On the next level it is the OFW who leaves the country altogether, for a wage that is again significantly higher, not only relative to the wages in the regional areas, but in the urban areas of the Philippines too. During holidays a massive exodus from the cities occurs where these workers travel back to their families in the provinces. Complete with anything that they can carry with them to take to the family back home as presents. OFWs do this too. It is best to avoid traveling during these times, especially Easter and Christmas, so as to avoid the sheer mass of people that one would encounter on one's journey. Planes, buses, boats and every other form of transport are jam-packed with people during these times, in addition to the perennial and ever-crowing roosters, the crates of mangoes and the large bottles of mineral water and food snacks that are the traveling companions of Filipinos on the move.

When caught up in the mass exodus of Filipinos moving from city to province, or wherever, there is almost always a good atmosphere and the Filipino takes all of the hassles and discomforts of traveling in their stride. For the foreigner, who is generally used to traveling in comfort, it can be a trial traveling with so many people and squashed into a small area of space. There are none of the comforts of home, and the usual dirty, smelly 'CRs' are all that may be available to you on a boat or by the roadside. But at least Filipinos are clean and friendly, and will tolerate any hassles with resignation and good humor. For anyone who wishes to experience the sheer numbers of the population on these islands, and the inadequacy of government services to deal with them, one other way apart from traveling by ordinary bus and boat around the country, it to stand in the queue for an NBI clearance in Manila. The National Bureau of Investigation issues police clearances to individuals who require it as part of a job application, or a passport for instance, and the OFW as part of the preparations for their travel overseas would have had to visit an NBI office. Every week day in Manila a queue forms outside of the NBI offices in Manila. And when I say a queue, I mean a *big* queue. If you is not there by 7a.m. then you will be left at a considerable distance away from the main office, having to wait for hours for the queue to inch its way forward. No queue jumpers here! I accompanied a friend on this endurance test. We went there very early and already others were waiting for the offices to open. The line of people, by 9a.m., stretched back as far as the eye could see. I did joke that out of the what looked like six thousand or so people waiting, only fourteen actually had any business at the NBI office. The rest of the people present were relatives or friends of the fourteen. In the Philippines you go *everywhere* with relatives or friends. Security guards kept a close eye on proceedings and strictly enforced the designated lines. There has been a big drive in the last few years to limit the activities of what is called 'fixers'. These are individuals who are paid to obtain documents and clearances by proxy for the individual who needs to acquire them. So the individual who needs a clearance document would give a fixer all of the necessary signed application documents and the fixer would do all of the queuing and undergo the hassles of getting the documents or clearances on behalf of the individual. The government is trying to prohibit this practice and the security guards keep a close eye on proceeding to make sure that fixers are not in operation. While there was a ban on fixers, the queue was serviced, as usual, by other wandering traders, selling food, drinks, ball point pens with which to complete one's application forms, and anything else that one might require. One security guard who was on duty the day I was in the NBI queue with my Filipino friend was particularly authoritarian in his manner, and barked out orders to applicants, and strictly enforced the orderly queuing. One of the applicants played a trick on him and everyone present had a good laugh. At least in such situations matters are tolerable when everyone is in a good mood. For Filipinos it is entirely normal to have to put up with deprivation and discomfort to get what they want and need. The OFW, like everyone else who requires an NBI clearance, would have got theirs in the end. Hopefully, it was worth it, and their life and work overseas were happy experiences.

Overseas Filipino Workers are the heroes of the nation. They travel to every corner of the globe, face every danger, and endure great pain, and all this to provide assistance to their families back in the Philippines. This mystical bond of the Filipino family that is so deep is what drives them. OFWs cry a lot, laugh when they can, and find solace and companionship with other Filipinos wherever they are. They dream of returning home rich and highly esteemed, and pray to God that they will continue to endure their hardships.

Chapter 5

Crime, Politics and the Church—Filipino style.

KEY POINTS: The civil structures of Philippine society are fragile and political influence over the judicial system is problematic. Despite constitutional precepts to the contrary, the organs of Church, State and the Military often enmesh.

ON THE 9TH March, 2010, a 14 year old high school student from Cebu, who also served as an altar boy at his local church, was out on an errand. He was walking to a vegetable stall at 8a.m., accompanied by an 8 year old companion. He possessed an old cell phone that was in a poor state of repair. He had to use a small stick to tap out text messages on the phone, because the keys were not operating correctly. He came to the attention of three men on a motorcycle who were passing by at the time. A neighbor of the victim reported that the three men passed by three times on their motorbike, observing the boy. Assuming that the way he was using his phone indicated that he possessed one of the more expensive touch-screen models, the men decided to stage a hold-up. The 14 year old had already placed the cell phone in his pocket and panicked when the men, who were wearing helmets, jackets, and who had covered their faces with T-shirts, confronted him. On attempting to run away he was shot in the back of the head by one of the robbers. He died later that day at the Vicente Sotto Memorial Medical Centre, Cebu.(1) It was later revealed that the murderers of the boy, on being captured by the police, expressed strong remorse for the crime. They said they had been seeking money to buy alcohol. Senseless crimes such as these abound in the Philippines, and in many other nations of the world too. This strongly Catholic nation, whose people seem for the most part gentle and tolerant, has a high homicide rate and an endemic drug and alcohol problem. As in other countries, the drug and alcohol problem exacerbates the crime problem. The government colludes in this. I was shocked to see an advertisement poster in the Philippines for an alcoholic beverage that had the phrase, prominently displayed in large letters, "It tastes so good you'll get hooked." Well, that perhaps is the plan. The company manufacturing the drink earns their profits, the government skims off its taxes, but the ordinary Filipino perhaps does become "hooked", and thereby suffers a life of alcoholism. And then his family suffers too. In tiny letters, at the bottom of the poster, were the words 'Drink moderately.' Why is such advertising allowed? Alcohol in the Philippines, and again also in many other nations, is an out of control problem, and causes huge economic and personal damage and suffering. The use of the drug 'Shabu' is widespread in the Philippines, it being the drug of choice of over 90% of Filipino drug users. This methamphetamine drug is highly addictive and can significantly alter the behavior of the user, and make them impulsive and irrational. Unfortunately, it is easily produced in make-shift laboratories.(2)

Making up another part of the homicide statistics is the murder of journalists in this nation. Journalism is globally a dangerous occupation, and many reporters are killed while covering wars, civil unrest, or investigating the malevolent deeds of those in political power. Within the Philippines it is a significant problem, and journalists, and anyone else, have to tread carefully in regards to what they may wish to investigate and report. On June the 13th 2011, an Associated Press article entitled 'Filipino journalist slain, 4th killed this year' appeared.(3) It reported on the murder Romeo Olea, a 49 year old radio commentator, who was known for his hard-hitting style on his radio show. He was murdered on his way to work. His wife stated that the journalist had been receiving death threats. He was shot while riding his motorbike on a deserted stretch of highway. The article goes on to state that the Philippines is one of the most dangerous countries for journalists, and few convictions occur subsequent to the murder. Only Somalia and Iraq are considered worse than the Philippines in terms of impunity of prosecution subsequent to the murder of reporters. There have been a reported 145 media killings since 1986, but fewer than ten people have been convicted since that time in regards to these crimes. News articles and media commentary that criticizes local politicians for alleged corruption and irregularities is considered to be the main reason for these murders. In the few cases where the actual killers are caught, they are often found to be hit-men and the mastermind remains free from prosecution. Again entrenched corruption and dysfunctional law enforcement are seen to be the main reasons for the failure to bring to justice the murderers. In 2009 a dreadful massacre occurred in the southern Philippines where at least 31 journalists, who were part of a group of 57 people traveling in a vehicle convoy, were murdered. Journalists have a highly important task to perform in a democratic society, and that is to bring to light any matters that may be of the public interest. They are the guardians of a true democracy. Their presence ensures that the public is informed about what is actually going on and brings to account politicians and public officials in whom, as members of the public, we place our trust and our money in the form of taxes or fees. The public has a right to know what happens to the money and resources that are entrusted to officials of local or national governments. I cannot ever remember an Australian journalist being murdered within Australia while engaged in his or her work, or as a result of political corruption. It simply does not happen there, or very, very rarely. And if it did happen there would be a huge outcry, and the there would be nothing spared in bringing the killer to justice. The same should occur in this nation. The murder of journalists is an evil that strikes at the very heart of a civil and a democratic society. It is unacceptable and it is highly damaging to the reputation of the Philippines as a safe, civil and democratic society.

Like the Church, and its enmeshed relationship with the government, there is a poorly defined separation between the judicial system and the body politic within the Philippines. The Republic of the Philippines is not a police state. One can walk around freely in most areas without being subject to arbitrary questioning or detention or harassment by the police. Certainly as a foreigner that has been my experience. Within the Philippines, one may say in private what one wishes, and it is no secret here that some politicians are corrupt, that the political system is dysfunctional, and that you need money to 'grease the palms' if you want to get something done, or even to occupy a specific occupational position. This is discussed openly between friends and between neighbors and is common knowledge. But to publicly criticize specific individuals and to publicly reveal facts relating to corruption can put one at serious risk. In contrast to other nations then, while one may express in private whatever one wishes, the media in the Philippines, or more exactly, the journalists covering the stories and doing the investigative journalism, put themselves at great risk.

The Republic of the Philippines, like other nations, has dark stains on its history. Mentioned above is the 2009 killing of a group of journalists and civilians in the Southern Philippines. Those alleged to be responsible for this crime are currently being tried in court. During the Vietnam war an event referred to as the 'My Lai massacre' occurred, where many innocent civilians were killed. The massacre, which took place on the morning of March the 16th 1968, was a watershed in the history of modern American combat, and a turning point in the public perception of the Vietnam War. In the course of three hours more than 500 Vietnamese civilians were killed in cold blood at the hands of US troops. The soldiers had been on a "search and destroy" mission to root out communist fighters in what was fertile Viet Cong territory. When the story of My Lai was exposed, more than a year later, it tarnished the name of the US army. Most Americans did not want to believe that their revered GI Joe could be a brutal murderer.(4) Cambodia is a land that has as its national religion Buddhism. This is a gentle religion, who's adherents try to avoid even the killing of an insect, and in all things take the "middle path", the way of moderation, and in all matters strive to be contemplative. During the rule of the Cambodian dictator Pol Pot, millions of Cambodians were murdered during a savage reign of butchery that was the direct result of his political and ideological fanaticism. The combined effects of forced labor, malnutrition, poor medical care and executions resulted in the deaths of approximately 21 percent of the Cambodian population. In all, an estimated 1,700,000–2,500,000 people died under his leadership.(5) Germany, referred to as the Land of the Poet and the Thinker, unleashed the dark side of human nature during the rule of Adolf Hitler and the National Socialist Movement. More than six million Jews and hundreds of thousands of other, what the regime viewed as 'undesirables', including homosexuals, political opponents to the regime, and the intellectually disabled' were murdered. The Nazis referred to the intellectually disabled as *'Defektmenschen'* or literally 'defective humans'. The civilized veneer of human behavior often cannot hold in check dark and evil impulses, and the savagery, that is part of human nature. The reason why I mention the above is so that we can discuss *in context* what happens within the Philippines. That is, in the context of what happens in other nations, and in the context of history. It is very easy to think in black and white terms. To say, "The Philippines is all bad", or "The Philippines is all good." This book is not a cheerful travel log, calling the Philippines a travel paradise. And neither is it a book of disasters. There are good things happening in the Philippines and there are bad things happening in the Philippines. It is a book about the *reality* of the Philippines, exactly as it is, as best as I can tell it. It is very important to talk about the bad things because they are the things that we have to change. We cannot ignore them. We have to deal with reality.

The senseless murder of Filipino journalists raises a very important question and that relates to the unhindered operation, or otherwise, of a free press with a nation. And this in turn relates to the basic question of what constitutes a democracy. We now have to ask the question: Is the Philippines a democracy? This is a critical question, if not for the very reason that most people assert that the Philippines *is* a democracy. Are they correct? Let us examine this question in detail. What is a democracy and does the Philippines have a right to claim to be one?

Firstly, we must define our terms. We can think of democracy as a system of government with four key elements: 1) A political system for choosing and replacing the government through *free and fair* elections. 2) The *active participation* of the people, as citizens, in politics and civic life. 3) *Protection of the human rights of all citizens.* 4) A rule of law, in which *the laws and procedures apply equally to all citizens.*(6) (Italics mine.) From the source that I use, the above four criteria are supplemented by other criteria that are given as the hallmarks of a democracy. They include: Voters must be able to vote *in secret, free of intimidation and violence.* (Italics mine). The people are free to criticize their elected leaders and representatives, and to observe how they conduct the business of government. There is *freedom and pluralism in the mass media. Democracy is a system of rule by laws, not by individuals.* The law is fairly, impartially, and consistently enforced, by courts that are independent of the other branches of government. *Office holders cannot use their power to enrich themselves. Independent courts and commissions punish corruption, no matter who is guilty.* (Italics mine). So, I have outlined in this book certain facts and events that are troublesome and problematic if we are to view the Philippines as a democracy. A democracy requires a free and independent media. I have outlined in this chapter the brutal killings of Filipino journalists. A democracy requires that voters be free of intimidation and violence. National and local elections in the Philippines are characterized by outbreaks of violence, that often the police find difficult to contain. More of that later in this chapter. A democracy requires that office holders not enrich themselves through the use of their power. And so it goes on. Such criteria, if we accept them as providing a valid definition of what a democracy is, do not fit with the political realities of the Philippines in 2011, or in years past. Later in the chapter I relate the issue of certain regions in the Philippines operating in a way that is consistent with feudalism. Now, let me clarify one thing. To me personally, it does not matter as to whether you call a nation a democracy or not. If one looks to Singapore, as we have done in Chapter 3, one can see that it could never have called itself a true democracy. But then *who cares?* Singapore is a rich, dynamic and free society. Unlike the Philippines it has a myriad of rules and regulations *that are strictly enforced.* And it is this model, this operating system, this *pseudo-democracy*, that has emerged as a first world nation, and all of its citizens have shared in its success. I mention in another part of the book the quotation from Deng Xiaoping: "It doesn't matter if a cat is black or white. As long as it catches mice, it is a good cat." For Singapore, the model of a pseudo democracy has worked, and worked very well. It was the cat that caught the mice. But what of the Philippines? We cannot call it a democracy, because the reality of what is happening here is not consistent with the criteria that we may use to define a democracy. This is again where the Philippines gets itself into difficulties, by accepting as gospel everything that flows from the almighty USA. The "Manifest Destiny" of the United States was originally a concept used to justify its continental expansion.(7) This proved hugely successful and the rugged individualism, extraordinary drive and work ethic of the pioneer is the stuff of legend.(8) Once the settlers conquered the continental USA, the concept of Manifest Destiny had an inertia and an inherent dynamism that allowed it to broaden to include a global, ideological expansion. Democracy, along with Coca Cola, Hollywood movies, and other American products, services and ideas were exported worldwide. What is exported from the USA are particularly American concepts, yet we have tried to fit them in, and make them work here in the Philippines, in the context of an Asian cultural matrix. The huge irony is of course that America, in a lot of cases, never established democracies, only pseudo-democracies, and in its obsessive attempts to contain the perceived expansion of communist ideology actually led to the undermining and sabotaging of democratic processes in some nations.(9) This has continued with the most recent nonsensical war driven by the American Neo-conservative agenda regarding Iraq. Chasing fictitious weapons of mass destruction, and supposedly bringing democracy to the people of Iraq, America invaded a sovereign nation. They were aided and abetted by my native country, the United Kingdom, by a labor leader named Tony Blair, who really should have known better than to participate in American folly. The only problem I have with the concept of America taking democracy to Iraq is that is that I do not know of any organized voting or polling that took place in Iraq, to ask the people in a democratic way if they wanted to be invaded. Such is the nature of political reality and American double-talk in the 21ˢᵗ century. As an aside, please do not assume that my criticism of the USA is in any way implied support for Saddam Hussein. I have been a member of Amnesty International for many years and am well aware of the brutal and murderous way in which Saddam ruled. Let us return to the original question, is the Philippines a democracy? The real answer is that in some ways it is, and in some ways it isn't. It has democratic institutions in place, but *in practice,* these clearly do not always function as they should.

The existence of true democracy in the Philippines is a fiction. But that is really not the point. The real point is that the Philippines, if it wants to eradicate the poverty of its masses and have a viable future, is going to have to come up with political and economic solutions that are appropriate to its own circumstances and needs. It needs to free itself from the cultural baggage of a brief liaison with an imperialistic power called the USA. The truth is that America never supported true democracy in the Philippines. It was all a sham. This was clearly illustrated by the following quote, made by then Vice President George H. W. Bush in 1981 (the father of the President who initiated the Iraq War), 'We love your adherence to democratic principles and to the democratic process, and we will not leave you in isolation.' This was made during the Ferdinand Marcos third term inauguration of June, 1981. He won the election to extend his rule by a massive margin. The main opposition parties boycotted the election, they would have seen it as pointless to participate in what was a foregone conclusion.(10) The key words, the code words, and the American-duplicity-double-speak-understood-by-all-dictators-who-are-friends-of-the-USA-words were, '. . . and we will not leave you in isolation.' From America, the real message was always, "Do what you like, just *call* yourself a democracy, and get the communist bastards." That's alright if one is honest about it. The communism as practiced in some ways and in some states is brutal, undemocratic, (as opposed to a *true* democracy) and an insult to human rights. What was America to do? Be nice? Be kind? Sit back while another Stalin comes to power in a communist state and spreads the dark side of communism to every corner of the globe, trampling on people's human rights. A military boot on the face and an AK47 aimed at the head. The liberal democracies of the planet have to be vigilant and have to use their power if that is justified in clear self-defense of their land and their (true) democratic values. But Iraq was *never,* in any way, a direct threat to the liberal democracies of the world. Saddam had no weapons of mass destruction, and he had no direct connection and no direct involvement with the terrorism or the ideology of Al-Qaeda. He was secular, and had nothing in common with the radical religious fundamentalism of Osama Bin Laden. They were as different as chalk and cheese, as the old English saying goes. The only possible defense that I could bring to the Bush administration is that within the political speeches of Saddam he did make indirect references to weapons of mass destruction. But for anyone who truly understood Iraq, and the Americans patently didn't, those speeches were a ruse on Saddam's part to keep Iran, his mortal enemy, in the dark about what he might have in regards to weapons, and weapons of mass destruction. It was a verbal deterrent, but aimed squarely at Iran. For American governments in such situations, where they engage in deceit, and for their support of nations such as the Philippines under Marcos, it was what I call "Mushroom Democracy." Its principal is. "Keep the people in the dark, and feed them bullshit." Just in the same way one cultivates mushrooms.

Internally within this nation the people, the government, the Church, the military and the Police have to censure, condemn and bring to trial those of its countrymen who use power and influence in a destructive and evil way. Political models and the use of power may be used in a pragmatic way, but the murder of journalists, priests engaged in human rights work, and others who exercise their human right to free speech is never, ever justified. Dictatorships sometimes work, but they must be benevolent dictatorships. For some, the global battle is for ideological superiority, as it was in the days of the communist threat. Today the ideological threat is fundamentalist Islamic ideology. It is a pernicious doctrine. It is just the same military boot on the face and an AK47 aimed at the head, only with the pretence of this representing Islam. As practiced by the Taliban it is vile. Gays are executed, girls are forbidden to go to school, power is exercised arbitrarily. There is no independent thought. No independent judiciary. No free speech. It is Hell on Earth. Except for the ideologues who live it and believe in it, and who hold the reigns of power. The debate rages on about how we deal with this threat, and win the "hearts and minds" of those who may fall under its influence. For the hawks in America, when engaged in ideological battles with either communists or the Taliban, the answer is simple, "Grab them by the balls, and their hearts and minds will follow." They have tried to grab them by the balls in Afghanistan, but the Taliban are resurgent. It's not clear how Afghanistan will end up, but all of the ammunition wasted there has come to naught in producing real security from the fundamentalist Islamic ideological threat. Ideological battles can not be won solely with military power. Part of the problem has really been the disastrous foreign policy decisions of America, and the fact that in recent history they have not been able to distinguish between what is a real threat and what is not.

The proliferation of legal and illegal weapons is problematic within the Philippines. Weapons are reportedly easily obtainable on the black market, and guns are produced in back street gun shops in some major cities. Legally, only Filipino citizens can own a firearm. Foreigners are prohibited from doing so. Filipinos are required to obtain a gun license in order to legally possess a weapon to keep in their home, and a special 'Permit to Carry' license must be obtained if the weapon and ammunition is to be carried outside of one's residence. In contrast to the United States of America, a gun license in the Philippines legally registers only one firearm, and records on the license the serial number of that particular weapon, whereas in America the firearms license holder can purchase as many weapons legally on sale as they may wish. The gun laws within the USA do vary from State to State, but in the Philippines are nationally consistent. There is then within the nation the day-to-day impulsive and senseless crimes and killings committed by the petty criminal, who is simply after money, to use for alcohol or for drugs or gambling. This is exacerbated by a widespread drug and alcohol problem, and the easy availability of guns on the black market. However, again for the sake of perspective, the homicide rate in the Philippines is just below that of the USA. There are also the killings and crime related to the chronic, low-level anti-government insurgency that exists throughout the archipelago. The New People's Army (NPA) groups, known as "Sparrow Units" were active in the mid-1980s, killing government officials, police personnel, military members, and anyone else they targeted for elimination. They were also supposedly part of an NPA operation called '*Agaw Armas*', (Filipino for 'Stealing Weapons'), where they raided government armories as well as stealing weapons from slain military and police personnel. A low level civil war with southern Moslems, Al-Qaeda sympathizers and communist insurgents has led to a general break down of law and order in some parts of the nation. There is always an upsurge in violence at the time of Philippine elections. Marred by widespread fraud elections in the Philippines often take place in an atmosphere of intimidation and fear. Due to the proliferation of guns shoot-outs between rival politicians or their supporters can occur, or it may just come down to plain-old fisticuffs. The presence of armed insurgent groups is an extra ingredient in the explosive mix. During the last national elections the National Police identified 558 of the country's 1,634 cities and municipalities as areas of concern, requiring extra security forces. 118 of the hotspots were located within predominantly Muslim autonomous regions in the southern Philippines where various armed groups operate. The Police are faced with a difficult task because often some of the private armies of the local political warlords have more weaponry than the local police.(11) The key to understanding Philippine politics is to understand that the nation remains in many ways a feudal system. Families with land, power and wealth control many of the regions of the nation. The problem for the Philippines, as we know, is that, disastrously, the middle classes have shrunk, therefore there are fewer people with increasing disposable income to buy land and to shift the balance of land and wealth away from the elite. It has been estimated that about 150 political clans control the body politic within the Philippines, from local government to congress, the senate and the presidency. In a fascinating article in the Philippine press, Manuel F. Almario discusses this issue. It is entitled 'Why feudal lords still reign in PH'.(12) In the article Mr. Almario discusses the reign of one of the political families in the Philippines. A reign that has led to the city in which they hail from being widely regarded as a success story, in terms of efficiency of services and a low crime rate. The vice-mayor of the city is the father of the current mayor. The politician in question is quoted in the article discussing this very issue of feudalism, and the relationship of the people to the ruling classes. Mr. Almario goes on to write about the, clearly evident, layers of Philippine society, which essentially exist at the top as as a ruling elite, then an aristocracy, then the diminishing middle class and at the bottom the masses of the populace. The above article that I mention is important, for it allows us an insight into the political realities of the Philippines, and the nature of political rule here. It captures the ambivalence that Filipinos have towards politicians and those in power. Further, it also highlights the excellent standards of Filipino journalism that exist in this nation.

The projection of power and political control from the central organs of government is weak in many of the regional areas. They may be highly democratized and progressive in Manila, but the control of the government does not extend to many regional areas. The archipelagic structure of the nation makes political rule problematic. Additionally it can be argued that the political system of the country is not appropriate or suitable for such a geographical morphology. On April 29th, 2008, it was reported that Senate Minority Leader Nene Pimentel was the principal author of a Senate resolution calling for a debate on charter change seeking, '. . . a revision of the Constitution to shift from a unitary to a federal system of government. The resolution was signed by 11 other senators: Senate President Manny Villar and Senators Jinggoy Estrada, Francis Pangilinan, Edgardo Angara, Rodolfo Biazon, Pia Cayetano, Juan Ponce Enrile, Francis Escudero, Gregorio Honasan, Panfilo Lacson Jr., and Ramon Revilla Jr.' It sought to convene both Houses of Congress into a constituent assembly to amend the Constitution, before the end of then-President Arroyo's term in 2010. It proposed to convert the country into a federal union of 11 states: Northern Luzon, Central Luzon, Southern Tagalog, Bicol, Minparom (Mindoro, Palawan, Romblon), Eastern Visayas, Central Visayas, Western Visayas, Northern Mindanao, Southern Mindanao and BangsaMoro.(13) The unitary system of government, as exemplified by the Philippines, is characterized by a form of government in which power is held by one central authority. Conversely, a federal system is characterized by a form of government in which power is divided between one central and several regional authorities. Federal governments often evolved out of confederations. A federal system has specific advantages. To take the analogy of radio waves, we have already mentioned that over distance the political control exerted by the government appears to attenuate, or weaken. With radio waves, the remedy for the attenuation of a signal, where one wants to transmit over long distances, would be a repeater station. This is a device whereby the signal is captured, strengthened and then re-transmitted. The signal is thus amplified and can be received strongly in local regions. The other issue is of course, and to use another example from radio electronics, that central governments cannot always be in tune with local interests and local issues, or have a true understanding of the local milieu in which the body politic of the region operates. Regional or State governments are in a position to retransmit the signals of a central government, with some fine tuning added. The reason that warlords and feudalism exists in parts of the Philippine is for the sole reason that the lack of effective political power by the central government creates a political vacuum. Feudalism and warlords exist because of this political vacuum, and their ability to move, operate and strengthen themselves within the local milieu. The political unity of a nation would not be necessarily any less under a federal system than it is under the current unitary system. This is because, in effect, there exists now this de facto multiplicity of political power anyway, indeed this de facto federalism, but with the power falling to the warlords, political clans and feudalist structures. With these entities there is little accountability, and little consistency with the central government policy and planning framework.

It is all very well to provide analogies and to discuss academically this issue. The crucial point is of course, how would such a system if adopted in the Philippines function *in practice?* We are aware of the nations with a federal system that are highly successful and stable political entities. We can list the USA and Australia for instance. But whether the success of these nations would translate to success in the Philippines is another matter. The disadvantage of a federal system is that the political and governmental bureaucracy that it engenders is huge. The thing that can be said with certainty is that the power and the influence of the central government throughout this nation is clearly not uniform, and in some regions is very weak. As we know, as at the time of writing this book in 2011, the government remains unitary in nature. It is not clear if the system of government will ever change to a federal system. That, in any case, will be for the Filipino people to debate and to decide.

I choose to live in the Philippines and I have never been the victim of any serious crime. I receive a pension from Australia, and live very comfortably. In fact, the only crime within the Philippines ever to befall me was the theft of a pair of training shoes which had I had left on my doorstep overnight. I find it amazing, that due to the depths of poverty and despair here, that this is all I have ever had stolen. As with other nations crimes often occur randomly and especially with the foreigner being so conspicuous, they can be targeted. For the foreigner obviously common-sense considerations apply. The same common-sense principles that would apply in any other nation.

There is within the Philippines specific regions that are under the control of politicians who have a very hard line towards crime. There are cities and regions where the local politicians have allegedly taken to extrajudicial measures to eradicate crime, and with reported significant success. One uses the word 'success' here in terms of any crime reduction that has occurred. In terms of human rights issues, and upholding the due process of law, extrajudicial measures can never be considered 'a success'. Some local politicians allegedly give free reign to the police or to vigilantes to hunt down and kill those engaged in serious crime. In one major city it was reported that criminals were so afraid of the vigilante groups that there were cases where individuals who knew they were going to be targeted once they were released from jail actually requested that they remain locked up in the relative safety of prison. Extra-judicial sentencing and killing is certainly not a new phenomenon within the Philippines, and its use continues to this day. By its very nature it would be extremely difficult to quantify this phenomenon. As discussed in the opening chapter, there is a high homicide rate in the Philippines and criminals may come to a sticky end due to various reasons such as coming into conflict with an associate or another syndicate, or just having too many beers one Saturday night and getting into a gunfight with an acquaintance over a gambling debt. In any case, if the deceased is a known criminal the police are likely not to expend any great effort on investigating the case. Where crime is directed towards innocent persons the police will attempt to apprehend those responsible. If their local intelligence is good, and it usually is, suspects are usually cornered quickly. This is because, unlike the West, where it is so much easier to live alone or live anonymously, in the Philippines more or less everyone is part of the social matrix, and a person's movements and behavior are usually observed.

In Chapter 4, when discussing the OFW, it was reported that Filipinos have fallen victim to piracy in international waters while working as seamen. The Philippines too has a piracy problem in its own waters. This is hardly surprising due to the number of islands that constitute the nation. It is a further economic hindrance to the nation, in which the transfer of goods and services, due to its archipelagic form, is already sluggish and sclerotic. In 2007, it was reported that a Filipino pirate leader and one of the men in his group were killed in an operation involving police and the military in a remote area in the southern Philippines. Piracy in the region was said to be rampant, and this was hampering the economic development of the province concerned. One of the important local industries was affected where seaweed, which is converted into a substance that is used as a natural preservative, was not able to be shipped to Cebu for processing, because of pirates abounding in the local waters.(14)

In regards to being a foreigner in the Philippines there are many places that one may go in relative safety. I have lived in Cebu, and in a provincial town in the Bicol region for example, happily and without incident. Family and friends are very protective. The police and the military I have always found to be helpful. However, there are some regions that I would not travel to. General Santos City and Davao City have a reputation for being safe. Some areas of Mindanao, such as the ARMM (Autonomous Region of Muslim Mindanao) is considered not suitable for tourism.(15) Same nation. Different world.

In summary of the crime and security situation in the Philippines the following may be said: There is an ongoing threat of terrorist activities in the Philippines, particularly in the Mindanao region. Bombs have exploded in public areas. Although mentioned is this specific area, Mindanao, anywhere in the country is at risk of terrorist activity. Justifiably one could say that this also relates to every other nation. There is nowhere on the planet that can be considered as totally safe. Kidnappings have occurred both in urban areas and in remote areas within the Philippines. Kidnap-for-ransom of business people has been frequent. Deaths have resulted from some kidnappings. Manila is a hot-spot for crime and unsuspecting tourists have been drugged and robbed. Visitors to the country are advised not to accept offers of food, drink or transportation from strangers. As a foreigner taxi drivers may attempt to charge exorbitant rates. Personally, when using taxis I insist that the taxi driver use the meter. On seeing a foreigner a driver may attempt to circumvent using the meter and quote their own exorbitant prices. If the driver does not engage the meter on entering the taxi, I insist he stop and I get another taxi. For those that simply engage the meter and take me directly to where I wish to go I always make sure I give a tip. Ferry accidents can occur, due to bad weather, overloading or poor maintenance of the boats, or sometimes a combination of all three. One must be observant and not board vessels that appear not to be seaworthy, or are overcrowded. I have already mentioned that pirates operate in the sea waters of the Philippines, putting commercial and private seafarers at risk of armed attack. The Canadian government, for instance, on its website, gives an official warning against travel in the the Autonomous Region of Muslim Mindanao (ARMM), which includes Basilan, Sulu, Tawi Tawi, Lanao del Sur, Maguindanao and Sharif Kabunsuan, as well as the Zamboanga Peninsula, Zamboanga del Sur, Saragani, Lanao del Norte, Davao del Sur (excluding urban areas of Davao City), South Cotabato, North Cotabato and Sultan Kudarat. In these regions there is a serious threat of kidnapping against foreigners.(16)

As mentioned, there is a chronic low-level insurgency within the nation. The intensity of this conflict varies from region to region. The most serious civil unrest and disruption occurs in the region of Mindanao. This is principally fueled by Muslim separatist groups who wish to establish an independent state within the Philippines. The conflict here is driven by religious ideology, and there are extremists who present a threat to foreigner and native Filipino alike. Kidnappings, bombings, assassinations and direct confrontation with the national military forces are common occurrences, and there is the subsequent fleeing of the civil population, who are caught in the middle of the conflict. These displaced people of the civil population (Internally Displaced Persons, or IDPs, as mentioned in Chapter 4) flee to other areas of the Philippines that are safer, and often settle in squatter areas within, and surrounding, major urban population centers. In other parts of the Philippines, this low-level conflict has been driven by the New People's Army, and other splinter, reportedly communist-orientated groups, that foment civil unrest and disruption, and also engage in kidnappings, extortion, and bank robberies to fund their activities. The boundaries are sometimes not clear, as to what constitutes the purely ideologically driven groups, and those who may be described as bandits simply engaging in criminal activity. Reportedly, there are Marxist and Maoist oriented groups operating, but for them the ideological world has passed them by, with Communism, Marxism, Trotskyism and Maoism all essentially deceased ideologies in the contemporary world.

During the Marcos era there existed a symbiotic relationship between the central government and the communist-insurgency groups. During the cold-war era, with the Soviet Union providing moral, if not material, support globally to communist insurgent groups, the United States supported morally, militarily and financially any leader who was anti-communist. U.S. President Franklin D. Roosevelt once reportedly commented to an aide, who advised him that a certain Latin American dictator whom the US was keeping in power, was a "son of a bitch". "He may be a son of a bitch, but he's *our* son of a bitch" was the reported reply of the President. The quote may be apocryphal, but it vividly reflects the actual thinking of the USA at that time.(17)

The world was polarized, and nations were either in the communist or the capitalist sphere of influence, and each nation, the United States and the Soviet Union, would do anything to maintain their ideological territory and keep their economic interests safe. History inexorably marched towards the dissolution of the Soviet empire. Like many previous empires of history it collapsed principally due to internal factors, and an external unyielding, increasingly efficient and prosperous global capitalist system. How a politician operated within a respective superpower's sphere of influence was not really of any consequence or concern. The same principle clearly operated in the case of Ferdinand Marcos. The communist bogey-man justified any form of political repression. This then, was the geo-political matrix in which Marcos came to office, and which allowed him to consolidate his political power. The Philippines at that time hosted U.S. forces, principally Subic Bay Naval Base in Luzon, and Clark Air Base, located near Angeles City. These bases were the largest overseas military installations of the US Armed Forces, and were considered at that time as absolutely essential for the projection of U.S. power and influence into the Asian region. Washington and Manila had a co-dependency relationship, and each one used the other to their advantage in whatever way possible. It was a game, and Marcos was a highly skilled political player. US Presidents came and went, serving perhaps their maximum of two terms allowed under the US Constitution. Marcos was in for the long haul. He controlled the political system, the political system did not control him. There were no limits, and in true Filipino fashion, no one in his entourage cared much about limits or boundaries anyway. The US went its own merry way, not getting itself involved in what was happening in Manila. There was plenty of Intelligence on what was going down in Manila, there were CIA operatives all over the place, but in Washington they didn't want to know or to see, or to hear. Plausible deniability was the key phrase and guiding principle. Manila was the main station for CIA operations in Southeast Asia, it was a very friendly environment, and the *status quo* was just fine.

Let's take a hypothetical briefing session with one hypothetical President of the USA and a hypothetical presidential aide called Mark. The day starts at 7a.m.

Mark:	"Good morning, Mr. President."
President:	"Good morning, Mark. What's happening today?"
Mark:	"Well, Sir, you are meeting at 10a.m. with Ferdinand Marcos."
President:	"Is that right? The guy's from Indonesia, right?"
Mark:	"No Mr. President, he's from the Philippines."
President:	"I'll be darned. At least I was close. What kind of assets do they have? Do the Philippines have a strategic role in our overall plans."
Mark:	"Well, Sir, it's a large group of islands. But when you talk about it as a nation, we refer to is in the singular. So better to ask, Sir, what kind of assets does *it* have?"
President:	"God damn it, Mark. Am I the President of the United States or am I in Grade School. Cut the crap, them or they or it. Just tell me the assets, Mark."
Mark:	"Big assets, Sir. Strategically important US naval and air bases. High quality electronic Intelligence facilities. Lots of human assets. But problems. Communists rebels in the north, Muslim rebels in the south."
President:	"So I have to meet this guy, Marcos?"
Mark:	"You do, Sir. He's important to us."
President:	"Damn, I'll have to make notes."

The president reaches over his huge, well polished Oval Office desk and picks up a shiny, new, sharply pointed pencil. He then grabs a note pad that is beautifully embossed with the White House emblem.

Mark looks over his shoulder as the President starts to write. A thought flashes through his head, "Oh shit, he's gonna start writing notes. Shit, I hope he doesn't use them during the meeting. We'll have to issue another clarification. He can't get a damned thing right."

The President starts writing. Mouthing the word 'Philippines', he writes 'Phillipines.' Mark becomes agitated.

Mark: "Sir, Mr. President. He nervously clears his throat. It's actually spelt 'Philippines', with a single l and two p's."

President: "God damn it Mark! There you go again. Are you a Grade School teacher or a presidential aide?" The President throws his pencil down in exasperation. "Just tell me about this guy Marcos."

Mark: "Because the Philippines is so strategically important, Sir, we have CIA crawling all over the place. Bad reports, Sir. The guy is very smart. Very capable. Anti-communist. But corrupt. He's siphoning money overseas and jailing political opposition at home. He likes power and he likes money. He'll be sticking around one way or another."

President: "Is that right? So we need to protect our assets there, stop the commies, and he's the guy who will ensure that happens?"

Mark: "That's right, Mr. President. He's very valuable to what we're doing."

President: "Thanks, Mark. That's all I need to know. Has the speechwriter got the speech down?"

Mark: "Yes, Sir. Ready to go."

President: "Thanks, Mark. In future, just cut out the Grade School teacher crap. By the way, can you spell Mississippi?"

Mark: "Yes, I can, Sir." Mark spells out "M-I-S-S-I-S-S-I-P-I."

President: "Got ya, you son of a bitch! You've spelt it wrong."

The President can't contain his glee.

President: "Get me a coffee and the baseball scores from last night. All this foreign policy stuff is giving me a headache."

The only American president to show any real concern about the Marcos regime was former President Jimmy Carter. Carter was a born-again Christian and from a different mold than the other presidents who

179

have inhabited the Oval Office. He was a man who avoided cussing and swearing, and seldom raised his voice. His aides reported that he had a laser-like stare, and he would use that to silence anyone who invoked his displeasure. Carter was considered by many, due to his stance on human rights, as "soft." But he was no fool, and he would use American might if he had to. However, unlike many others, he saw the short-sightedness of supporting unequivocally regimes that abused human rights. If America had principles, and it said it had, then it had to promulgate those principles in a clear and *consistent* way. That was his viewpoint, and he ran into a lot of resistance and ridicule because of that. However, nothing changed in terms of the aid the Philippines received. He lost his bid for reelection for a second term, and was succeeded in Office by Ronald Reagan. All of the other administrations were effusive in their support for Marcos. Even though they knew what he was up to, and that the agenda was not democratic. Again, that might have been acceptable if there was no deceit and the US demanded clear limits be set, and the defenseless were protected. But they did not even do that. All of the power and leverage that the US had, but they did nothing, except idly stand by and give praise and unlimited support. Because of his excesses, and the excesses of those he placed in key positions around him, the Marcos regime fell. If the US had acted earlier and made clear conditions it may not have come to that. There was just no one around to say "enough is enough". Sometimes people, even dictators, need to hear that, so they know where the boundaries are.

Using the communist insurgency as a pretext, on the 21st September, 1972, Marcos declared martial law within the Philippines. The political dictatorship of Marcos, his crony capitalism, and the clear lack of betterment in the lives of the poor within the country, provided a steady stream of recruits to the communist insurgency groups. Essentially, its members had nothing to lose. For the most part, they were dirt-poor and politically disenfranchised. As history unfolded Marcos was eventually removed from power by the 'People Power Revolution' in 1986. A man with a brilliant mind, and a superb political operator, he worked tirelessly, and in his day to day life was extraordinarily self-disciplined. He preferred simple meals and beverages rather than sumptuous fare that may have been on offer, however by the end of this rule it is estimated that US$5Billion to US$10Billion was taken by him from the country, and laundered through various overseas bank accounts.(18) Fleeing to the United States at the end of his rule, to Hawaii, he faced an ignominious end, after a period of rule that had so unmistakably molded the Philippines during a formative period in its history. While still in Office, at the height of the political chaos that had been unleashed, at 3:00 p.m., February 20, 1986, Marcos talked to United States Senator Paul Laxalt, asking for advice from the White House. Laxalt advised him to "cut and cut cleanly". It was the best advice that could have been offered. And it was perhaps the only clear advice and the only proper directive that the US had ever given him. He died in 1989, while still dreaming of returning to his homeland and re-claiming political power. I had visited the Philippines many times during the rule of Marcos. The middle name of my daughter is Imelda, she was named after Imelda Marcos. The Marcos rule had so much of a Philippine tragedy. Golden dreams and bitter heartache. It all ended in tears. For everyone. Filipino brilliance and that same old damned curse of never being able see the boundaries. It could have all ended differently. The momentum, the direction, the progress and the confidence of the nation had been lost from those early days in the 1960's, when the Philippines was the second richest nation in Asia. The question at that time should have been, "How can we consolidate our position and the economic gains that we have made." The other nations of Asia started awakening, like Singapore, who got its act together and left the Philippines in the dust as it raced ahead economically. Other factors came into play. The Philippines started to export its best and brightest people, not the layabouts, and there are plenty of those, who should have been on the first boat out. The population of the nation exploded. The demographics were all wrong. Capital inflow became capital outflow, to overseas bank accounts. Complacency in the political ranks and demoralization in the populace set in. Power corrupts and absolute power corrupts absolutely. And when you put into key positions people who are friends, or family, or the friends of family, or the family of friends, then you don't get the right people for the job, and no objective evaluation either of suitability or of performance takes place. And that is still happening now. Even in 2011. This is the weakness of Filipino political thinking and political culture. It can lead to disaster. And it did.

What took place in Philippine history is the facts that we can read in our history books. There is often an attempt, by many nations and by many people, to rewrite history. The emotions and the immediacy of the period of history in question are gone, and a different perspective is gained. Things *can* be balanced and rounded and adjusted and smoothed at the edges, and reconciliation, and healing, can and should take place. But the core truths can never be allowed to be forgotten. If we forget those we run the risk of repeating our history, and our mistakes. That is all. Honor everyone. Remember the principles of human rights, of 'life, liberty and the pursuit of happiness.' But the facts have to stand as they are, and always be remembered. For the good of all.

Swept to power in his place was Corazon Aquino, the mother of the current President, and widow of the assassinated politician Benigno 'Ninoy' Aquino Jr. She was a woman of great conviction, honesty, heart and high moral and ethical standards. She embodied the hopes of a nation tired and cynical of the political system then operating. She was smart and she was homely. She once answered brilliantly, in responses to Ferdinand Marcos taunting her that she had no experience with which to lead a nation. "It's true. I have no experience in lying, cheating and stealing." Marcos, as stated before, was a brilliant political operator, but Aquino instinctively knew how to meet him head on and deftly disarm him of his political rhetoric. This was psychological judo *par excellence*. Marcos must have been fuming and probably thought, "who is this upstart, this *woman*". The male cronies of Marcos and the military always considered politics and running the country as man's work. Sadly, it is the entrenched political and economic interests that control the levers of power within the Philippines and real, fundamental change in the way things operated was never achieved, despite the best intentions by Corazon Aquino. The family dynasties of political power and wealth remain, with exceptions such as Manny Pacquiao, the world boxing champion and government representative, who fought his way to the top from an impoverished background.

It was on August 23rd 1983 that I was in Melbourne, Australia, visiting the home of my parents. The television was on, my father always liked to watch the television news programs. The news had just broken of the senseless and tragic assassination of Benigno Simeon 'Ninoy' Aquino Jr. It is one of those events that is etched in one's mind, and one always remembers it, and the circumstances of where one heard the news. It was the same when U.S. President John F. Kennedy was assassinated. I was only a small boy at the time of JFK's murder, but I still remember the newsflash and where I was at the time. The jolting news that the charismatic bearer of great hope is now dead. And then the world becomes a darker place. For those foreigners visiting the Philippines, Manila International Airport is now named in Benigno Ninoy Aquino's honor, and this will be their first reminder of the troubled political history of the nation. 'The Filipino is worth dying for' he so famously stated. And die for the Filipino he did. This bearer of great hope was shot in the head as he disembarked a plane at Manila Airport after returning from exile in the USA. As is usual in Philippine politics and crime the truth is hard to find, and the facts as to who ordered the assassination have never been established beyond doubt. Another man, a purported communist assassin by the name of Rolando Galman, was present at the time and was shot on the tarmac just after Aquino was assassinated. Aquino was being escorted by soldiers assigned by the government to protect him. It was reported, in a subsequent investigation, that the soldiers who were directed to safely escort him off the plane did this and got him safely to the tarmac, but the alleged killer, Galman, was waiting to allegedly fire the fateful bullet. After the Marcos government was overthrown, 16 defendants were found guilty and sentenced to life imprisonment, but it is still not known definitively who planned the assassination or who pulled the trigger.(19)(20) Ferdinand Marcos was a highly intelligent, controlled man with a superb mastery of all things political. Had he directly chosen to eliminate Aquino it is unlikely he would have done so in such a blatant, public and brutal way, and he would have had full knowledge that to have committed such an act would have brought retribution upon himself. Various persons have been named as the mastermind behind the horrendous assassination, but it is likely that we will never know the truth. At the very end of his rule, when the disintegration of his support in the military occurred, a stand-off took place between the civilian population and those in the military opposed to his rule versus his loyalists. Marcos stated that he could have ended the open revolt against his rule, and used the forces still at his command, but that it would have been a bloody event. He was exactly correct, and many a dictator, unlike Marcos, would have engaged in open massacre in an attempt to hold on to power. He had no hesitation in jailing his opponents, but brutal, premeditated murder was never his style. The problem with dictators, as with Marcos, was that they often surround themselves with 'yes-men' of varying degrees of intelligence, competence and foresight. In all probability it was one of those 'yes-men' who ordered the assassination of Ninoy Aquino, in an attempt to "protect" the Marcos regime, and this unleashed the forces that swept Marcos from power. Marcos is gone but politics Filipino style inexorably moves on, and with it the same old inattention to boundaries and limits.

Inviolable. It's an interesting word. Words can have a very clear and precise meaning, or they can be subject to obfuscation. Let's look at this word 'inviolable' and its application to the relationship between the Philippine body politic and the Catholic Church. Although the Philippine Constitution asserts there must be an 'inviolable' separation between Church and State, it is clear that this precept has never been followed strictly. The word 'inviolable' is defined as 'secure from assault or trespass.'(21) Synonyms for this word include 'holy', 'sacrosanct', 'sacred' and 'untouchable'. Words that the Church, of all people, should understand. The church acts out of a position of power and authority in the Philippines, and in typical Filipino style, the boundaries between it and the government can all get a bit confused and blurred. The example here relates to the sense of entitlement that some members of the Church seem to display in the Philippines, and how this linked in with political patronage and, of all things, the national lottery competition.

The Philippine Charity Sweepstakes Office (PCSO) is tasked with the administration and overview of the Lotto Sweepstakes that are run in the Philippines. Part of their charter is to distribute the profits of this enterprise to charitable causes. In 2011, an investigation had begun into exactly how these funds were used and distributed. On buying lottery tickets in the Philippines one has to be careful to keep the tickets from being damaged or torn. Despite the PCSO collecting huge amounts of money via the lottery system, it has no player registration system in place. In Australia, for instance, one can register with the lottery provider and receive a plastic lottery card, which records the lottery transactions and lottery ticket numbers and details. If one then wins, but is not able claim the prize, the prize money is sent automatically in the form of a check to the winner. Due to the player having electronically registered the purchase of the ticket the player does not have to concern themselves with the paper tickets becoming torn or damaged or defaced. One may be forgiven for thinking that the PCSO may have considered how best to invest some of its huge profits back into the service that it provides its customers. However, it would seem that excess funds were earmarked for other acquisitions. It has emerged that Catholic Church bishops asked the former President Gloria Macapagal Arroyo for Sports Utility Vehicles. At least seven bishops were dragged into the PCSO funds mess that was being probed by the Senate Blue Ribbon Committee, after they received SUVs that were funded by sweepstakes money. One of the bishops petitioning for a vehicle was entirely open and frank in regards to what he wanted, asking for '. . . . a brand-new car, possibly a 4x4 which I can use to reach the far-flung areas of Caraga (region),' he wrote in his February 8, 2009 letter to Arroyo. 'I hope you will not fail to give a brand-new car which will serve as your birthday gift to me.' In the same letter, the bishop assured Arroyo of his 'constant support' for the former president.(22) Reportedly, in response to the petition from the prelate, former President Arroyo had made the written directive 'for appropriate action, please'. What constitutes 'appropriate action' may be subject to debate. The bishop's request, and the government's, and PCSO's, response, are illustrative of the cozy and enmeshed relationship that has existed between the Church and State for years. The petition from the bishop, and the response, were actually "normal" behaviors in the context of this prevailing culture. The Catholic Church of the Philippines certainly has political leverage, and it knows it. This is one of the key lessons of the People Power Revolution that swept Ferdinand Marcos from power. And the Church will use such leverage to its own ends, as has been made clear time and time again. The PCSO scandal is one example of this. Later the PCSO director revealed that P6.9 million of the charity's funds were allocated for the purchase of utility vehicles for certain prelates. A Philippine Senator, who was present during the government hearing into these matters, cited a Constitutional provision stating that public funds must not be used to give favors to any specific religion. The Philippine press reported that one of the bishops, who received a SUV as a 'gift', also allegedly told the 2011 current President, President Aquino, to resign, with the president having served less than a year in office. Reportedly 'dissatisfied personalities' were already plotting to remove Aquino from office.(23) The fact that this is reported to have been said by a bishop is simply astounding. The bishops involved in the PCSO scandal later apologized. This apology received some analysis in the newspapers, one of which, in an editorial, expressed concern at the sense of entitlement that these bishops seemed to display. Reported also was that the Catholic Bishops Conference of the Philippines promised to reexamine its working relations with the government, and to incorporate 'the highest ethical standards.'(24) So it should. One would certainly expect the 'highest ethical standards' from the Church.

In this day and age it is sometimes difficult to know exactly what sort of lifestyle priests and prelates lead. For some prelates their existence is clearly very comfortable, and they enjoy and have no hesitation in inappropriately exercising the political leverage that they have. The same applies to some priests, who seem to live a lifestyle that is not quite consistent with a traditional role. One cannot tar everyone with the same brush of course, and there are members of the clergy in the Philippines who are selfless, dedicated, and work very hard for their parish and their flock. I always try to find a sense of balance and perspective in all things, and from the sense of entitlement and political shenanigans(25) of some religious prelates I turn to the case of an individual priest who engaged in heroic human rights advocacy work, which in certain areas of the Philippines can be extremely dangerous. The individual concerned payed for his work with his life. I titled this chapter 'Crime, Politics and the Church—Filipino style', because sometimes all three elements, with their otherwise divergent agendas, can within the Philippines mesh, as in this case. The nation is not alone in this regard, and the same type of situation can occur in Latin American nations also. Father Cecilio 'Pete' Lucero, aged 48 years, was the parish priest of St Joseph the Worker Church in Catubig, in the Eastern Visayan region. He died after about thirty gunmen, (yes, the article that I sourced this from states thirty gunmen), opened fire on his car as he was traveling along the national highway in Northern Samar province. The priest directed the central diocese's Human Rights desk, and had been receiving death threats for some time. It was another brutal slaying that sadly has happened so often in the Philippines. With utter callousness and barbarity, and showing no inhibition in harming a man of the cloth, the priest was initially wounded by several rifle shots, and then one man walked up to his vehicle and shot him in the head. The police reportedly had no leads on who the killers might be, although a local bishop stated several groups had been threatening the priest. He traveled frequently to investigate alleged human rights abuses and had angered both the military and the insurgents with his work. Police in the Eastern Visayan region organized an investigative body that will look into Father Lucero's murder, the Philippine National Police (PNP) announced today.(26)

These are the priests and clergy that sacrifice all for their flock and do not shy away from engagement in human rights advocacy. A role which in many parts of the Philippines may lead to one's untimely demise. For any who think that all priests and clergy live a quiet life of entitlement and comfort, such cases as this shake us out of our human tendency to generalize. In regards to the role of the Catholic Church, it has a right, as does any person or any other institution, to an opinion and to be consulted, but it does not have a right to dictate the agenda, not in a modern-day democracy in any matter of governmental policy. As we have also read above, some members of the Catholic clergy have not the slightest inhibition about openly seeking material goods that they feel they want, and also threatening the elected President of a nation with excommunication from the Church due to him responsibly formulating a national birth control and family planning program.(27) Church officials are also prone, as we have read, to openly attempting to undermine the rule of a democratically-elected president and discussing his removal from office. Astonishing but true. As with everything else in Filipino life the boundaries and the limits are often never set, or as in this case, where the presence of the word 'inviolable' is clearly there, they are just simply ignored.

Chapter 6

The fate of the Republic of the Philippines— overcoming obstacles and facilitating change.

KEY POINT: To create economic success in the Philippines, cultural change is needed.

FOR ME, IT has been a long journey and a long association with the Philippines. At first working with Filipinos resident in the United Kingdom in the 1970's and then first arriving in the Philippines in 1981, and periodically thereafter. Residing here from 2011 onwards, I have seen most facets of Filipino life and culture. It has been a fascinating experience. The Filipino has the superficial inclination to Hollywood and to all things Western, but is at heart an Oriental, and at times deep and inscrutable. They can sometimes keep what is in their hearts hidden from others. They react in ways consistent with concepts relating to loss of face, respect for elders and veneration of the family. They are a gentle soul but can react with ferocity if their family or their honor is threatened, or if face is lost. Like every other human on this planet they have needs and desires, but these needs and desires are shaped and expressed and filtered according to the unique cultural template and cultural mix that the Philippines possesses.

The fate of the nation is problematic, and there is a serious danger that the economic and political situation within the Philippines will further deteriorate. The exploding population will place even greater demands on an already burdened economy, an economy that does not function efficiently. The nation has poor infrastructure, it is handicapped by its geographical morphology, it is facing threats from multiple fronts, such as climate change, and it has a shrinking middle class. In addition to this, as if that was not enough, the population has cultural and behavioral traits that markedly hinder global economic competitiveness in the 21st Century.

We mentioned previously the fact that Ferdinand Marcos came to power in the matrix of a divided world, with two superpowers vying for control and influence over the planet, and its natural resources. Marcos, as we mentioned, was a superb political operator and had the United States tied around his finger. By showing his anti-communist credentials there was, basically, nothing that he could not get from the US. He colluded with the US and created the fiction that the Philippines was a democracy. The pay-off for the US was that communism was kept at bay, and the pay-off for Marcos was unlimited political power, and almost unlimited wealth. The Philippines hosted strategic defense force bases here that allowed the projection of US power into the Asian region. It was a valuable ally and asset in the power game between the two superpowers. The world today is very different and changing all of the time, and at a rate that is breathtaking. Filipinos, and everyone else, have to understand the current and future state of play and the forces that are operating geopolitically. This is critically important, because these forces will either work in the favor of the Philippines or against the economic and political progress of the nation. The United States stills maintains a military superiority that is unparalleled. There is no other nation on this Earth that comes close to matching the military hardware and military effectiveness of the US. That, however, will change.

The overriding military lesson of World War II was that in conventional military conflict air superiority is the critical factor. And the US has a military air superiority that is unquestioned. But the Americans have a problem, and that is, that there is a growing mismatch between their military superiority and their economic superiority. In blunt terms, the United States of America, although still astonishingly powerful, is in economic decline. As this decline continues there will be an inevitable weakening of its military power. Other nations will, by necessity, fill the subsequent vacuum. In contrast to the decline of the USA, there is an awakening economic and military giant, and that giant is in close proximity to the Philippines. The country is, of course, China. There is no reason to suppose that the decline in the economic power of the USA will reverse itself. One of lessons of history is that world powers, superpowers and plain old empires come and go. They fade into a genteel existence, seemingly happy to exist without the burden or responsibility of administering and controlling lands that are far away. The examples are obvious, especially to the Filipino. Spain, of course, and other great sea-faring nations such as Portugal. The British Empire, that global superpower of its time, on whose conquered lands of the Earth the sun never set. The Romans, the Greeks, the Aztecs of South America, all faded in their glory and power. The USA will fade in influence and power too. America has had a mystical belief in its place in the world, its 'Manifest Destiny', as it is called. Its role, or so it was perceived, was to spread democracy, capitalism, and its way of life firstly across its continent, and then to all corners of the globe. It was fated to reign supreme in business. It did this with astonishing efficiency and success. Every possible consumer item was manufactured in this land and exported worldwide. The American industrialists were revered. Ford, Getty, Du Pont, Westinghouse. American individuals and companies that were icons and had enormous wealth. American business models, like their military technology and capability, was unparalleled. Not only on Earth but into the heavens too, did it spread its ideology and its technology. The Apollo program took Americans to the moon, beating the Soviets in a politically-inspired space race with the former Soviet Union. America did this because it worked harder, it worked smarter, and it thought more creatively, than any other kid on the global block. And it also *believed in itself* and its Manifest Destiny. The key to its success, especially with its race to the moon, was its unquestioned technical superiority. The Americans succeeded in creating the necessary miniaturization of computer equipment that was necessary for the moon landing, something that the Soviets were not able to do at the time. The Soviet Union was a police state, and the state-controlled media of the USSR (Union of Soviet Socialist Republics) used to trumpet the usual grandiose propaganda about the successes of the Soviet Union, and the failures of everyone else. Its steel production figures were always a cause for great celebration, until the world shifted into the post-industrial era, where successful economies were principally science and knowledge based. These new economies, the new wave, relied on the free flow of information, without censorship or bureaucratic interference. The Soviet populace used to joke, in reaction to the incessant boasting of the Soviet propaganda machine: "Soviet microchips. They are the *biggest* microchips in the whole world." How true this was, and it was the principal reason that they failed to put a man on the moon. I mention all of this is for a reason. And it something that the Philippines must understand. In the coming years the success or the failure of the Philippines cannot rely on its relationship with the USA. Big brother USA will be gone as a world force. The Philippines has in many ways always considered itself a *de facto* 51st State of the United States of America. But American power and influence is waning. And at some point America is just not going to be interested anymore. This is the reality of empires in decline. The Philippines must always understand the geopolitical realities of its region and of the world in general, and maneuver itself to take advantage of global trends and economic currents. It manifestly failed to do this with the recent tidal wave of economic globalization, that shift to a global purely capitalistic system of economic activity. I mentioned in Chapter 1, while discussing cultural variations, that Filipinos have a lesser degree of *individuation* relative to other nations; relative to Australians, for example. The cult of the lone hero has always existed in the USA. This rugged and successful individuality is in marked contrast to the populace of Japan, for example, where there is more of a collective consciousness, consensus thinking and an *extraordinary capacity to self-organize*. The Philippines has never been fully able to detach itself from the Americans, to achieve national individuation, and to see itself as primarily an Asian country with an Asian populace an Asian cultural heritage. The other cultural norms and values and templates of Spain and of America were superimposed. This attachment to the USA is very strong on a psychological level within Filipinos. To the Filipino, America is a mystical land, a land with unbounded material wealth, it is a land of self-realization, and a big brother who will protect it no matter what. The Filipino has an extraordinarily strong attachment to America, but as the very nature and power of America changes, so must the dynamics of this relationship. The reality is that the world is ever-changing, and a new set of geopolitical circumstances will bring with it the necessity for adjustment, and the absorption of new ways of thinking and behaving, that are adaptive to the circumstances of the era we are in. This was the key to success of the 'Four Tiger Economies' of Asia. That, and their astonishing capacity to drive themselves, and to focus on the task and the vision that they had set themselves. It is not only evident in these Asian economies, but also in that industrial powerhouse of science and engineering, and strong attention to detail, Germany. At the end of 1945 Germany was in absolute ruin. World War II had ended, and the dictatorship of Hitler and the National Socialist German Workers Party (the Nazis) suffered defeat at the hands of the Allied powers. There was little remaining of the infrastructure of Germany. The allied bombing raids had decimated its cities. The old German nightmare of becoming encircled and attacked from East and West, a war on both fronts, had become reality. This was fully explicable in the context of the disastrous political and military decisions that Hitler had made. Prior to his death, by suicide, when Berlin was encircled by advancing Soviet and Allied troops, he issued an order to his armaments minister, Speer, that all remaining industrial complexes, bridges and other infrastructure items be destroyed, so that they would not fall into Allied or Soviet hands. Speer had more sense than to carry out such a bizarre directive, and did not act on it. In any case Germany, as stated, was already in ruins. Within a generation Germany, or more strictly speaking, West Germany as opposed to the communist East Germany (the country is now reunited), became an industrial powerhouse exporting world wide products that we associate with superior engineering quality, such as Mercedes Benz and BMW motor vehicles, and BASF and Bayer chemical engineering industries. It is a rich, highly industrialized, and democratic nation. As an aside, it must be said that this was a superb triumph also of American diplomacy, financial aid and political skill. It was the Marshall Plan (or otherwise known as the European Recovery Program) that was key to the effective recovery of Europe after the World War II. The moral of the story is that nations can transform themselves and redefine their place in the world. *Should they wish to do so.*

The People's Republic of China, some 30 years ago, decided its fate for itself, and chose to embark on a modernization and industrialization program that was incredibly successful. The Chinese also made decisive and highly effective policy decisions in regards to its population. It brought its population rapidly under control by introducing the one-child policy. When the Chinese elect to do something, they do it with decisiveness. The Chinese during the 1960's and 1970's went through a huge and destructive political upheaval that was referred to as 'The Cultural Revolution'. After these convulsions had subsided, and the nation was released from its self-absorbed, ideologically-driven period of chaos, new Chinese political leaders emerged that were ready to take a different path. These men were pragmatic, and they were to set China on a course to economic and military might. Deng Xiaoping was one of these politicians and he was highly pragmatic. He once said, "It does not matter if a cat is black or white, as long as it catches mice, it is a good cat". He was referring to the economy of China, and his readiness to use any economic system or model that would advance the interests of his nation, and allow it to realize its power and destiny on the world stage. His intention to move China away from the grossly inefficient Marxist economy was evident when he stated, "Socialism does not mean shared poverty." According to politicians like Deng, China would emerge from its stagnation and backwardness, and it would do so with such ferocity that the Philippines and the world would shake.

In the next thirty years the world is going to change politically, technologically and economically in such a way that we as humans will be shaken to our very core. Change and technological progress is occurring in a exponential, not a linear, manner. Computer power will increase exponentially, and the revolution in biotechnology will advance without pause. Is the Philippines ready to ride this wave, and to align itself with the opportunities that these revolutions will bring? Not at this point in time. Its internally competing factions and interests, political and economic, work against themselves and the nation. There is no internal synergistic alignment of forces or interests within this nation. The feudal lords that exist in various parts of this nation work for their own interests, as do the political clans, as do the separate religious groups. Same nation, different world. Political discourse in the Philippines is highly conflictual in nature, and family or clan centered. It is not nationally consensual, as in the more successful democracies. There is a lot of energy, money and attention wasted in attempting to hold the nation together. The critical infrastructure item of the knowledge, information and technological based era, the Internet, is poorly developed in the Philippines. The Philippines is not going to catch the next wave of the latest technological revolution. It is not placed to do so. The best and the brightest of the Filipino graduates are mostly lost to overseas nations. Investment in this nation is paltry. There is not a culture of excellence, of attention to detail, of academic achievement and research. It has very bright and talented people but nothing to hold them here. Filipino culture dictates that professional advancement is dictated by family ties or by 'greasing the palms'. Bribery and who you know takes the place of objective selection for a professional position. This breeds demoralization, inefficiency and allows incompetence to flourish. This is the culture, it's what is normally done. Everyone knows it. The Philippines is in many ways crippled by this culture, just as it is crippled by adverse meteorological events.

To focus again on China, this nation is already probing and using its military and economic might, and testing out the resolve of other nations. While writing this chapter the Spratly Islands in the South China Sea were an on-going issue of significant concern. The Philippines, China and four other nations having overlapping claims in whole or part around the Spratlys. So here we have a potential flashpoint for conflict.(1) Not only is the Spratlys a potential area of conflict, but lurking quietly in the background is the issue of Taiwan, another potential flashpoint on the doorstep of the Philippines. Taiwan, or the Republic of China, is an island in the Pacific Ocean and located off the southeast coast of the People's Republic of China. During the Chinese civil war in 1949 Chiang Kai-shek and his nationalist forces fled to Taiwan. Establishing a base there the island was transformed into an economic powerhouse over the coming decades, with an uneasy background tension ever present between the People's Republic of China and the island state. It is one of the economic 'Four Asian Tigers', along with Singapore, Hong Kong and South Korea. The People's Republic of China considers Taiwan an integral part of China. It states that Taiwan is an inviolable part of the People's Republic of China. And when the Chinese say "inviolable", they mean it. Unlike in the Philippines, where the Constitution states that the separation of Church and State is inviolable, but as we have seen both parties continue to have an enmeshed relationship. Taiwan is armed to the teeth, and backed up in its stance of *de facto* independence from China by the USA. That is enough at the moment to keep China at bay. But the Chinese are very smart people, and they are patient. If any political vacuum becomes evident in the region, the Chinese will move to fill it. China is a tiger, and it is hungrily pacing back and forth eying its prey. It is unashamedly hegemonistic. Nothing will shake its resolve. Standing next to its prey is someone carrying a big gun, the USA. The tiger is rational and logical and engages in a risk-benefit analysis. For now the risks outweigh the benefits of attacking the prey. It will wait. In time the protector with the big gun is going to become weaker and less able, or less willing, to protect the tiger's prey. This is what the Philippines must realize. The days of being in a cozy and snug relationship with the worlds greatest superpower will pass. The might and influence of the USA will wane, and then the Philippines is going to find the world a lonely and frightening place. This will have internal political and economic, ramifications also. This is precisely why I mention it. The geopolitical matrix that was apparent in the era of Marcos is gone. It will never repeat itself. The Philippines has to wake up, and it has to change. It has to adapt, and it has to shed a lot of useless cultural baggage from the past. The first of these is the nonsensical superficiality of a Hollywood culture that has Filipino children steered into never-ending talent shows, rather than engaging in academic study and plain old reading and writing. Karaoke singers, child actors and Whitney Houston wannabe's offer no future for the Philippine nation. Look to the Chinese and the Taiwanese and the populace of Hong Kong. They are on your doorstep. They have a life-long drive to academic achievement and economic success that is breathtaking, and that is why they will rule the region, and perhaps the world. I make no apologies for writing what I write. Others may well disagree in my analysis, but I must at least give an honest opinion.

The geopolitical environment in which the Philippines finds itself is obviously critical to its future. Like Australia did under the leadership of John Howard, the Philippines must determine where the economic flows and currents of the region are, and position itself to take advantage of these. What needs to be remembered is that the Philippines, due to the Spratlys, *has already an area of divergent interests and conflict with the emerging Superpower of the region*. The relationship with the USA was always straightforward and uncomplicated. It was essentially, "Let us, the USA, keep bases in your land. You keep the communists out, and then you can do what you like, as long as you talk the talk." To 'talk the talk', is to *claim* to be a democracy. This was never overtly stated. It didn't have to be. Marcos was brilliant and he picked up on the rules of the game straight away. In contrast, the relationship with China will be problematic, and the Philippines must realize this, and adjust to this. It is not the friendly big brother, the good old US of A. China has its own interests, its own agenda, and its own way of doing things. In the 21st century, trade and economic growth is the glue that holds nations in civil partnerships. China benefits from the consumer economy of the Philippines, it is a place that they can export their products to. That's important. So war in the region is not likely at this point. The balance of forces, and the need for continued trade to allow China to consolidate its economic power, and subsequent to this its *military* power, is the overriding consideration for China at this point. But make no mistake about it, China will bide its time, and move when it sees the opportunity to do so. The Philippines could learn a lot from China in terms the way it operates, but it has never shaken itself from thinking that America is all things. In terms of the defense alliances and partnerships that the Philippines must forge and maintain, I always have a reflexive thought in regards to this, "Ah, if only NATO (the North Atlantic Treaty Organization) were a *global* security pact." (2) (3) As we know, SEATO, (the South East Asia Treaty Organization) of which the Philippines was a founding member, has been since 1977 defunct, but NATO has shown itself to be highly efficient effective, durable and adaptable.

Change is essential in order to turn the ship of state around, and to steer it into the slipstream of global economic growth. Change has to occur on a number of levels. Firstly, those in governmental office need to consider and facilitate cultural change. We live in a world where precision, accuracy, speed and efficiency are the benchmarks of an effective economy and society. In the sleepy and lazy days of the 1960's and the 1970's, nations could plod along and rely on an agricultural base for their economy. Those days are gone. The Philippines enjoyed a status of being the 2nd wealthiest nations in Asia at that time. But time has passed by, and the Philippines squandered the lead that it had. The 'Tiger Economies' of the region have awoken, and have pursued their economic goals with a ferociousness and a hunger that is breath-taking. Within a generation they have left the Philippines, in relative terms, floundering. The economies of today, the successful ones that is, are knowledge and technology based. The "solution", up to this point in time, to the economic problems that have beset this nation, has been to export the cream of its labor force to earn foreign income. All well and good, as the inflow of funds is a stimulus to the economy. When its not collected, embezzled, and sent back to a Swiss or US bank account, that is. However, the major and unsustainable drawback to this is that it robs the country of the specialist workers that are needed to form the middle classes, and to provide the technical expertise necessary for the development of the nation. One cannot have a knowledge and technology based economy when one is exporting all of one's technical and science professionals. The Philippines is therefore in a catch-22 situation. Without its overseas workers and the money they remit to the country it would experience a significant economic reversal. But while overseas their expertise provides no direct scientific and technical expertise to the Philippines directly for the nation building that is required. And required for longer term economic growth. This too, in turn, is dependant on good political leadership and governance. These factors must come together in order for real, sustainable gains to be achieved. For the owners of this nation, the Filipinos, it will be entirely up to them as to what they will make of their country. If Filipinos feels that matters are all in order, then all well and good. Then change is not necessary. However, for many, the need for advancement, for progress, for economic security, for self-realization, for *a future* for themselves and for their children will spur restlessness and disillusionment with the *status quo*. Then things clearly will have to change.

The author lived in apartment block in a regional town the Philippines. The neighbors were tremendous and we lived like a big family. As a foreigner, I was treated with unfailing respect and hospitality. As is usual in the Philippines children were everywhere, gorgeous but noisy, and frequently the neighbors would gather in the common area of the apartments to have a drink and talk. Observing this behavior for a few nights running I asked on passing one night, as everyone was consuming alcohol, what the occasion for celebration was. "Nothing", was the reply. We laughed. Celebrating nothing is a common occurrence in the Philippines. I was not able to recall on any occasion an adult sitting quietly in the common area reading a book. This is actually one of the most frightening things that I have observed in the Philippines. There is not a widespread thirst for knowledge. Children actually pattern there behavior, not so much on what they are told to do, but rather on what they see their peers and adults doing. I have discussed in previous chapters the issue of languages in the Philippines. I have also mentioned that I have a Filipina teacher friend who speaks English flawlessly. The key to her success in this area, relates to her parents instilling in her a love of books, and of reading and writing. And the books were in English, one of the official language of the Philippines. English is a global language, it is the common language of pilots for instance, and it is the business language of the 21ˢᵗ Century. Its global reach stems from the influence and power of the former British Empire, and from the on-going global enchantment with Hollywood and American culture.

The key to mastering this language, like any, is through reading, and through writing, and through practice in conversation. Its utility and global reach is the reason why it is important. It's not a "better" language that Tagalog or Bisayan. There is no such thing as a better or superior language, just as there is no such thing as a better or superior culture. The key point and the importance is in its *utility*. It is a world language. Proficiency in it will allow a Filipino to interact globally. Filipinos are often handicapped because they are often reluctant to practice their English. Many of them don't read enough. They are "shy", they do not grasp opportunities that are available to them. They do not use people, whom they might find as neighbors, such as myself, as mentors and as guides. This trait, this "shyness" and reticence is endearing and cute, but it is a handicap in terms of learning. And it is a part of the cultural mindset of the Filipino that is maladaptive in terms of success in a global economy. When Filipinos are "exported" overseas, they have to use their English then. They have no choice. But the whole point is about using English here in the Philippines, and attracting economic activity to this nation. In regards to my comments about people not tending to engage in reading in the Philippines, before anyone states that it's difficult to buy or obtain books here because everyone is so poor, then I reject such a statement emphatically. The reason being that there always seems to be money available, and supply arrangements made, for alcohol. Living in a small regional town in the Philippines I saw very little reading going on but there were a number of shops that sold second hand books, for a price that would have been the equivalent of a few beers. It's the choices people make, their lifestyle, and what they are motivated to do that is the key issue.

While living in the apartment it was also of interest to see how Filipinos worked, and to be involved in the dramas surrounding attempting to get someone to clean my apartment. I mention this because it illustrates the attitudes that Filipinos can display and their behavioral traits. I had previously thought that there is such a demand for work in the Philippines that to get someone to do the simple task of cleaning an apartment would be like organizing a drinking session in a brewery. That is, it would be the simplest thing in the world. How wrong that proved to be. Firstly, at the suggestion of the apartment owners, two of his relatives who stayed with him, and who were students, cleaned they apartment. They did a good job, but after a couple of months stated they were unable to continue as it was just too much working for the apartment owner in addition to their studies. We attempted to find someone else and a local lady offered to do the cleaning and the laundry. This lady was paid monthly in advance and for spending approximately one to two hours cleaning twice per week and for washing one laundry basket full of laundry twice a week she received PHP2,000—per month. This was a reasonable sum by local standards. Once in a restaurant in the town where I lived, a friend happened to ask one of the waitresses what her wages were. She stated she received PHP1,500—per month. This was for working 8 to 10 hours per day, six days a week. Paying a cleaning lady what would be considered in relative terms so well I thought there would not be any problems in retaining this person. Sadly, matters did not work out. Her attendance at the appointed hours we had agreed on to do the cleaning did not always take place. This was despite having been paid in advance. Her erratic attendance was tolerated for a while, but got too much in the end, and she also began complaining that she was too busy elsewhere. Another lady was sought to perform the services required. It was suggested to us that another local lady, who had a family and was unemployed, might wish to work for us. She was reportedly desperate to get work. It was agreed she take the job. The lady who had, erratically, worked for us agreed to show her the cleaning routine. This was very straightforward. It was a small apartment shared by two persons who were extremely clean in their habits. If the occupants had been diesel mechanics who brought their work home, and who had six teenage children, 3 dogs and a cat that always shed its fur, one could understand the cleaning challenge that this would present. But this was not the case. Problems occurred more or less straight away. She never turned up at the appointed time and we had to text her to chase her up to get her to attend. After about two weeks of this she again failed to turn up at the appointed time and day. As usual, there was no text from her explaining her absence. On sending her a text it was reported that there was 'an emergency at the school'. This did not ring true as she had no association with the school. Actually she probably did, but as is the habit of Filipinos, we can try to find humor in such situations. I was getting fed up with this and she was asked to commit to this job, or to advise she did not wish to continue. I just wanted to know one way or the other. She advised through a third party that she did not wish to continue. No reasons were given and she had never indicated that there was actually any definable problem with the job. The saga of finding an apartment cleaner continued. Getting more involved and lengthier than the production of the movie Ben Hur, another cleaner was sought. This time a local male was suggested to us. He had a family and only otherwise worked part time. This guy seemed willing and ready to work. He was exceptionally reliable, punctual and worked hard. He was paid PHP1000—in advance for 4 cleaning sessions and to do the laundry. A little while into this arrangement he asked for another "cash advance" in regards to his wages. He had already received an advance for another four sessions, and was not due to receive another PHP1,000—at that time. In seeking a "cash advance" he seemed to be confusing his employer for the local bank or ATM machine. Or maybe he thought I was one of the billionaire Getty family, and rolling in money. Or maybe he thought I was a close family member. Anyhow, this request was refused. It was explained to him that only PHP1,000— would be given at a time in advance. Another time he protested that his electricity bill needed to be paid, and sought again an advance on his wages. That is, an advance on top of a previous advance. The answer was again no. It was explained to him that there was no connection between his work, his employer and his electricity bill. As is usual in the Philippines, the boundaries all get a bit blurred. He continued to do a very good job cleaning and he was paid without fail in advance for four cleaning sessions. He then asked that "snacks" be provided for him when he attended to do his cleaning sessions. This was done. Snacking is a Filipino custom and to deny anyone their 'snacks' would be tantamount to mistreatment. Despite the previous advice to him that he would receive wages in advance for the cleaning sessions, but only to the amount of PHP1,000—he persisted in asking for extra advance payments. A text was received one day asking for a further advance of PHP500-. This request was refused for the same reasons as previously given. He then texted back to ask if PHP250—would be ok. It was on of the few times where I have encountered texting being used in such a direct and specific manner. But when it come to matters of 'pera' (money), the motivation is there. His negotiating skills did not stand him in good stead, because again my reply was, sorry but no. I was then advised by a third party that this man did not want to do the cleaning anymore. Questioned as to why he wanted to stop work, the answer was that he needed money but that as he was refused a further advance (that is: the advance on top of the previous advance), so he did not want to continue anymore. On hearing this my response was along the lines of, "Okay, let me get this right. This guy desperately needs money, right? He is paid for the simple task of cleaning an apartment and doing some laundry PHP1,000—in advance for four cleaning sessions, right? But now, although he desperately needs the money, he is not wanting to do the job anymore. There must be some logic in there somewhere, but I'm darned if I can find it!". And so after two months he advised that he would not be continuing with the job. Some Filipinos work tirelessly, are very good workers, and are very good at what they do. But finding good helpers can be problematic too. I do the cleaning of the apartment myself now. It's good for the soul to do such work and it allows me to avoid any dramas. As regards my laundry, one of the helpers in one of the other apartments offered to do it. She is paid PHP150 per laundry basket. I wanted to pay her in advance or pay her each time, but she refused the money, saying she wanted it to be saved. That this would be money put by for her, her little side job, and her little savings fund. The first time she asked for payment was after she had done 5 baskets over a period of a few weeks. The moral of the story is that you can never quite work it all out. Filipinos will always surprise you. Some will frown on a foreigner engaging in such menial tasks as domestic cleaning, but I've never been one to worry about what others think. There is nothing demeaning about physical labor. Some Filipinos seem to have the greatest difficulty doing the simplest tasks for any length of time, growing tired of the work. Others will work their proverbial butts off, and be embarrassed and hesitant to accept the money offered. A lot of the Filipino men, after getting married seem to fall into a pattern of laziness. The wife or older children or "helper" (what is referred to in the West as a maid) take care of all the domestic chores and responsibilities. The men just take to drinking and talking with their buddies for hours on end, when the cockfighting session has ended that is. They don't seem to have much interest in any physical or intellectual pursuits. The children who live locally will walk past these groups of men, who idle their time away, drinking and talking. Such adult role models fail these young children.

I mention the above, and I have recounted the experiences that I have been through, because often politicians are blamed in the Philippines for all of the wrongs and failures that have beset the country. The corruption too is used as a convenient excuse to avoid the collective responsibility that citizens must take. In the Philippines there is none of widespread burning drive to succeed, to make money, and to achieve academically that there is in the other countries of Asia. Especially the 'Tiger Economies'. It is not by chance that they have reached the level of economic development that they have. It is through exceptional planning and drive and sacrifice. Their populations also have a high degree of capacity for self-organization, and an exceptionally strong work ethic. Or so we may say anecdotally. We must also remember that Filipino workers *are* highly regarded globally. This is the success story of the Philippines. But when you are overseas you *have* to work, and you have to adapt. There is no choice. We have seen that the OFW goes through great danger and sacrifices much to provide to those in their homeland. But back in the Philippines some party on as though there is no tomorrow, and when it comes to work, they don't want it or can't cope with it. Even when it is available and at decent wage rates.

The Philippines is not alone in having to face critical choices in regards to its future, and being subject to the enormous challenges that the 21st Century presents. That nation that Filipinos look to with continual wonderment, the United States of America, recently had its credit rating reduced from a AAA to AA+. Never in my lifetime had I considered such an event possible. This utterly astonishing turn of events was in part induced by the disastrous political decisions of former American administrations, the principal one being the absurd decision to invade Iraq. This venture, this multi-trillion dollar abject waste of American taxpayers money, was initiated for purely ideological decisions, *not* for any national security reasons. The fiction that was promulgated that justified the invasion was that Iraq possessed weapons of mass destruction. It was all about the US and British Intelligence agencies presenting various pieces of information that the American and British governments then wove into a questionable whole. The outcome had been decided previously, on a political level. It was essentially, 'we want to get Saddam. Make a connection that will justify this.' The Intelligence had to fit the foregone conclusions of the Bush administration. In 2008, the American Senate Intelligence Committee, after conducting hearings, found that the Bush administration had, "misrepresented the intelligence and the threat from Iraq."(4) We know that Saddam used chemical weapons against his own people. He was a brutal dictator. But then, there are many brutal dictators worldwide. The USA has supported some of them. The Iraq war satisfied the neo-conservative agenda, it boosted the coffers of the military-industrial complex, but it defaced the image of America. And it put the economy of that nation further into unsustainable deficit. It was a disastrous political, economic and moral decision. Filipinos may bemoan their own politicians, and sometimes quite rightly, but compared to other politicians worldwide they are often no worse. What Filipino politicians are alleged to have squandered and wasted is but a tiny fraction of the astronomical sum that the administration of George W. Bush squandered on the Iraq war. The cost of the Iraq war has been estimated at US$3 trillion dollars. That is when everything, including all of the disability pensions of the combat veterans, and all of the armaments, and all of everything else that was wasted, and the budgetary problems it created, are taken into account. (5) I have mentioned in this book that Ferdinand Marcos is alleged to have salted away between US$5 to US$10 billion. The United States, through nonsensical political decisions, such as the decision to invade Iraq, wasted during this war an estimated US$3 *trillion*. A US trillion is 1 followed by 12 zeros, so 3 trillion is 3,000,000,000,000. The equivalent in Philippine Pesos (PHP) is 3,000,000,000,000 then multiplied by the prevailing exchange rate at the time of writing, that is, PHP43 to US$1. So the equivalent amount of Philippine Pesos wasted in Iraq was PHP129,000,000,000,000. PHP129 trillion! That's an awful lot of money. To put it another way, the GDP of the Republic of the Philippines in 2010 was US$188.7 Billion. Therefore, the amount of money wasted in Iraq was the equivalent to almost 16 times the Gross Domestic Product of a whole nation, the nation of the Philippines, in the year 2010. This money literally went up in smoke with the use of armaments, it paid for benefits for the families of the American war dead, is to be paid in on-going disability benefits and rehabilitation for the American wounded and disabled, disappeared into the pockets of corrupt Iraqi government officials, paid for the massive logistical effort that was required in supporting all of the troops there, will pay for the interest on the government bonds that are issued to cover the budget deficits, and paid for everything else that was required to sponsor a war. Further, just how can one calculate the *emotional cost* that was borne by those families that lost loved ones, or those wounded, or who lost friends? But for the United States of America, and its ally, the United Kingdom, making war is in their blood. They have a ready supply of 19 year olds to put into battle, (that was the average age of the conscript killed in that previous totally senseless war, Vietnam), a huge military industrial complex that benefits from the opportunity to sell, and to test out in actual battle, their weapons systems, and influential neo-conservatives that stand in the wings and provide rabid encouragement to all of this. They want to recreate the world in their own image, into a 'true' democracy with liberty and freedom. *Whether you like it or not.* They want the world to be better, but it's their definition of better. Being of British descent I say the above with shame, but it is a fact. Especially in the Middle East, the British acted with disgraceful duplicity during the 'golden years' of their empire there. Some of the current problems of the Middle East are a structural result of their occupation and meddling. The United States, in particular, has wasted so much human life, so much money, and so much good-will, by engaging in disastrous and wasteful overseas conflicts. All for spurious ideological reasons. The Vietnam war was an example in recent history that I've mentioned above, the Iraq conflict was another. Osama bin Laden was, in the end, killed by the Americans, in a highly skillful and clinically executed military operation. But then, all the evidence shows that Osama bin Laden plotted, funded and encouraged the senseless attack by a group of criminals on the World Trade Tower in New York. Innocent people were killed, Osama bin Laden gloated over that.(6) He gloated over civilians, sons and daughter and husbands and wives, going about their normal lives and going to work in the World Trade Center, and then being murdered. They were innocent victims. They did not deserve to die and they did not need to die. It was senseless. And it gave the American neo-conservatives all the excuses they needed to go on a rampage that killed more innocent people in Iraq. I won't waste any sympathy on Osama bin Laden. He who lives by the sword shall die by the sword. And anyone who threatens the liberal democracies of the world and the freedoms that they possess is an enemy, especially when they represent fundamentalist religious ideology, whether Christian or Islamic or whatever. The liberal democracies have to protect themselves, but in the right way and against the *actual* threat that is there, not the *perceived* threat or the *fictitious* threat. The Americans will still carry on regardless with their bizarre and counterproductive foreign policy. Palestine is threatened with a veto of its bid to join the UN. Another injustice and another episode of double standards. Another slap in the face for the Arab world. Nothing more and nothing less. No wonder America is in decline. The reason why I point this out is that Filipinos should not feel that they are the only ones betrayed and disadvantaged by incompetent politicians and disastrous political decision-making, by poor governance, or by government deceit. It happens with great regularity, and on a greater scale, worldwide. *And by the very nations and powers that we look to for example and guidance.*

It is not just in the Philippines that we have the myth, that it is always external factors, or events, that are the real threat. This is also perpetrated by other nations, such as the USA. For the last decade we have all been taken on an absurd and ridiculously expensive ride by the conservative forces in the USA who are waging a so-called 'War on Terror'. As stated above, part of this involved the invasion of a sovereign nation by the name of Iraq. By some gobbledygook logic the neo-conservatives in America managed to create a spurious and totally false link between the brutal and senseless act of a criminal gang hijacking aircraft to crash into the World Trade Towers in New York and the

Pentagon, and the regime of Saddam Hussein in Iraq. The icing on the fictitious cake was, as mentioned before, the idea that Iraq possessed thermonuclear weapons capable of mass destruction. The number of Americans on average killed by terrorist acts yearly would average about the same number of Americans killed by bee stings. *Americans kill more Americans than anyone else. The real enemy is within.* The Second Amendment to The United States Constitution, proclaims that it is '. . . the right of the People to keep and bear arms . . . ' This constitutional sentence has led to the countless deaths of Americans, *at the hands of fellow Americans.* The Founding Father's of the USA would have had their reasons as to why they would allow the civil population to usurp the functions of a civil police force and the military. Those are the entities which should be exclusively the ones tasked with the protection of the citizenry of a nation. Obviously the unique historical circumstances of the framing of the Constitution explains this. Saddam Hussein, as far as I am aware, was never responsible for the death of one single American. He was a brutal rogue, but he reserved his butchery for his fellow Iraqis who threatened his rule. The only ideology that Saddam Hussein understood was the ideology of Saddam Hussein. He was strictly secular, but he played the Islamic card like any other self-obsessed despot in the Middle East. He was completely narcissistic, and would never have antagonized the Americans by involving himself in acts of terror against the USA. He did provide rewards and verbal encouragement to those who committed senseless terrorist acts against Israelis. This was to allow him to play the Arab pan-national hero and increase his status in the eyes of other Arabs. However, there is no evidence that he ever himself arranged these terrorist acts, or provided any direct support. Like all brutal men everywhere he would get others to do the dirty work, but always set himself up to take the glory. In the Philippines, as in the USA, the real threat has always been within. The current bogey-man of the USA, in 2011, is Iran. The Iranians are likely involved in the process of manufacturing nuclear weapons, as a reflexive attempt to protect themselves from a possible invasion by the USA, who would have considered it once they had finished with Iraq and spread their mayhem there. After the invasion of Iraq, the nations of the Middle East were thinking, "Who's next?" And then followed, logically, "We need to get some big deterrents in place." Nuclear weapons do that job well. The Iranian government has a dreadful human rights record, and engages in the most senseless and barbaric human rights violations, such as the stoning of women who are alleged to have engaged in adultery, or executing homosexuals. However, it is not a war-mongering nation. For the Iranians the possession of nuclear weapons would be for defensive purposes, a deterrent. They don't plan on actually using them on anyone. Although the President of Iran, Mahmoud Ahmadinejad, has made some utterly irresponsible and inflammatory statements along the lines of wanting Israel wiped off the map. This is stupid, senseless rhetoric that only plays into the hands of the hawks and the right wing ideologues in the USA and Israel. Despite all of the political rhetoric, principally created for internal political reasons, to detract the Iranian populace from the shortcomings of the government there, Iran is a peace-loving nation. It is not a nation that has repeatedly gone to war. That dubious honor falls to the USA, the United Kingdom and Germany. These are the nations that are aligned with the Philippines. Read your history books. Read the *facts*. There is one thing that must be stated unequivocally at this point, and that is that there *is* a real terror threat. Of that we can be in no doubt. The problem is, and the whole point about the above mentioned issues, is that the Americans got it wrong about *who or what the real terror threat was*. This is extremely dangerous, because it blinds and distracts us, and takes away resources from combating the *real* threats that are there. The planet is awash with nuclear fissile material. Some of it reportedly obtainable on the black market. The world is also awash with fanatics and criminals who would be ready to use this fissile material. We have to be extremely vigilant. *And we have to get the Intelligence right*. We cannot afford to make foregone conclusions, and to manufacture Intelligence to suit political policy or prejudice. The stakes are just too high. After terrorists engaged in a senseless and criminal act of steering jet aircraft into the World Trade Centers and the Pentagon, the Bush administration and everyone else was in shock. Subsequent US Senate hearings established that the terrorist acts occurred in the first place as a result of a failure in US Intelligence. There were all sorts of suspicious characters wandering in and out of the USA prior to the event, and a group of them were taking up pilot training at an American flying school. Just as an example of the information that is reported to have been collated *prior* to the terrorist attacks, I cite the following:

March 2001—Italian intelligence warns of an al Qaeda plot in the United States involving a massive strike involving aircraft, based on their wiretap of al Qaeda cell in Milan.

July 2001—Jordanian intelligence told US officials that al-Qaeda was planning an attack on American soil, and Egyptian intelligence warned the CIA that 20 al Qaeda Jihadists were in the United States, and *that four of them were receiving flight training.*

August 2001—The Israeli Mossad gives the CIA a list of 19 terrorists living in the US and say that they appear to be planning to carry out an attack in the near future.

August 2001—The United Kingdom is warned three times of an imminent al Qaeda attack in the United States, *the third specifying multiple airplane hijackings.* According to the Sunday Herald, the report is passed on to President Bush a short time later.

September 2001—Egyptian intelligence warns American officials that al Qaeda is in the advanced stages of executing a significant operation against an American target, probably within the US.(7) (Italics above mine.)

The criminals that engaged in this mass murder had been training as pilots in the USA under the very noses of the American Intelligence services, and according to the information above, there was clear advance warning of what was going to take place. Emerging from this event, the Bush administration wanted a link between Saddam Hussein and the terrorist act. The 'neo-cons' had been gunning for Saddam for a while. Now there was a perfect excuse. Saddam's lair was in the Middle East and strategically highly significant. From one intelligence failure to another, the neo-cons manufactured the link between Saddam and the terrorist attacks. He was supposed to have met, at some point, with a terrorist leader in Baghdad at one time or another, and also Saddam was supposed to possess thermonuclear weapons of mass destruction. The neo-cons put 2 and 2 together and got 5, that is, Saddam had met a terrorist and he has thermonuclear weapons of mass destruction therefore he must be planning to use them on the USA. The Intelligence had to fit their conclusions, which in any case were based on false premises. Saddam might have met a terrorist at some point or another, but this claim was found to be dubious in any case. Saddam had met Donald Rumsfeld too, in December of 1983, while Rumsfeld was US Special Envoy to the Middle East. At that time Saddam had started a senseless and brutal war against Iran, and the Americans were concerned that Iran would win, and that its radical Islamic ideology would grow in strength and influence in the Middle East. Rumsfeld later became US Secretary of Defense, and was instrumental in driving the US to go to war against the man had had previously been shaking hands with. Rumsfeld, in 1983, at the time of his meeting with Saddam, was part of the American administration that gave support to Iraq in '. . . the form of technological aid, intelligence, the sale of *dual-use and military equipment* and satellite intelligence . . . '(8) (Italics mine)

What, the Filipino reader might ask, has this got to do with us? Well, it has pretty much everything to do with the Philippines. There is always some political, some economic or some historical connection with the Philippines and the other nations of the world. The Philippines participated in the unjustified invasion of a sovereign nation, that is Iraq. This nation, the Republic of the Philippines, was part of the Multi-National Force that engaged in a war in Iraq. It's participation was admittedly minor. It sent 51 medics, engineers and other troops, and withdrew these on July 14th, 2004. While there, 3 Filipino soldiers were wounded. Fortunately none were killed.(9) So Filipinos ought to know about this, as part of the history of their nation. Also in the news, as I am writing this book in 2011, is the drama of the downfall of another dictator by the name of Colonel Muammar Gaddafi, of Libya. Now, what has this got to do with the Philippines? Well, while Ferdinand Marcos was in power, Imelda Marcos visited Gaddafi in

Libya twice, in 1976 and 1977. The Philippines was seeking engagement from Gaddafi in brokering talks with the Moro National Liberation Front, the Muslim separatist group that has been engaged in armed struggle with the government of the Philippines.(10)

The issue flowing from this is that when discussing terrorism and Intelligence issues, it is important to know that the Philippines is a significant nodal point in terrorist planning, movements and past and potential future attacks. Across the nation there are many radical groups, from Islamic fanatics, to loony-tune Maoist ideologues, to plain old oddballs, who feel hard done by. No nation is actually safe. Timothy James McVeigh was a born and bred American. On April 19, 1995, he perpetrated a terrorist act on American soil, referred to as the Oklahoma City Bombing. He detonated a truck bomb in front of a public building, and the attack killed 168 and injured over 800 of his fellow Americans. Prior to the attack on the World Trade Center, it was the most lethal terrorist incident on American soil. Timothy McVeigh was not a Muslim, and he was not a Communist. He was a good ol' American gun-toting boy who just happened to be disaffected with his government, and his grudges led him to the perpetrating of mass murder. Within the Philippines the weighting of the terrorist threat falls to the southern regions, although it could occur anywhere in the nation. The significance of this cannot be underestimated. Some authorities refer to this region as 'a second hub for world terror.'(11) The island of Mindanao, and particularly the adjacent and remote Sulu Archipelago, where the militant organization ASG (Abu Sayyaf Group) maintains bases, could become a safe haven for *jihadi* cadre who have fled Afghanistan. The al Qaeda influence appears to be channeled through regional and local organizations such as JI (Jemaah Islamiyah) and the ASG. In many cases they have cooperated in the form of ad hoc arrangements of convenience, such as helping procure weapons and explosives. Security difficulties are a major impediment to foreign investment and to the economic development of resource-rich Mindanao Island.(12) In addition to the two groups mentioned above there is also the Moro National Liberation Front, (MNLF), the Moro Islamic Liberation Front, (MILF), and the New People's

Army, (NPA). Apart from the NPA, which operates in the northern Philippines, the other groups operate primarily in the south of the nation, where most of the country's Muslim minority live.(13) Under the Constitution of the Republic of the Philippines, foreign troops are not permitted to engage in a combat role on the soil of the Philippines. There are however American troops posted to Mindanao that take part in 'training exercises' with Filipino troops.

But also beyond this, there is the fact that anything and everything that happens on the geopolitical stage is of significance, and may well have some strategic significance, to the Philippines. The Philippines is dependant upon the importation of almost all of its oil. It is dependant upon the importation of huge amounts of rice, and it is dependant upon favorable employment conditions for its OFW's, some of whom reside and work in politically unstable regions of the world. Further to this, the Philippines has to be aware of all of the economic and geopolitical factors that can influence it favorably or adversely. These external factors may link with internal factors and cause a favorable or adverse alignment. If, for any reason, there is tension or conflict in the Middle East, or with any of the other oil producing nations the price of oil will increase. Because the Philippines has to import almost all of its oil, this will have a flow-on effect to the internal economy. The jeepney and bus owners will have to put their prices up to pay for the increased gasoline prices. The passengers pay more and have less disposable income for other goods or services. The economy stagnates or goes into recession. The Philippines must be ready to maneuver itself into strategically advantageous positions based on prevailing conditions and factors. It chose to take part in the invasion of Iraq, presumably due to a reflexive need to follow big brother USA, wherever it goes. It really needs to think independently about these issues. Germany refused to commit troops to Iraq. Obviously, their Intelligence assessments were far better than the American's. In the end the Germans were right. Going to war in Iraq was folly. Some people did actually benefit from it, that is, the corrupt Iraqi officials who siphoned off huge amounts of US dollars sent to rebuild Iraq, and the US military-industrial complex at home benefited too. Uncle Sam always pays up front, and the American taxpayer is left with the trillion dollar bill. The Philippines must start to think independently about the world, the events of history, and where the economic tides are flowing, in order to position itself to its best advantage. This is what Singapore did, and it's what the Chinese are doing right now. As has already been stated, the Philippines lives in the neighborhood of potential flashpoints, those being the Spratlys and also Taiwan, and it is dependant on oil from another flashpoint, the Middle East. It has to be aware of all that is taking place in the region and in the world. To anticipate any threats, and to take advantage of any opportunities.

To return to internal challenges, for the Philippines it is time to stop pretending that a central, unitary government can rule this geographically fragmented nation. The Philippines needs to move to a strong, federally structured system of government. It will then be time to bring the Diaspora of its OFW's back to their homeland, and not to send them away in the first place. To build the nation here. To provide technical and scientific input, to build the proper infrastructure that the nation needs. It is time for proper governance. For Filipinos to accept the value of the concept of conflict of interest, to apply this, and to begin to utilize universally the principles of good and ethical governance. Just a simple step such as the acceptance of conflict of interest guidelines would have incalculable value. It is time above all to introduce proper and effective birth control and family planning, and to aim towards the demographic parameters that are required to build an economically viable nation. Economic progress and prosperity do not happen by chance. It is time for the Catholic Church to be reminded of its proper place, and reminded of the inviolability of the boundaries between the Church and the government. The President of the day, and those in power, will have to confront their own compatriots about these issues. They will have to go to battle against the prevailing culture. Without winning that battle no change will take place, and the stagnation will continue. For the Philippines to become a prosperous and dynamic nation, it seems to me, as I have said, that some things are going to have to change. Brave Filipinos have made an attempt in this direction. I know of local mayors who have introduced Western business practice standards, and who insist on attention to detail, on punctuality, on formulating a vision, and who drive their staff to high performance standards. There is no other way. No other path to prosperity. There have been national initiatives along these lines, with the former President Gloria Arroyo proclaiming a Punctuality Week. Proclamation No. 732 was promulgated and this declared the period from the 21st to the 27th of November as 'National Consciousness Week for Punctuality (Respect for the Value of Time) and Civility (Respect for the Rights of Others).'(14) There is an organization called 'Organized Response for the Advancement of Society, Inc.' (ORAS), which initiates such ideas and actions. More power to them. During the stated week there were various program activities, and talks in national and local offices and schools emphasizing the Presidential Proclamation, and the value of time and the respect for the rights of others. This is the stuff of nation building and cultural change. Lots of small changes can have an accumulative and synergistic effect.

In the past 20 years the tide of business activity and wealth has shifted to the Asian region. The giants of the region have woken from their slumber, that is China and India. The 'Tiger Economies' of the region have placed themselves in a position to ride the wave and sail in the slipstream of this gigantic economic growth that globalization has unleashed. The Philippines has missed out on this opportunity. I sometimes wonder what that intellectual giant of Filipino life, Dr. Jose Rizal, would make of his nation were he to return here, to magically awaken from his repose. He would certainly rue the lack of intellectual pursuits of the population as a whole. He would no doubt be puzzled by the superficiality with which the Filipino pursues fame and fortune and the Hollywood lifestyle. He would be appalled by the corruption, and no less by the clerics who interfere in the legitimate political functions of a modern state, and threaten the President of the day with excommunication due to him formulating rational family planning policy; that human right of every man and woman on this planet. I'm sure Rizal would find it all quite strange. He was a man of great ideals, and he had a great love for his Filipino compatriots. The Filipino *beyond* his immediate family. I am quite certain that Rizal would say that some things have to change. He was a selfless man. He was one of the most intelligent men in history. And he had a great *social* intelligence. Why don't I see Filipino adults reading his works? Books by Rizal or about Rizal, or about anything for that matter.

Margaret Thatcher, the former Prime Minister of the United Kingdom, transformed the face of that nation through her policies and the stamping of her ideology on the political and economic landscape of the nation. For anyone who says that a strong political leader has to be a man, look to the example of Margaret Thatcher. This lady had an iron will, an energy, and a determination that would leave many a man floundering. This lady was *tough*. She was a buddy of Ronald Reagan, that charismatic American President, who was referred to as the Great Communicator, and who preached an unashamedly right-wing, anti-communist message. Of course Reagan met Marcos while he was in power. Ronald Reagan's style was the antithesis of Margaret Thatcher's. He had a laid-back, sunny Californian disposition, and was able to see and formulate a grand vision, but he liked to leave the detail to others. On starting his presidency he set the tone by telling his aides, "Don't bring me problems. Bring me solutions." That seemed like a logical place to start. He was a master at designating duties, and went his own affable way during the working day, He was everyone's favorite uncle, and had none of the obsessive drive of most of the other Presidents in US history. Unashamedly right wing he had it in for the communists. Once referring to the now dissolved Soviet Union as an "Evil Empire", he, along with Margaret Thatcher, drew the line in the sand, and faced down communist hegemony. The Philippines was always a useful ally in this big geopolitical chess game. Subsequently, the Soviet Union collapsed under its own bureaucratic and inefficient weight. The fragmentation left us with Russia, and the other states that it had previously incorporated into its empire going their own separate ways. Free at last. Russia, like England in the United Kingdom, was always the pre-eminent force of its region, and by force assimilated its geographical neighbor into its body and identity. But it was a stolen identity. Such is the way with empires. Russia was probably glad to give up its economic burdens like Cuba anyway. And to free itself from having to listen to the frequent hours long, rambling speeches of Fidel Castro. This interesting and colorful character was a thorn in the side of America for decades. The left wing *intelligentsia* of the world, and the young students of the radical left in Paris or London, have an orgasm when they hear his name. Castro no longer smokes cigars but in his younger years he like to puff on a good old Cuban *Cohibas*. The *Corona Especial* specifically. He survived numerous assassination attempts or at least plots, one of which included the plan to give him an exploding cigar. There was also an attempted invasion of Cuba by Cuban exiles, supported by the American Central Intelligence Agency. It ended in disaster, and was a big embarrassment for the USA. Castro was a cool cat, and he had, like a cat, many lives. He was fated to survive, while all of the American presidents who cursed him ceaselessly finished their one or two terms of political power and faded into a financially comfortable obscurity. Things got dangerously out of hand during the Cuban missile crisis. The Soviets decided to place some nuclear missiles in Cuba. That is, right on the doorstep of the USA. In the Kremlin the conversation probably went along the lines of: "Comrade, what are we doing today? We have finished reading the glorious steel production figures for this month, and our glorious scientists have made the biggest microchip in the world." Reply: "Comrade, we are the best in the world. The glorious revolution and Soviet power will conquer the world. Let's put a few nuclear missiles in Cuba." Reply: "OK, but does that mean we have to sit through another five hour, mind-numbing speech given by Castro? My ass is still sore from sitting so long last time. I think I'll shoot myself if I have to listen to that crap again." Reply: "Comrade, don't you know *anything!* We'll just *tell* him this is what's going down. Get a subordinate to attend the speech. We'll just focus on getting the nuclear missiles down there." J.F.K. had no choice but to face the Soviets down and demand the removal of the nuclear weapons. The conversation in J.F.K.'s White House office would have contained a lot more expletives than the conversation in the Kremlin. In the end, after a very tense confrontation, the USA won. The Soviets didn't. The missiles went. Castro remained. The subordinate tasked to attend the speech of Castro is probably still in Cuba, and probably listening to the same speech. J.F.K. was assassinated. By a fellow

American. J.F.K.'s killer, Lee Harvey Oswald, like Timothy McVeigh, was not ideologically indoctrinated, although he had defected to the Soviet Union for a brief period of time. He was basically just odd and disaffected. Castro was the hero of the Cuban Revolution, and always spoke of it as a dynamic, eternally progressive movement of change. But all he ever really did was to fossilize his own leadership and entrench his own power. While talking for hours about the struggle for, and the glories of, political liberation, he jailed homosexuals and anyone who had a contrary opinion to his. Some hero. Some liberator. However the Cubans do have a first-class health care and education system, and that to their credit. It is a significant and important achievement by any standard, and at least his populace have universal access to high-quality effective services such as these. That cannot be said for his long-time enemies across the water, the USA. Castro's colleague in the early days of revolution was the charismatic Argentinean, Che Guevara. Che is a cult figure, and radical-left revolutionary icon. His image can still be seen in the West and in the Philippines. The bearded, handsome man with the beret, looking wistfully into the distance. You can see it on the T shirts that hip Filipinos wear. The students who have wealthy parents and who are studying at UP (University of the Philippines), as well as the NPA (New People's Army) in the mountains of Luzon. It is the photograph taken of him by Alberto Korda, entitled 'Guerrillero Heroico.' This has been declared 'the most famous photograph in the world.'(15) The mythos and image of socialist revolutionary Che, printed on T shirts that are made in the labor sweat shops. These are run by fat-cat capitalists who earn a 1000% profit on every garment. Ironic, but then irony is everywhere. Comrade Che would be turning in his grave if he knew in what way his image is being used.

The Soviet Union's stranglehold on the free exchange of information, (it was a police state), was one of the reasons for its downfall. The world moved into the information age, and technical information, indeed any information, was the new international currency. If the free exchange of information and technical expertise was not allowed, then those Soviet microchips were going to stay mighty big. And then progress would not be possible, because the world was now in the post-industrial era. It was all about micro-technology then. Now its all about nano-technology. Reagan's vision and untarnished image did come undone with the Iran-Contra affair, where his administration was found to have secretly directed his government to provide funds to a right wing group of insurgents in Latin America, and at the same time engaged in secret negotiations with Iran. When you are a pragmatist you find yourself with some strange bedfellows. His ideological soul mate on the other side of the Atlantic Ocean, Margaret Thatcher, had her own set of problems and her own national issues, beyond the global vision that she shared with Ronald Reagan. In the United Kingdom in the 1960's the Labour Party, the political organization that was to the left of the political spectrum, equivalent in some ways to the Democrat Party in America, was the main political opposition to the Conservative Party. The Conservatives were Mrs. Thatcher's party. They were to the right of the political spectrum, the equivalent of the Republicans in the States. The Labour Party in the United Kingdom in the 1960's was represented by such Prime Ministers as Harold Wilson. It was a party that represented the "working class", the ordinary British worker, as opposed to the upper classes and industrialists. Harold Wilson was the hero of my father. The Labour Party tried to bring a fair distribution of wealth within the nation, and set fair wages and conditions for workers. It also believed in the retaining of nationalized industries. These were run by the government and owned by the nation, but were for the most part inefficient and cumbersome. The Labour Party had a problem, and that was that the party, and the Trade Union movement that it was affiliated with, had been infiltrated by Communists, Trotskyisks, Maoists, and just about every ultra-left wing ideological grouping on the planet. For a lot of them the agenda was not progressive change, but out-and-out revolution and the overthrow of the capitalist system. The Trade Union movement in the 1960's and the 1970's in the United Kingdom was very powerful, and it exercised this strength in ways that were damaging to the economy. It called strikes, it resisted any effective reforms, and the loony-tune Trotskyisks and Maoists, who somehow believed that their extreme political ideology had some relevance in today's world, attempted in whatever way they could to sabotage the fundamentals of a democratic and capitalistic United Kingdom. Their

219

ideology taught, in all the obscure ideological books that they used to read, that it was the end days for capitalism and they were happy to hasten its demise, in whatever way they could. It was in this turmoil, this context, and this culture, in which Margaret Thatcher ascended to power. And to this lady such shenanigans were a red rag to a bull. To Margaret Thatcher, the power that the Trade Unions exercised, and the radical ideologues that had attached themselves to it, were hampering economic growth in the United Kingdom, and preventing the introduction of policies that would, in her view at least, lead to a more economically powerful and unashamedly purely capitalistic United Kingdom. The reason why I mention this is to make the key point that sometimes political leaders need to go into conflict with their own population in order for change to take place. She was never a populist. She did not consider herself to be elected to be nice. Margaret Thatcher took on the Trade Union movement in the UK and decimated it. She stripped them of political power, and she introduced economic reforms that she felt were necessary to place the United Kingdom in the slipstream of globalization. She was ready for a fight, and she would go in, boots and all.

Political leaders are elected and do one of two things. They either see it as their role to maintain the *status quo,* or they consider themselves as elected to make changes. Could a President in the Philippines ever betray their own class? The elite of the nation. Dilute its power and its interests. Would such a leader in the Philippines ever be *allowed* to do that? Margaret Thatcher was a leader who felt she needed to make changes, whatever the cost. She came from a working class background, but this did not deter her from taking on her own class. She took those that resisted her vision and her policies head on, and she won. Some had felt that she was too rigid, too focused, too unforgiving in her policies. Her economic policies that brought the rampant inflation of that time under control, also had the effect of increasing the levels of unemployment. It was suggested in the popular press that she needed perhaps to make a U-turn, just like a vehicle does on the highway, to head in the other direction. Mrs. Thatcher would have none of this. "To those of you that say we need to make a U-turn in our policies, there is only one thing I will say. No. You turn!" (A play on the U of the original phrase). Even the Soviets were wary of her, and they referred to her as "The Iron Lady". She had a very nice husband called Dennis, who was an oil executive by profession. I'm absolutely certain he would have won none of the normal, domestic arguments that married couples have. Margaret Thatcher was a force to be reckoned with, and everyone knew where she stood. She was highly opinionated, and she was rigid, but if she set her mind to do something the job would be done. And rather than just tinker with macroeconomic policy, she knew that to get real economic results and efficiencies, she had to change the working culture of the UK, and this she did. The British Trade Unions were in her view paralyzing the economic dynamism of the nation, and therefore they would damn well have to go. The landscape of Britain was changed markedly by Margaret Thatcher, and she had also significant influence on international events. For her, the *status quo* would never do.

The Philippines is a nation requires change, and its leaders need to confront those practices that are hindering the nation, and leading to its continued economic decline relative to other economies. Change is required on every level. On the political level, on the economic level, and on the cultural level. The current trending of this nation's economic performance is downwards. Since the 1960's, apart from isolated little bursts of economic dynamism here and there, such as that displayed under the government of Ramos, it has been all downhill. I have cited clear indicators of this. The middle classes have shrunk. Poverty has increased. The intelligentsia, the professionals and the technicians are being exported, to help others nations build *their* nations, to look after *their* sick, to safely deliver *their* babies, to create *their* computer software and to do *their* Research and Development. The Philippines supplies the education for these OFW's, and then loses them when they are at their most economically productive. Nice one. For the other nations, that is. But apart from that there are cultural factors at work too, and the Filipino leader who wants to change this nation, and change its economic performance, needs to change these too. It is no use simply tinkering with the macroeconomic issues, as important as these are. I mention these adverse cultural factors in this book. The lackadaisical business practices, the cronyism, the lack of punctuality, the preoccupation with drinking and gambling, the lack of focus, and the lack of precision. These are all cultural and mindset factors in the Philippines that work against the economic efficiency of the nation. For any political leader who wants true change, and wants the Philippines to compete in any real way with the other economies of Asia, they are going to have to go into psychological battle with their own population. To change these cultural traits and the mindset, which are essentially hindrances. If the leadership and the populace feel that they don't want that to change, that is fine and that is your choice. But the consequences are clear. The probability is that further economic decline is going to occur. If you do not like my opinion, you are fully entitled to hold a contrary view, and a contrary opinion. That is your human right. But I am obligated to give an honest opinion. I am driven to give this opinion partly out of a sense of anger. I have seen and felt and smelled and touched the poverty of the Philippines. I personally do not think it's acceptable for children to be malnourished, educationally disadvantaged and to run about in rags, with the only real distraction being the time they spend rummaging in garbage dumps for anything they might find of value. This is happening in the Philippines. It's happening today. Right now. And it is unacceptable.

There needs to be far more emphasis placed on continual self-improvement and on adult education. There needs to be a change in the idleness that so many adults in the Philippines engage in, but seem to regard as acceptable. Role models are needed that reflect these traits and values. Effective public education programs are essential. One has to remember that the culture of a nation, the behavioral traits of its people, and the values and attitudes embedded within the psyche of the nation, are malleable structures. They are not 'hard-wired' into our brains. They form the 'software'. Culture can change, and my conclusion is, that in the Philippines it can and it should. Otherwise you are not going to be competitive. And that is what, in today's world, it is all about. One may look at a nation and its culture in exactly the way one would look at a large corporation. Changing organizational culture is a huge task. It has been embedded in the thought pattern and the behavior of the population over a long time. People get used to it. People really need to see a need for change, and have a desire to engage in the process of change. But it's possible. There are three major steps involved in changing an organization's culture.(16) Firstly, before an organization can change its culture, it must first understand the current culture, or the way things are now. Secondly, once you understand your current organizational culture, your organization must then decide where it wants to go, define its strategic direction, and decide what the organizational culture should look like to support success. What vision does the organization have for its future and how must the culture change to support the accomplishment of that vision?

Finally, the individuals in the organization must decide to change their behavior to create the desired organizational culture. This is the hardest step in culture change.(17)

For Filipinos, it has always been the family first. This is the greatest strength, and the greatest weakness, of Philippine society. Families provide love, and support and help and social contact, and care for us and nurture us and are always there for us. For the Filipino, though, it means that its family members that have to be in positions of power or advantage or control. The political and financial dynasties in this nation are examples of this. As mentioned before, conflict of interest is a very poorly understood concept in the Philippines. The consequence is that people get into key positions, not on merit or performance, but on what is almost a hereditary right. And that means that judgment and decision-making is badly impaired. Accountability is avoided. Decisions and outcomes are focused less on the common good. The Philippines is more akin to a monarchy than a Westminster style of democracy. Just changing this one aspect of Filipino culture, by introducing clear conflict of interest guidelines, and by forbidding the employment or engagement of any family member in one's political organization, would have incalculably positive outcomes for the nation. The secret is that the Philippines is awash with talent. A lot of good talent is wasted, because they are not part of a political family or dynasty, and will therefore never get the opportunity to serve in key positions. The further problem for the Philippines is that it has never industrialized, it has never created a science and knowledge-based economy, principally because it has exported its technicians and professionals, and it has absorbed from the brief period of American colonization only the most superficial and economically useless elements and icons of American culture. That principal icon being Hollywood. Economically useless outside of America that is. But there is no direct economic benefit to a third world country like the Philippines in wanting to be Hollywood. Wall Street business acumen, entrepreneurship, drive, creativity and individuality have never been absorbed into Filipino popular culture. The Philippines has been let down in the past by its political leadership. But the populace itself must take responsibility for change, because it is also the populace that maintains the culture and presents the role models for the next generation. I mentioned at the very beginning how critical the morphology, or geographical shape, of this archipelagic nation is. The free flow of physical goods is hindered, and especially so in this nation, as the Philippines has a poor physical infrastructure and inefficient transport systems. We live in the 21st Century. In the last 20 years another dimension to commerce has evolved and that is e-commerce. In the blink of an eye information can be transported, exchanged, bought and sold via that global mesh of electromagnetic waves and signals, the World Wide Web. Software development, creating e-books, website design and construction, website hosting, are just examples of the types of activities that are possible using the internet. The significance of this is that these types of activities, and the use of the internet, *transcend any geographical and physical barriers that might be in place.* This means that a Filipino developing a piece of software in Davao is on a level playing field with someone developing a similar piece of software in Berlin. In fact, the individual in Davao has an advantage, because wage rates for employing someone to assist with software development is cheaper in Davao than in Berlin, and so are the local goods and services that might be required in producing the software. The creation, the storing, the application and the transmission of software is not dependant or hindered by geographical barriers such as water between the islands of a nation, or any other barriers. And this is why the Philippines, if it is to prosper economically, must become a knowledge and science based economy. This means in turn that certain changes must take place. It means that Filipinos must develop a hunger, a hunger for knowledge, for reading, for technical research. And it means that the Philippines must stop exporting its technical IT and scientific graduates. It means that the Philippine government must encourage, facilitate and support entrepreneurship in technical areas. The Philippines needs the equivalent of a Silicon Valley. A prestigious place of research and development for IT, for software, and for hardware devices that will be critical in supporting the next wave of technology. In regards to popular culture, we need to place far more emphasis on intellectual talent and achievement. Entertainment is fine, but it is not going to pay the way for the Philippines in the years ahead. The Filipina Whitney Houston or Filipino Justin Bieber wannabe's may well be dreaming of stardom and having fun, and so might the audience, but the likely end result is perhaps a stint in a Tokyo night club. If you're lucky. Filipinos always want to be an imitation. Why not be the real thing, in an individual way? True artistry is the expression of individuality, not the imitation of an American pop singer. Filipinos can achieve much, much more than this. But the popular culture encourages them down this track of imitation. In terms of economic development the other nations of Asia are leaving the Philippines for dead. And we know why, the reasons are outlined in this book. If the Philippines wants a viable future for the population at large, it's time to get *serious*, and to inculcate the same focus, drive and precision that is evidenced by our Chinese and Taiwanese neighbors. *Should the Philippines want to.* Not only *can* we learn from the Chinese, but we *need* to learn from them. Overseas investment is sorely needed in the Philippines, but its not occurring, for the reasons I have already mentioned in this book. It is needed especially for infrastructure projects that will effect the more rapid transit of goods and services. I include under the heading of infrastructure, as well as roads and bridges, the internet also, and an efficient and reliable mail system. At the very heart of a dynamic economy, and the generation of wealth, is the free and unhindered flow of goods and services, thoughts and ideas. And in addition, creative expression and inventiveness. The

Philippines can do it, the only question is, do they want to, and will the leadership be at hand.

There is another thing that I must say before this book comes to an end. It is that the easiest thing in the world is to be what is referred to as an 'armchair critic'. That is, someone who has no responsibility for any of the matters they are discussing, none of the burdens of elected office, none of the headaches and challenges of running a nation, and has no responsibility for the consequences of any proposed actions. Currently, that falls to the President of the Republic of the Philippines, Benigno Simeon Aquino III. It is hard for me to imagine the responsibility that lies on his shoulders. He acts, I am sure, not only out of his own dedication to this nation, but in memory of both of his parents. One of whom was brutally murdered before he could challenge for the Presidency, and the other who was elected into Office as a consequence. I am not sure if that makes it harder for the President or easier. In any case, the burden of Office is onerous, and I am cognizant of that fact. Writing a book is very challenging, demanding and is hard work. But it is nothing compared to the responsibility of presiding over a nation.

For me the association and the bond with the Philippines will continue. I am a Westerner that has been planted in a culture that is kaleidoscopic in nature and shows faces of both the East and the West, of Hollywood superficiality and of Oriental depth and inscrutability. I find myself gradually absorbing these values and behaviors, and find my attachment to the nation of the Philippines, and its people, deepening. My life and my fate is inextricably bound with this nation. I have said most of what I wanted to say in this book, but there is always something to write about the Philippines. A pile of books the size of a mountain could be written about this nation. It is a fascinating place. Due to the values and taboos imbued in Philippine culture, one is expected to tiptoe around certain issues and facts so as not to be disrespectful or cause loss of face. But I owe it to you to be blunt and honest. Then we know exactly where we stand on an issue. The other sinister side of this issue is that it may be dangerous to tell the whole story, to detail the political corruption, to highlight certain behaviors of Filipino politicians and their associates.

Behaviors that in the West would result in immediate dismissal from office, and would not be tolerated in a civil society that claims to live by the rule of law, are tolerated in the Philippines, because political power is wielded in a different way to that in the West. That is the reality. The mindset is different. I have never been threatened or felt threatened in the Philippines, and have always felt completely free to do and say what I want here, but I am a foreigner, and could be told, quite rightly, to mind my own business. However, as Corazon Aquino once said "You, the foreign media, have been the companion of my people in its long and painful journey to freedom". Filipinos yearn still to be free. To be free from poverty, and from the bonds of a hopeless future. The truth must be told, because it is the truth that sets us free.

I have a love and a passion for the Philippine nation that is deep. I am addressed as *"Kuya"*. I accept the honorary title! Just don't call me *"Lolo!"* I think about and care for the Philippines just as a *kuya* thinks about and cares for his brothers and sisters and his family. A lot of what happens here angers and frustrates me, because things *could* be different and the Philippines *could* be a lot better, and people not have to suffer and live in poverty. I hope and pray that change will come. Perhaps when a foreigner provides an alternative frame of reference, then an alternative and a choice becomes available. It is partly about changing the level of consciousness about such issues. But to actually enact change will be the choice and prerogative of the Filipino people. I cannot help you with that.

While traveling one day on Masbate Island, I stopped at a store outside of Masbate City, to buy some refreshments, and take a rest from the journey I was on. The Filipino store owner and I engaged in conversation, and he was eager to show me the kiln that he used to bake bread. Every day, he told me, at 3.30 a.m., he would commence his work, to bake the fresh bread for his customers. We talked about our respective nations, and I mentioned that Australia was a very rich country, in comparison to the Philippines. The store owner replied, "The Philippines is rich too, only the people here don't know how to use that wealth". *He is exactly right.* In all of my time here, this is the truest and most insightful statement I have heard anyone say about the Philippines. His wife then mentioned that a lot of the local population just engage in drinking and gambling, and that is exactly right too. The Philippines has squandered its wealth, and squandered its time, and continues to do so. On every level of society. Other economies in Asia have raced ahead in economic terms, with only a fraction of the resources that the Philippines has at its disposal. These 'Tiger Economies' are extremely focused and extremely motivated and hungry for economic success. And just in case anyone says, "But the Philippines is a disaster-prone country", then one can reply with the fact that so is China, it follows closely behind the Philippines in disaster events, but its economy races ahead. Their mindset is different and they have a focus, a drive and a hunger for economic success that is extraordinary. Only through that can economic success come.

The Republic of the Philippines does have so many factors working against it. It is ravaged by storms and earthquakes. It has a dysfunctional political system, and poorly defined boundaries between the Military, the Church and the State. It has a high level of corruption, at every level of society. It is geographically fragmented. This is precisely why the planning and execution of national policy by the government has to be precise and executed well. There is simply no room for error. It is also one of the reasons why many would favor a federal governmental structure for the nation. The current unitary system is ineffective for projecting influence and control to all regions of the nation. A strong federal government, and strong state governments, may provide better regional control. As we have said there are risks with this, and it would depend on how well such a change is executed. Also, it would depend on how well the state governments each become government entities with transparency, efficiency and effective execution of federal government policies. That is, how it all is made to work *in practice*.

When I first had the idea for this book I did think of the title immediately, 'The Unlucky Country'. However, after spending my time in the Philippines, researching, experiencing, thinking and discussing the country with others, I have come to the conclusion that the Philippines is actually not unlucky. The title of this book is a misnomer, but I have retained it nonetheless, because a lot of people *think* of this nation as unlucky. But luck, or lack of it, cannot explain the problems and the poverty of the Philippines. China suffers a lot of disasters, almost as many as the Philippines, but as I have said, it still races ahead economically. India is a corrupt nation, but India also races ahead economically. We have discussed in this book the real reasons for the poverty that exists in the Philippines. A very important one is that the Philippines has failed to control its population, and its population demographics. Another of the problems, and one of the causes of the condition the nation is in, is that it has exported its best and brightest. The technical and scientific graduates, and the health professionals, for example, have left for greener pastures overseas. Some of those Filipinos left here are clearly not export quality. Filipinos with a lackadaisical and irresponsible attitude. For the OFW's, some of them live lives of danger and of deprivation. At the same time some of their compatriots at home party on like there's no tomorrow. One of my charitable commitments is to sponsor the Filipino grandchild of a man I met through my church activities in Cebu. He explained to me last year that his son-in-law, the father of this grandchild in question, is actually employed, but drinks and gambles his money away. Others are left to pick up the burden and the responsibility. Bishops of the Church in this nation, in this year of 2011, were being driven around in brand new SUV motor vehicles, that they petitioned for themselves from the former President, in one case as . . . 'your birthday gift to me.' The vehicles the Bishops got cost over a cool 1 Million Pesos per set of wheels. Nice. Call me old fashioned, but I just don't think it's right that Bishops should be driven around in brand new SUV's, while Filipino children are working in garbage dumps, and women are dying in childbirth. Bishops were also threatening the President of the day with excommunication for proposing a family planning and birth control program, and discussing rumors of his removal from office. This year, like every other, almost 5,000 women in the Philippines will die as a result of the complications of childbirth.(18) The Church will look after its own interests and its own people. The masses have to fend for themselves. Fortunately, there are some heroic priests and nuns in the Philippines that don't follow the unfailingly dogmatic line that comes from the Vatican, and they actually *care* about their flock. They too probably risk excommunication. But if excommunication comes because of caring for people and fighting for their human rights, for their dignity, and for the true alleviation of poverty, then God is on your side. Be spiritual, not religious. 5,000 women dying every year because of the complications of childbirth is not acceptable. When the publicity about the Bishops SUV's occurred the vehicles were quickly given back. Passed on out of their hands like hot potatoes. It was a shameful episode for the Church. Hopefully the SUV's have been sold and the funds used for maternal health care, or for ambulances as in the original intention of the PCSO.

I have during the course of writing this book stayed in the best hotels in Makati, and I have stayed with a poverty-stricken family in one of the poorest regions of the nation. I am sponsoring two individuals through High School from that region, and it is always wonderful to get down there to see them. There is nothing heroic in this, in choosing to stay in the same conditions as a family that is dirt-poor. I have a *choice* as to where I live. For them they have no choice. They are desperately poor, and they are likely to stay that way. There is nothing but poverty for them. And this will likely repeat itself for the next generation, and perhaps for the one after, unless something changes. In coming to the conclusion of this book one might ask, what is it that I *feel* about my experiences, about the poverty and the problems of the Philippines? The feeling that I have is one of anger. Anger at those who have stolen money from the nation and stashed it in overseas bank accounts. Anger at the Catholic Church. Anger because things *could have been different*. Most of the poverty in the Philippines can only be viewed as *an injustice*, because with proper birth control and family planning programs, and with proper governance, and with the ceasing of the nation exporting its best and brightest, the fortunes of the nation and the poverty rate would have improved years ago. The real enemy of the Filipino has been the Filipino himself. I have said that the Filipino will do anything for their family, and they will. We have to admire this. But towards their compatriots they can show the most dreadful disregard. The Filipino journalist who is doing his job, who is maintaining one of the pillars of a true democracy and a free society, that being the right to investigate and to report on matters that are in the public interest, is murdered by being shot in the head. The Filipino who perpetrates this crime does this with no regard for his fellow-Filipino, no thought for the suffering of the family of the journalist, no thought for the democracy of this nation and the principles of a civil society, and no thought of any interest beyond himself and his immediate family. In addition there is no thought about the future of this nation and its betterment. Sing the national anthem with your hand on your heart, go to Church and be seen in front of the people kneeling to pray, call your compatriot *brad* or *pare*, pretend, pretend, pretend. All the while robbing the nation and murdering your countrymen, and guaranteeing the rest a life of poverty. The masses are distracted and numbed by their poverty. They are compliant and pious as a result. The ruling powers, the Church, the State and the Military, who should be separate but are enmeshed, can then get on with their own agendas. The figures relating to the embezzlement of public funds are astronomical. *Walang bigayan. Walang bigayan,* big time. There is a tangled web of embezzlement. It's part of the 'culture.' The political *modus operandi*. The way of doing things here. The total amount sitting in overseas bank accounts is, without doubt, astronomical. We can't quantify it because the perpetrators have been so skilled at what they do. For a nation that calls itself Catholic and religious there is a huge disregard for the Ten Commandments. Had the Filipino journalists who have been shot dead reported something that was untrue, or unjustifiably offensive, then whoever it was so affected by this, has the right in a civil society to redress the issue in a court of law. To issue a charge of slander or libel. This is the process and the right of redress in a civil society. In a just and civil and fair and compassionate society. The sort we would want for our children and our grandchildren. Or he would have been forgiven, as befit's a 'religious' nation, a 'Catholic' nation. This brutal and senseless murder of journalists, and of priests engaged in human rights work, does not happen in nations that are truly democratic. Or if it does those responsible are brought swiftly to justice. This is a stain on the fabric of Philippine society. It is unnecessary and inexcusable. And it is an insult to all ethical and caring and decent Filipinos, who form the vast majority of the people of this nation. The real enemy lies within. Call yourself a democracy, or call yourself religious, but it doesn't change the behavior.

The Philippine nation must face and formulate its own fate and destiny. No one can help it unless it reformulates its goals, and values, at a grass-roots level. Sadly, if current trends continue, if change does not occur, then the Philippines is doomed to at least another 15 or 20 year cycle of poverty and under-achievement. That much is clear. But there is a choice and there are alternatives. I can only hope that change will be embraced and that change will occur, constructive, measured, real change. Only then will the Philippines unleash its incredible potential, and the Diaspora of overseas Filipinos, driven by necessity to earn money overseas, will end. And then the nation will focus on building itself with the large pool of talent that it possesses. There are progressive and forward-thinking Filipinos here who are instituting change and incorporating best-practice concepts, in business and in civil administration. There are brave priests and nuns who see the needs of the Filipino as their first concern and priority, not unthinking allegiance to the Vatican and its tyrannical dogma. We should support and honor them. There are modern day Filipino individuals, such as Manny Pacquiao, who display an incredible mindset, and personality traits that the Filipino really needs to embody in order to take the world head-on, without being intimidated or "shy". To display incredible will, self-discipline and drive, to become number one in a tough world. To have a mindset that is conducive to economic success, and conducive to shaking the Philippines from its economic slumber.

There are some things that can be changed, and some that cannot. The Philippines was given by fate its unique shape, or morphology, its composition of over 7,000 islands which works against its prosperity in so many ways. Adverse weather events are also beyond our control, although it can be argued that there is a link between global warming, and the increase in the amount of CO_2 released into the atmosphere, for example by coal-fired power stations in the Philippines. Beyond these factors there are things that we can change and we can control. This relates to the corruption within business and institutions, the dysfunctional political system, the resistance of appropriate birth control measures by the Catholic Church, and the mindset of Filipinos. All of these factors are cultural and behavioral in nature, they are man-made, and therefore changeable, should individuals and the collective whole take responsibility for facilitating change.

Carl Gustav Jung was a Swiss Psychiatrist. He was an intellectual giant of a man. He gave us the terms introversion and extroversion in relation to personality types, and many, many other psychological concepts. He once said, in relation to his teaching duties as a psychiatrist, 'True art is creation, and beyond all theories, and that is why I say to beginners (in psychiatry) "learn your theories well, but put them aside when you touch the miracle of the living soul." The miracle of the living soul of the Filipino has been hidden under a layer of imposed culture from Spain and from America. It's time for the Filipino to break out from these cultural impositions, and to find and express their own individuality, to became creative in a truly Filipino way. You can *use* foreign cultural concepts and information and knowledge to do this, but don't *depend* on them. And make space for your own soul and its unfathomable creativity. It is also time to recognize the realities of economic life and survival in this era, that Filipinos must aggressively compete on the economic world stage. Just like Manny Pacquiao does in the boxing ring. In exactly the same way.

The experience for the foreigner of living in the Philippines is being faced with a culture and an experience that is kaleidoscopic. One sometimes feels that one really want to ask Filipinos "What do you want? What do you really want". For some it seems that there is no concern for tomorrow, no motivation to change, and no plan. Some are supported by relatives who are OFWs and they see no need to change this cozy arrangement. Others are insightful and see the condition their nation is in. The task for change will fall to them.

On finishing the writing of this book, the very first thing I will do is to head out on a motorbike to the wide open spaces, and the rolling hills, of my beloved Masbate Island, in the Bicol region of the Philippines. It is the geographical heart of the nation. I will ride past pastures and rice fields that have been tilled and harvested for millennia, with which the Filipino farmer shares a mystical bond, and a life that is intertwined with the spirits and superstitions of his forefathers. My head will clear and, distracted by this magical landscape, I will forget all of the pressures and responsibilities and worries of my life. The green pastures will spread before me, as if to infinity, and the farmer will be bowed over his crop, seemingly in homage to that which sustains him and his family, and gives them life. His children will be riding the caribou, that patient and plodding beast of burden of the Philippines, helping their father in a way that is half work and half fun. Finishing his work for the day, as the sun sets in a magnificent blaze of splendor, the farmer will return to his Nipa hut, to live his family life the way it has been lived for countless generations. Life for him will essentially not change, the only question is if it will change for his children, or for his children's children. Perhaps this farmer, while engaged in his daily task, in this ritual of giving to the land, and of taking from it to sustain his life and that of his family, will look up and see me passing. Noticing it is a foreigner he is likely to wave a greeting, and were we to engage in conversation he would likely ask me where I am from. That is a good question. Where am I from? What winds of fate carried me here and what will be our collective future? Is it destiny that has brought me here today, or only the rational and informed decisions that I have made? So many questions, but that is the whole point. It is the questions that makes us human, and a part of the Divine, not the answers. We ask these questions in exactly the same manner, whether from the East or from the West. He sees me as a foreigner, but I have, no doubt, absorbed much the culture of the Philippines, and over time it has modified my thinking and my behavior. So I don't know if I am still truly a foreigner, because living in the Philippines has changed me. It has changed my identity, and it has changed my values.

The future for the nation, it must be said, does not look bright. The seasons, and the inexorable change from rainy season to dry season, used to be predictable. Many years ago, one had never heard of global warming, and there seemed to be a reassuring permanency and predictability about the cycle of the seasons and the weather. But in recent years there has been a capriciousness in the weather that has never been seen before. The booming urban areas and their huge consumption of energy and resources are changing the face of the nation, and the planet, for ever. And the very seasons that we thought were changeless, and the very rains that the farmer needs for his crops, are now less predictable. The booming population is ever-hungry. Hungry for food, hungry for energy, hungry for novelty, hungry to see and do and taste and experience. They also produce, in addition to the CO_2 released through the burning of coal to feed their need for electricity, huge amounts of waste and garbage. The direct consequence of this, and this relates particularly to the Philippines, is that the air and the soil will become more polluted, and the country will become more crowded, and more indebted to the rest of the world, as it has to import more food and more oil and more consumer products. All without food and energy security. The Philippines is in a precarious position. But, take heart Filipinos. The story of your nation is not yet over, and the future is open and unformed. Other nations have been in the same situation, and have transformed themselves within a generation. They have performed economic miracles, and so can you. Should you choose to do so.

NOTES/REFERENCES/BIBLIOGRAPHY

For all references that I have used in this book I have collated and used in a way that is consistent with the provisions of Fair Use, as exists under Copyright protection laws. I have intended to fully acknowledge sources. Please contact me if there has been any omission to acknowledge any source or any correction needed.

Introduction.

(1) Shape of the State. State Morphology by Matt Rosenberg

http://geography.about.com/cs/politicalgeog/a/shapestate.htm

(2) Australia has in its history been subject to devastating cyclones. The northern Australian city of Darwin, in the Northern Territories, was devastated early on Christmas morning 1974 when hit by the tropical weather depression that was given the name 'Cyclone Tracy.' As the eye of the cyclone passed over the city between midnight and 7.00 a.m. on Christmas morning torrential rain fell and the winds were officially recorded at 217 kilometers per hour. This was prior to the Bureau of Meteorology ancmometer being destroyed. Houses and other buildings disintegrated due to the force of the cyclone. 65 people were killed (including 16 lost at sea) and many more were injured, 70 per cent of Darwin's homes were destroyed or suffered severe damage. All

public services—communications, power, water and sewerage—were severed.

http://www.naa.gov.au/about-us/publications/fact-sheets/fs176.aspx

National Archives of Australia. 'Cyclone Tracy.'

(3) http://www.indexmundi.com/philippines/population.html

(4) www.wikipedia.org/wiki/List_of_sovereign_states_and_dependent_territories_by_population_density

(5) www.wikipedia.org/wiki/Demographics_of_the_Philippines

(6) http://en.wikipedia.org/wiki/History_of_the_Philippines

(7) www.wikipedia.org/wiki/Languages_of_the_Philippines

(8) *ibid.*

(9) *ibid.*

(10) http://josecarilloforum.com/forum/index.php?topic=1622.0

'Let's be firm on whether the name "Philippines" is singular or plural.'

Jose Carillo's English forum. July 25, 2011.

I like to independently check sources whenever possible, and the relevant part of the interview relating to the issue discussed can be found on the US Department of State website at: http://www.state.gov/secretary/rm/2011/06/167187.htm

(11) *Ibid.*

(12) http://www.icn.ch/projects/philippines-tuberculosis-remains-a-major-killer/

Online article. 'Tuberculosis remains a major killer in the Philippines.'

Chapter 1

(1) Online article on 'Culture' at http://en.wikipedia.org/wiki/Culture

(2) A.T. Church, 'Filipino personality' (Philippines: De La Salle University Press, 1986 pp 10-12)

(3) Tirupathi, Karthik. 'Punctuality: The Japanese way of business'. www.Redcliffe.com. India Abroad. Online article—'India as it happens'. February 21, 2007.

(4) Nelson, Peggy B., (1959) 'Sound in the classroom' ASHRAE Journal 45 22-25.

(5) Wakefield, Julie, (June 2002) 'Learning the hard way' Environmental health perspectives 110.

(6) Online article 'America's Forgotten Children' and video from Al Jazeera television. http://stream.aljazeera.com/story/americas-forgotten-children.

(7) Martin Heidegger was a German existentialist philosopher who wrote, among other works, the classical treatise 'Being and Time'.

(8) 'Heidegger,s philosophy of authentic existence and the Filipinos: social dimensions' KINAADMAN An Interdisciplinary Research Journal, Holy Name University, Tagbilaran City, Bohol, Philippines.

(9) World Health Organization 2009. 'Suicide rates per 100,000 by country, year and sex'.

(10) Statistical data 'Homicide rates per nation' as recorded per www.chartsbin.com

(11)'The Concept of Saving Face: an introduction to the concept of face in Asia' by Greg Rodgers. Online article. www.about.com

(12) *ibid.*

(13) US-based technology and social media news blog www.mashable.com in a report dated 18th. August, 2010, citing collated data from Reuters, the New York Times, CTIA.org, UPI.com, Pew Research, Kvue.com, Matzav.com, and Portio Research.

(14) http://www.gmanews.tv/story/198832/philippines-still-text-messaging-champ-us-study GMA News online article, August, 2010.

(15) www.techie.com.ph 'RP ranks second in number of Facebook users in Asia'. Online article dated 19th January, 2010.

(16) Manila Bulletin Newspaper. Online article http://www.mb.com.ph/articles/275145/gloria-diaz-declared-persona-non-grata-cebu by Rowena Joy A. Sanchez September 1, 2010.

(17) *Ibid.*

(18) *Ibid.*

(19) *Ibid.*

(20) http://en.wikipedia.org/wiki/Filipino_language—the Wikipedia entry here states that a citation in reference to this entry is needed.

(21) *ibid.*

(22) *ibid.* Wikipedia cites as a source: Paraluman Aspillera (1993). 'Pilipino: The National Language, a historical sketch'. from Basic Tagalog for Foreigners and Non-Tagalogs, Charles E. Tuttle Publishing Co., Inc., Tokyo.

(23) *ibid.* Wikipedia gives the source of this statement as 'J.U. Wolff, "Tagalog", in the Encyclopedia of Language and Linguistics, 2006'.

(24) 'The relationship between hypertension and epistaxis is implicated. Epistaxis is more common in hypertensive patients, and patients are more likely to be acutely hypertensive during an episode of epistaxis.'

http://www.nurse-ocha.com/2009/02/epistaxis-nosebleeds.html

(25) 'Actress says sorry for bikini show'. Online article by Rizel S. Adlawan, February 19, 2010. http://www.sunstar.com.ph/cebu/actress-says-sorry-bikini-show.

(26) *Ibid.*

(27) *Ibid.*

(28) *Ibid.*

(29) www.abs-cbnNEWS.com Online article entitled 'Boy abused in 'Willing Willie,' DSWD says' by Jojo Malig. Posted at 03/28/2011 Manila, Philippines, with a report from Trina Lagura.

(30) *Ibid.*

(31) *Ibid.*

(32) *Ibid.*

(33) http://www.catholic.com/library/gay_marriage.asp Online article dated 2004.

(34) American Psychological Association 'Statement on Homosexuality' 1975.

(35) Online article ABS-CBN News. 'Vice Ganda's Facebook fans reach 1 million'. http://www.abs-cbnnews.com/entertainment/03/21/10/vice-gandas-facebook-fans-reach-1-million

(36) 'The word "Novena" comes from the Latin word "novem" which means nine. So a novena is generally prayed for nine consecutive days—most often in preparation for a great feast day, or for a special prayer request or need. However, a novena can also be spread over nine weeks, with each day of the Novena being said on any day depending on when the day of a particular saint or devotion falls. For example, Wednesday is the day traditionally associated with devotions to St. Joseph so a weekly novena in his honor is usually done on a Wednesday.' From an online article found at: http://www.stjosephsite.com/SJS_Articles_novena.htm

(37) www.thephilippinescene.com 'Online article 'Priest found dead in motel room'.

(38) abs-cbnnews.com 04/16/2010 'Priests violate vows of celibacy'.

(39) Online article at Global Nation Enquirer, Agence France-Presse. http://globalnation.inquirer.net/6681/australian-arrested-for-sexually-abusing-girls-in-cebu

(40) 'Selective Sound Sensitivity Syndrome or 4S is an intense and immediate emotional and physiological reaction (possibly rage, frustration, sadness, or panic) upon hearing certain sounds—most prominently noises associated with oral functions such as eating, breathing, chewing or other noises such as typing sounds or pencils scratching.' Definition from the website: www.soundsensitive.org

(41) Wikipedia The Free Encyclopedia www.wikipedia.org/mindset Article on the definition of 'mindset'.

(42) Financial Times Lexicon. Online at: www.ft.com

Chapter 2

(1) Mount Pinatubo Eruption

'The Volcanic Mount Pinatubo Eruption of 1991 that Cooled the Planet'

By Matt Rosenberg, About.com Guide http://geography.about.com/od/globalproblemsandissues/a/pinatubo.htm

(2) www.wikipedia.org 'Mount Pinatubo Philippines'

(3) www.geonet.org.nz/volcano/alert-level 'Volcano Alert Levels'

(4) www.volcano-pictures.info 'Glossary. Caldera.'

(5) Mount Pinatubo Eruption

'The Volcanic Mount Pinatubo Eruption of 1991 that Cooled the Planet'

By Matt Rosenberg, About.com Guide http://geography.about.com/od/globalproblemsandissues/a/pinatubo.htm

(6) www.wikipedia.com 'Mount Pinatubo'

(7) www.youtube.com/all_comments?v=NQzGjGKdGvQ

Youtube comments section Mount Pinatubo Volcanic Eruption

(8) http://www.crcd.be/search/node/philippines

Center for Research on the Epidemeology of Disasters. 'Philippines.'

(9) World Bank Report.:

'Natural Disaster Risk Management In The Philippines:

Enhancing Poverty Alleviation Through Disaster Reduction.'

The World Bank National Disaster Coordinating Council.

(10) *Ibid.*

(11) *Ibid.*

(12) http://money.howstuffworks.com/personal-finance/financial-planning/9-odd-things-insured-by-lloyds-of-london8.htm

'Odd things insured by Lloyds of London.'

(13) World Bank Report.:

'Natural Disaster Risk Management In The Philippines:

Enhancing Poverty Alleviation Through Disaster Reduction.'

The World Bank National Disaster Coordinating Council.

(14) *Ibid.*

(15) *Ibid.*

(16) http://www.cred.be/search/node/philippines

Center for Research on the Epidemeology of Disasters. 'Philippines.'

(17) http://www.mb.com.ph/node/271081/rp-world

'RP world's most disaster-prone–study'

Manila Bulletin online.

By Dexter A. See

August 6, 2010.

(18) 'Millions Of Victims, Little Aid For Philippines Disaster Victims' by Staff Writers Manila (AFP) March 6, 2008 appearing on www. terradaily.com.

(19) http://beta.searca.org/kc3/index.php/feature/168-eu-fpavas-climate-change-component

The European Union—'Focused-Food Production Assistance to the Vulnerable Sectors' (EU-FPAVAS) 2010.

(20) http://www.newton.dep.anl.gov/askasci/wea00/wea00239.htm 'Average Global Lightning Strikes' Online answer given by:

David R. Cook Atmospheric Physics and Chemistry Section Environmental Research Division

Argonne National Laboratory

(21) World Bank Report.:

'Natural Disaster Risk Management In The Philippines:

Enhancing Poverty Alleviation Through Disaster Reduction.'

The World Bank National Disaster Coordinating Council.

(22) http://www.struckbylightning.org

(23) Email communication to author from Mr. Michael Putly, September 27th, 2011.

(24) http://en.wikipedia.org/wiki/Ozone_Disco_Club_fire

Wikipedia. 'Ozone Disco Club fire.'

(25) From WikiPilipinas: The Hip 'n Free Philippine Encyclopedia. 'The Ozone Disco Fire Tragedy.'

(26) *Ibid.*

(27) http://www.hungzai.com/ozone-disco-fire/ Online Ghost Stories. Present on website 29th August, 2011, anonymous contributor.

(28) Email communication from Hung at hungzai.com to the author, September, 19th, 2011.

(29) Dr. Carl Gustav Jung explained synchronicity as meaningful coincidences of seemingly highly improbable random events. "Synchronicity is the coming together of inner and outer events in a way that cannot be explained by cause and effect, and that is meaningful to the observer." Dr. Carl G. Jung. Quote sourced from: http://www. heureka.clara.nct/books/synchronicity.html

(30) Manila Bulletin Online Article By Jenny F. Manongdo December 20th, 2009. http://www.mb.com.ph/articles/234955/drowning-silent-killer-rp-kids

The findings were contained in an analysis on drowning of children conducted by Safe Kids Philippines, the Philippine Life Saving Society and the Department of Health entitled, "Child drowning in the Philippines: The silent killer speaks." As sourced from the above newspaper article.

Chapter 3

(1) www.wikipedia. Philippines.

(2) From an article by Aurea Calica, The Philippine Star Online, October 27th 2010.

(3) Online article 'Rice import quotas lifted', by Christine Avendaño. Philippine Daily Inquirer, 4th. August, 2008.

(4) Online article: www.asianews.it/news-en/Swamped-by-rice-imports,-the-Philippines-loses-food-self-sufficiency 29th August, 2010.

(5) Online article: '2010 oil import bill surged 40% to $9.96B' 'Higher crude prices blamed for rise from $7.11B' By Amy R. Remo. Philippine Daily Inquirer. 4th October, 2011. http://opinion.inquirer.net/inquireropinion/letterstotheeditor/view/20110410-330445/2010-oil-import-bill-surged-40-to-996B

(6) By Amy R. Remo Philippine Daily Inquirer, 4th October, 2011.

Filed Under: Energy, Oil & Gas—Upstream activities, import, Statistics.

(7) www.eoearth.org/article/Energy_profile_of_Philippines 'Energy profile of the Philippines'.

(8) Online article by Karl Wilson. Published Jun 30 2004 by INQ7, Archived Jun 30 2004 Philippines: 'Bataan nuclear plant costs $155,000 a day but no power.'

(9) A BBC Online News Report by by Kate McGeown 'Philippines opens Bataan nuclear plant to tourists.'

(10) *Ibid.*

(11)http://www.philstar.com/Article.aspx?articleId=660035&publicationSubCategoryId=63

The Philippine Star. Online article. Updated February 23, 2011, by Jess Diaz. 'Phl has world's highest power rates.'

(12) www.greenpeace.org/raw/content/seasia/en/press/reports/ bringing_calamities_to_communities Greenpeace report 'Bringing Calamities to Communities.' October, 20th. 2005.

(13) *Ibid.*

(14) http://www.jcmiras.net/surge/p160.htm 'Coal-Fired Power Plants in the Philippines.'

(15) www.sciencedaily.com/releases/2007/11/071114163448.htm

Online table 'Top-50 Countries with Highest CO2-Emitting Power Sectors'.

(16) www.greenpeace.org/raw/content/seasia/en/press/reports/ bringing_calamities_to_communities Greenpeace report 'Bringing Calamities to Communities.' October, 20th. 2005.

(17) *Ibid.*

(18) www.reef.crc.org.au/discover/coralreefs/bleaching/coralbleaching Online article on coral bleaching.

(19) www.greenpeace.org/raw/content/seasia/en/press/reports/ bringing_calamities_to_communities Greenpeace report 'Bringing Calamities to Communities.' October, 20th. 2005.

(20) www.naturalnews.com Online article 'The Mad Hatter Syndrome: mercury and biological toxicity.'

(21) www.greenpeace.org/raw/content/seasia/en/press/reports/ bringing_calamities_to_communities Greenpeace report 'Bringing Calamities to Communities.' October, 20th. 2005.

(22) www.mb.com.ph Online article 'Investment in renewable energy urged,' by Ellalyn B. De Vera, July 28,2011.

(23) www.worldbank.org.ph World Bank Online article 'Philippines: Growth need not come at the expense of environment.'

(24) www.greenpeace.org/raw/content/seasia/en/press/reports/ bringing_calamities_to_communities Greenpeace report 'Bringing Calamities to Communities.' October, 20th. 2005.

(25) *Ibid*.

(26) http://business.inquirer.net/5473/rich-countries-asked-to-help-philippines-expand-research-into-re Online article: 'Rich countries asked to help Philippines expand research into RE.' By Amy R. Remo, Daily Enquirer, June 28th, 2011.

(27) http://www.unfpa.org/rh/planning.htm

'World Health Report; and Meeting the Need, 2006, by UNFPA.'

'The Lancet's Maternal Survival and Women Deliver Series (2006/2007).'

(28) *Ibid*.

(29) *Ibid*.

(30) www.inquirer.net The Inquirer newspaper. Online article, 'Indonesia: A Family Planning Model for the Philippines?' By: Walden Bello.

July 16th, 2011.

(31) The Philippine Inquirer. September 30th 2010. 'CBCP reminds Aquino about excommunication.' By Philip Tubeza.

(32) *Ibid.*

(33) *Ibid.*

(34) http://answers.yahoo.com/question/index?qid=20110130180307AAPAn9X

Yahoo! Answers. 'Is there a foreign mail theft problem in the Philippines.'

(35) 'Philippines eyes to destroy P10M counterfeit goods in 2011.' by Danica Hermogones, July 1ˢᵗ, 2011. Inquirer.net

http://globalnation.inquirer.net/5168/philippines-eyes-to-destroy-p10m-counterfeit-goods-in-2011

(36) The data is from the nation master website and they source the data as from a the Fifth Annual BSA and IDL global piracy software study.

http://www.nationmaster.com/graph/cri_sof_pir_rat-crime-software-piracy-rate

(37) University of the Philippines School of Economics Professor Ramon Clarete. 'Piracy robs Philippines of software investment.' September 24, 2004. http://www.smh.com.au/articles/2004/09/24/1095961838408.html?from=moreStories

(38) *Ibid.*

(39) http://www.abs-cbnnews.com/business/08/13/08/rp-software-exports-hit-1-billion-2010 'RP software exports to hit $1 billion by 2010' abs-cbnnews.com, 13ᵗʰ August, 2008, AFP and Michelle Orosa.

(40) www.wikipedia.org 'Political Corruption'

(41) *Ibid.*

(42) http://en.wikipedia.org/wiki/Corruption_Perceptions_Index 'The Corruption Perception Index.' Wikipedia online encyclopedia.

(43) *Ibid.*

(44) http://www.dnaindia.com/money/column_is-corruption-good-or-bad-jury-is-out_1333247

'Is corruption good or bad? Jury is out.' By R. Jagannathan, January 11th, 2010.

(45) www.wikipedia.org.

Citing a BBC article, 'India lost $462bn in illegal capital flows, says report'. News: South Asia (BBC) http://www.bbc.co.uk/news/world-south-asia-11782795.

(46) http://www.financialtaskforce.org/2010/07/30/the-very-questionable-case-for-good-corruption/

(47) http://en.wikipedia.org/wiki/Embezzlement

Wikipedia online article. "Embezzelment.

(48) http://www.dnaindia.com/money/column_is-corruption-good-or-bad-jury-is-out_1333247

'Is corruption good or bad? Jury is out.' By R. Jagannathan, January 11th, 2010.

(49) http://www.adb.org/documents/books/poverty-in-the-philippines/chap6.pdf

Asian Development Bank. 'Causes of Poverty in the Philippines.' Chapter 6, Page 17.

(50)www.sustainer.org/dhm_archive/index.php?display_article=vn210singaporeed

The Donella Meadows Archive Voice of a Global Citizen 'Singapore Leads the Good Life Under a Benevolent Dictator'

(51) *Ibid.*

(52) www.globalconversation.org 'Singapore.'

(53)www.sustainer.org/dhm_archive/index.php?display_article=vn210singaporeed

The Donella Meadows Archive Voice of a Global Citizen 'Singapore Leads the Good Life Under a Benevolent Dictator'

(54) The International Dollar, also referred to as the Geary-Khamis dollar, is based on the twin concepts of purchasing power parities (PPP) of currencies and the international average prices of commodities. It shows how much a local currency unit is worth within the country's borders. It is used to make comparisons both between countries and over time. For example, comparing per capita gross domestic product (GDP) of various countries in international dollars, rather than based simply on exchange rates, provides a more valid measure to compare standards of living.

(55) GDP PPP definition http://www.gfmag.com/tools/global-database/economic-data/10299-the-worlds-richest-and-poorest-countries.html#axzz1ZWsBENBB

(56) CIA GDP PPP figures http://en.wikipedia.org/wiki/List_of_countries_by_GDP_(PPP)_per_capita)

(57) www.adb.org

'Philippine Development: Performance and Policy'

(58) *Ibid.*

(59) The Standard Newspaper Hong Kong

'Crony capitalism keeps Philippines stagnant.' By Karl Wilson.

February 24, 2006.

(60) www.asiaviews.org

Newsbreak Vol.4, No.7, April 12, 2004

By: Ricky Carandang.

Last Updated, Tuesday, 21 December 2010.

AsiaViews.

(61) *Ibid.*

(62) *Ibid.*

(63) *Ibid.*

(64)http://entertainment.inquirer.net/9671/paris-hilton-arrives-in-manila-missing-2-cell-phones-on-deplaning

'Paris Hilton arrives in Manila.'

Inquirer Newspaper. Online article by Mike Morelos, dated August 15, 2011.

(65) www.biztaxlaw.com 'Conflict of Interest.' Online article.

(66) Wikipedia, the free encyclopedia.

'Conflict of Interest.'

(67) www.doingbusiness.org 'Economy Rankings.'

(68) *Ibid.*

(69) http://en.wikipedia.org/wiki/Zimbabwe

Online article, 'Zimbabwe.'

(70) http://www.post1.net/lowem/entry/zimbabwe_hyperinflation_rate_hits_516_quintillion_percent_to_set_world_record_within_6_weeks

'Zimbabwe inflation rate hits 516 quintillion per cent.'

(71) http://shocking-news.org/economy/zimbabwe-the-state-of-hyperinflation/

(72) www.economywatch.com/world_economy/philippines/economic-forecast Online article. 'Philippines Economic Forecast.'

(73) www.wikipedia.org/Failed_state

Online article. 'Failed State.'

Chapter 4

(1) www.wikipedia.com

(2) 'Pinoy S&T workers leaving in droves.' By Helen M. Flores, February 15, 2011. The Philippine Star newspaper.

(3) *Ibid.*

(4) *Ibid.*

(5) http://www.malaya.com.ph/sep13/news7.html

Online article, 'DepEd adds 100 more schools for specialized science curriculum.' By Ashzel Hachiro. September 13, 2011.

(6) http://www.mb.com.ph/articles/322999/rd-will-be-driving-force-asian-century

'R&D will be the driving force of the Asian century.' By Michael Alan Hamlin. Manila Bulletin, June 17, 2011.

(7) http://www.philippinestoday.net/ofwcorner/July03/ofw703_1.htm

Online article, 'Risks high for Filipino seamen.' By Alecks Pabico, of the Philippine Center for Investigative Journalism. Mr. Pabico's article provides expert opinion and analysis in regards to Filipino mariners.

(8) *Ibid.*

(9) www.bbc.co.uk 'Piracy classes mandatory for Filipino seafarers.'

Online article.

(10) http://migranteinternational.org/

Migrante International. Migrante is an OFW welfare organization.

(11) http://www.migrationanddevelopment.net/research-publications/caring-while-at-risk-ofw-phenomenon-and-its-impact-to-the-filipino-family

'Caring while at risk: OFW phenomenon and its impact on the Filipino family.'

BANICO, Albert, Philippien Association for the Sociology of Religion (PASR),

An essay by Mr. Odine De Guzman of the University of the Philippines, who is an expert in the history and status of OFWs, is also cited in the above article as a reference source.

(12)http://en.wikipilipinas.org/index.php?title=Filipino_Women_ Overseas_Workers Wikipilipinas. Online encyclopedia. 'Filipino Women Overseas Workers.'

(13) www.pinoyoverseas.net

'OFW in coma racks up P2.4M in Dubai hospital bills.'

GMA News, July 28, 2011.

(14)http://ph.news.yahoo.com/malaysian-cops-arrest-2-suspected-killers-pinay-maid-054408950.html / GMANews Online.

'Malaysian cops arrest 2 suspected killers of Pinay maid.'

13 August 2011

(15)   http://globalnation.inquirer.net/news/breakingnews/ view/20110127-316938/Lawmaker-calls-for-probe-on-proliferation-of-OFW-drug-mules

Inquirer Newspaper. Online article.

'Lawmaker Calls Attention to Increasing Number of OFW 'Drug Mules'

By Lira Dalangin-Fernandez. Published on January 27, 2011.

(16) *Ibid.*

(17) The Daily Telegraph. August 15, 2011.

(18) Michael S. Serrill, Reported by Scott MacLeod/Al-Ain and Nelly Sindayen/Manila, TIME, October 23, 1995

www.time.com/time/international/1995/951023/justice.html

(19) *Ibid.*

(20) www.islamicaweb.com

Pakistan's Christian 'Sex-Slaves': A Case Study by Raymond Ibrahim

Raymond Ibrahim is a Shillman Fellow at the David Horowitz Freedom Center and an Associate Fellow at the Middle East Forum.

(21) *Ibid.*

(22) *Ibid.*

(23) *Ibid.*

(24) *Ibid.*

(25) www.philstar.com

Kuwait court affirms death sentence on Filipina maid

By Reinir Padua (The Philippine Star) Updated April 02, 2008

(26) www.telegraph.co.uk

'Filipina bride 'paid hitmen to murder pastor.'

By Richard Edwards

December 12, 2007.

(27) Inquirer Newspaper.

Tuesday, August 08, 2006.

'God has purpose for OFWs, asserts top-selling author.' By Blanche Rivera.

(28)http://sydney.edu.au/education_social_work/future_students/careers/teacher_salaries.shtml

'Teacher salaries.' (2011 rates.) (For the state of New South Wales.)

(29) *Ibid.*

(30) http://en.wikipedia.org/wiki/Internally_displaced_person

Wikipedia online encyclopedia. 'Internally Displaced Person.'

Chapter 5

(1) www.cebucity.org

News item concerning 14 year old boy murdered while on errand.

(2) http://www.stuartxchange.com/Shabu.html

From an online article on Methamphetamine use in the Philippines.

(3) 'Filipino journalist slain, 4th killed this year', June the 13th 2011. Associated Press article written by Teresa Cerojano.

(4) http://news.bbc.co.uk/2/hi/asia-pacific/64344.stm

BBC online news article 'Murder in the name of War.'

(5) http://en.wikipedia.org/wiki/Pol_Pot Wikipedia gives the following reference; 'The Cambodian Genocide Program". Genocide Studies Program. Yale University. 1994-2008. http://www.yale.edu/cgp/. Retrieved May 12, 2008.'

(6) http://www.stanford.edu/~ldiamond/iraq/WhaIsDemocracy012004.htm Stanford University Lecture, 2004. What is democracy?

(7) www.u-s-history.com/pages/h337.html 'Manifest Destiny.'

(8) http://en.wikipedia.org/wiki/American_pioneer

Online article; 'American pioneer.'

(9) See for instance: http://www.remember-chile.org.uk/comment/00-10-29lat.htm

(10) http://en.wikipedia.org/wiki/Ferdinand_Marcos

'Ferdinand Marcos.'

(11) http://asiancorrespondent.com/27264/mass-riots-expected-in-philippines-during-elections/ Asian Correspondent. Hybrid News Limited. Online article dated January 7th, 2010.

(12) http://www.manilastandardtoday.com/2008/april/29/antonioAbaya.htm Online article by Antonio C. Abaya. 'Federal fol-de-rol.'

(13) Manuel F. Almario. 'Why feudal lords still reign in PH.' Philippine Daily Inquirer Wednesday, July 20th, 2011. Spokesman, Movement for Truth in History.

(14) www.peopledaily.com.cn January 04, 2007.'Philippine military kills pirate leader.'

(15) http://safety.mindanao.com/2006/09/can-i-travel-to-mindanao-is-it-safe/ 'Is it safe to travel to Mindanao?' September 27, 2006.

(16) 'Travel Report Philippines' http://www.voyage.gc.ca/countries_pays

(17) Though the Somozas were generally regarded as ruthless dictators, the United States continued to support them as a non-communist stronghold in Nicaragua. President Franklin D. Roosevelt (FDR) supposedly remarked in 1939 that "Somoza may be a son of a bitch, but he's our son of a bitch." According to historian David Schmitz, however, researchers and archivists who have searched the archives of the Franklin D. Roosevelt Presidential Library have found no evidence that Roosevelt ever made this statement. Source: www.wikipedia.org

(18) List of the Top Ten of the Money Launderers www.toptenz.net

(19) www.time.com

(20) 'Who ordered the hit on Ninoy Aquino?' By Rodel Rodis,

INQUIRER.net August, 2009.

(21) Online dictionary www.merriam-webster.com/dictionary/inviolable

(22) 'Bishop's SUV a birthday gift from then-President Arroyo' Kimberly Jane Tan, GMA News, July, 2011.

07/06/2011

(23) *Ibid.*

(24) Editorial, 'Sorry, but they'll keep the SUVs' Cebu Daily News.

Wednesday, July 13th, 2011.

(25) Meant here as 'Secret activity or maneuvering'.

(26) 'Philippines: priest killed after receiving death threats.' Independent Catholic News. Online edition. Posted Monday, September 7, 2009.

(27) www.manilastandardtoday.com/insidenews Online article 'CBCP threatens to excommunicate President Aquino.' October 1st, 2010.

Chapter 6

(1) BBC online article 'Flashpoint Spratly.' http://news.bbc.co.uk/2/hi/asia-pacific/279170.stm

(2) See for instance: www.aviationweek.com Online article 'NATO's Global Partners by Nicholas Fiorenza, September 15th, 2011.

(3) For an overview of NATO see: www.nato.int

(4) Wikipedia. The online encyclopedia.

'The Iraq War.'

(5) http://www.washingtonpost.com/wpdyn/content/article/2008/03/07/AR2008030702846_2.html

'The Iraq War Will Cost Us $3 Trillion, and Much More.'

By Linda J. Bilmes and Joseph E. Stiglitz. Sunday, March 9, 2008. The Washington Post.

(6) http://www.telegraph.co.uk/news/worldnews/asia/afghanistan/1364905/Bin-Laden-didnt-expect-New-York-towers-to-fall.html

The Telegraph. December 10, 2011. 'Bin Laden didn't expect New York towers to fall.'

(7)http://en.wikipedia.org/wiki/9/11_advancedknowledge_debate#Intelligence_warnings

Wikipedia. The online encyclopedia. 'Advance knowledge debate. Intelligence warnings.'

(8) http://en.wikipedia.org/wiki/Iran%E2%80%93Iraq_War

America provided support in this form to Iraq during its war with Iran. Iraq had started the war by invading Iran, presuming that Iran would be in a state of weakness as a result of the internal chaos caused by the Iranian Revolution.

(9) Wikipedia. Online encyclopedia. 'Multi-National Force Iraq.'

(10) http://www.abs-cbnnews.com/nation/08/23/11/imelda-marcos-stands-gaddafi. ABC-CBNNEWS. By R. G. Cruz August 23, 2011.

(11) http://www.ipcs.org/article/terrorism/terrorism-in-philippines-combine-hard-and-soft-options-3221.html

Institute of Peace and Conflict Studies

Article by Panchali Saikia. August 19, 2010.

(12) *Ibid.*

(13) http://www.adl.org/terror/tu/tu_0404_philippines.asp

'The Philippines and Terrorism.' April, 2004.

(14) Online article of the Manila Bulletin www.mb.com.ph. 'RP celebrates Punctuality Week November 23, 2004'.

(15) Wikipedia. Online encyclopedia. 'Che Guevara.'

(16) Susan M. Heathfield in an online article on cultural change at the website www.about.com /humanresources.

(17) *Ibid*.

(18) http://www.likhaan.org/book/export/html/480 'Women Deliver Philippines. 2010'.